GCSE

SOCIOLOGY

Stephen Harris

 LONGMAN

LONGMAN STUDY GUIDES

SERIES EDITORS:
Geoff Black and Stuart Wall

TITLES AVAILABLE:
Biology
Business Studies
Chemistry
Design and Technology
Economics
English
English Literature
French
Geography
German
Information Technology
Mathematics
Mathematics: Higher Level
Music
Physics
Psychology
Religious Studies
Science
Sociology
Spanish
World History

Addison Wesley Longman Limited,
Edinburgh Gate, Harlow,
Essex CM20 2JE, England
and Associated Companies throughout the world.

First Published 1994
Second impression 1997

ISBN 0 582 22651.1 PPR

British Library Cataloguing-in-Publication Data

A catalogue record for this book is available from the British Library
Set by 19QQ in 10/12pt Century Old Style

Produced by Longman Singapore Publishers Pte Ltd
Printed in Singapore

Contents

EDITORS' PREFACE

Longman Study Guides for GCSE/Key Stage 4 are written by experienced examiners and teachers, and aim to give you the best possible foundation for success in examinations and other modes of assessment. Much has been said in recent years about declining standards and disappointing examination results. While this may be somewhat exaggerated, examiners are well aware that the performance of many candidates falls well short of their potential. The books encourage thorough study and a full understanding of the concepts involved and should be seen as course companions and study guides to be used throughout the course. Examiners are in no doubt that a structured approach in preparing for examinations and in presenting coursework can, together with hard work and diligent application, substantially improve performance.

The largely self-contained nature of each chapter gives the book a useful degree of flexibility. After starting with Chapter 1, all other chapters can be read selectively, in any order appropriate to the stage you have reached in your course. As well as the examination-type questions and answers at the end of each chapter, you will also find "Review Sheets" to test yourself on the content of that chapter.

We believe that this book, and the series as a whole, will help you establish a solid platform of basic knowledge and examination technique on which to build.

Geoff Black and Stuart Wall

ACKNOWLEDGEMENTS

I am indebted to the following Examination Boards for permission to reproduce their questions.
The answers given are not the only possible answers, and are entirely my responsibility:

Midland Examining Group (MEG); Northern Examinations and Assessement Board (NEAB);
Southern Examining Group (SEG); Edexcel Foundation (London) (ULEAC).

I would like to thank the many officers at the Examination Boards for their co-operation

I received invaluable critical advice from Grahame Coates on questions and answers and from Paul Lawrence on coursework. Rita MacIlwraith and her students at Pimlico School provided me with some useful answers.

Geoff Black, Stuart Wall and Linda Marsh provided encouragement and removed obstacles.

Melanie, Sarah, Lily and Prudence let me write in relative peace.

We are grateful to the following for permission to reproduce copyright material; the artist's agent for an "Alex" cartoon from *Daily Telegraph* newspaper (date unknown); Central Statistical Office for a Table from *Social Trends* 1988, Tables from *Social Trends* 1991 and 1993, adapted Tables from *Social Trends* 1987 and 1991, figures from *Social Trends* 1991 and 1993 and adapted figures from *Social Trends* 1985 and 1993; the Controller of Her Majesty's Stationery Office for an adapted figure from *Labour Force Survey* (HMSO, 1984) and a figure from *Tackling Crime* (Home Office 1989), both Crown copyright; the artist, Ken Cox for a "Kelly" cartoon from *Best* magazine 16.2.90; Future Publishing Ltd for a cartoon from *PC Plus* February 1988; Guardian News Service Ltd for a graph from *The Guardian* newspaper 22.12.88, an extract from the article "Crime puts women in state of siege" from *The Guardian* newspaper 13.2.90 and an extract from the article "Mad dogs and Englishmen" from *The Guardian* newspaper 23.1.91; Macmillan Ltd for a figure from *New Statesman Society Database 1987* (1987); Ewan MacNaughton Ltd for an extract from the article "Union decade of decline set to continue" from *Daily Telegraph* newspaper 6.6.91 and an extract from *Daily Telegraph* newspaper 6.8.91; New Statesman and Society for a Table from *New Society* 6.3.87 and a figure from *New Statesman/Society* (date unknown); Office of Population Census and Surveys for a figure from *Occupational mortality: 1970–72* (HMSO 1978); Olympus Books UK for a figure from *Sociology Update* by M Denscombe (1991); Pan Books Ltd for a figure from *The State of the Nation* by S Fothergill and J Vincent (1985); Rex Features for the headline and an extract from the article "Poll shock for Jim" from *The Sun* newspaper 27.10.78; Social Studies Review for a figure from *Social Studies Review* November 1985; Solo Syndication and Literary Agency Ltd for a "Mac" cartoon from *Daily Mail* newspaper (date unknown); Syndication International for the headline and an extract from the article "Jim's sweet win in the poll" from *Daily Mirror* newspaper 27.10.78; Yorkshire Post Newspapers Ltd for a photograph from *Yorkshire Post* newspapers September 1991.

We have been unable to trace the copyright holders in the following and would appreciate any information that would enable us to do so; an article from *Daily Telegraph* newspaper 11.12.90; a photograph from *Mastering Sociology* by G O'Donnell (Macmillan 1985).

Stephen Harris

GETTING STARTED: USING THIS BOOK

GCSE SOCIOLOGY

THE NATURE OF SOCIOLOGY

TOPICS AND SYLLABUSES

COURSEWORK

THE EXAMINATION

This book is divided into a series of chapters based on different sociological topics. I have chosen topics which are examined by the various boards. However any single question may require you to draw on knowledge from more than one of these topic areas. Sometimes the same ideas may be studied under different headings, e.g. changes in the age-distribution of the population are discussed in Chapter 2 on age groups but could be included in a question on the family, the welfare state, population or work. Some questions may deliberately invite you to use a wide variety of subject matter; e.g. a question on education may ask you to discuss other forms of socialisation which would allow you to consider the family, mass media and religion. It will therefore help to have a broad overview of the various topic areas as well as a detailed knowledge of particular topics. As you read each chapter you will be reminded of other chapters which are relevant to the topic being discussed.

Each chapter will contain the following

- **Getting Started:** a brief introduction to the topic and outline of key definitions.
- **Essential Principles:** a review of the main points of theory and practice in that topic area, with emphasis on sociological studies providing evidence for or against particular viewpoints.
- **Examination Questions:** Actual examination questions for you to practise before looking at the answers provided.
- **Answers to Examination Questions:** Full and outline answers to various questions. Most chapters will include an actual student answer with examiner comments so that you can see how others have tackled questions and what the examiner is looking for.
- **Review Sheets:** At the end of every chapter (or pair of related chapters) there is a Review Sheet which will help you to check your understanding of what you have read in that chapter. In this book the review questions will often involve you in using and interpreting tables or charts or in finding examples to illustrate particular ideas. These skills are a vital part of any Social Science and will be important in preparing you for the examination in Sociology.

In this chapter we will introduce a number of elements important to your study.

- The Nature of Sociology
- Topics and Syllabuses
- Coursework
- The Examination

Some syllabuses stress *themes* which cut across different topic areas. The last chapter deals with some of these, including SOCIALISATION, SOCIAL CONTROL, and SOCIAL CHANGE. This chapter should encourage you to try and draw on a wide range of knowledge.

ESSENTIAL PRINCIPLES

1 THE NATURE OF SOCIOLOGY

What is sociology ?

Sociologists may disagree amongst themselves about what they should study, how they should study it and how they should explain what they find out. However there is some general agreement that sociology is the study of human social behaviour. This section deals with the subject matter and methods of sociology.

What do sociologists study ?

Sociologists study human behaviour. There are of course other academic disciplines which also study people and describe humanity, such as art, literature and journalism. Sociology is different in that it concentrates on *social behaviour.* This means that:

1 we study people in *groups* rather than as individuals, whereas Psychology is more interested in individual behaviour.

2 we study not just behaviour itself but the *social meaning* given to behaviour; e.g. raising two fingers was used by Winston Churchill as a V for victory, yet today we use it more commonly as an offensive and obscene gesture. The behaviour is the same, the social meaning has changed. Different cultures use different gestures to insult others – do you know some?

> **66** Groups and social meaning are important **99**

What's different about sociology ?

Unlike political scientists and economists, sociologists do not restrict themselves to a particular area of social life. We are interested in everything! However new topics appear on syllabuses and old ones disappear. The family, education and work are old favourites. Health and developing countries have recently become more popular and food and falling in love have yet to enter the syllabuses or text books. If these seem trivial subjects you might ask yourself *why* you do not think them important. In any case we see war as an important human activity (just look at the News) but I know of only one popular textbook, by A. Giddens, which deals with it as a topic in its own right.

Biology, psychology and sociology

Biologists emphasise the importance of NATURE in explaining human behaviour. Modern developments in the understanding of genetics have helped to make their explanations more and more detailed and convincing. Biology does, however, also recognise the environment in which the human as a biological organism exists. A large part of this environment is man-made and can be seen as a *social creation*. The social environment would affect all of the three examples explained below: *Health* is adversely affected by industrial pollution but may be improved by health education and the availability of drugs in some societies but not others. *Child development* is influenced by the various kinds of family life that exist in any one society or in different societies. The frequency of *homosexual behaviour* in previously heterosexual men increases when men are placed in all male societies, such as prisons.

> **66** Even Biologists recognise the importance of the social environment **99**

Psychologists fiercely debate the relative importance of NATURE and NURTURE in explaining behaviour. Studies of identical twins have been used to measure the influence of nurture (or environmental) factors on psychological development in such fields as intelligence or mental illness.

Sociologists tend to under-emphasise nature and see human behaviour as best explained at the social rather than the individual level. CULTURAL diversity has been cited as evidence against the importance of nature in determining our behaviour. This involves showing that what is assumed to be natural, in fact varies from time to time and place to place. For example, gender roles may be clearly distinguished in some societies but not in others. There are clearly biological differences between men and women (and considerable similarities too) but the effects of these real or sometimes imagined differences have varied between cultures. In the 18th century, menstruation was seen as a healthy symptom and "bleeding" using razors and leeches was adopted as a cure for male ills. Yet in the 19th century it was seen as evidence of women's ill-health.

> **66** Nature and the individual are less important than social and the group **99**

Health

The biological approach

We normally see health and sickness as being different physical states. Biological definitions of ill-health suggest that something has gone wrong with the body whereas good health exists when the body functions normally. Causes of ill-health might be an accident or disease produced by a bacteria or virus.

Different approaches to
health problems

The psychological approach

Psychologists are interested in the relationship between the body and the mind. They tend to study the health of individuals. They might explain mental illness not only from a biological point of view but also by examining the family background of the individual.

The sociological approach

Sociologists are interested in the *social causes* of ill-health, such as poverty or dangerous occupations. They are also interested in why something becomes seen as being abnormal and unhealthy. For example, they might ask why madness, pregnancy, old age and even unhappiness have all become conditions which doctors might deal with.

There is, of course, common ground between all three approaches. The National Survey of Sexual Attitudes and Lifestyles, which is described in the methods chapter (ch 16) has produced data for the use of sociologists, doctors and government policy makers. The researchers were just as interested in physical behaviour as social meanings.

Child development

Can you identify the different approaches that a biologist, psychologist and sociologist might take to this universal occurrence? Consider what they might observe and measure and how they might explain it. You may be surprised when you have read about childhood in the next chapter to find out that some sociologists think that childhood only came into existence as a distinct phase of life fairly recently. Your grandparents may be able to remember the discovery of "youth" in western countries after the Second World War.

Homosexuality

In 1993 some biologists claimed that there might be a genetic difference between homosexual and heterosexual males. This encouraged the view that homosexuality is an abnormal health condition rather than a pattern of desires and behaviour. Up to the 1960s, psychiatrists in the USA defined homosexuality as a mental illness. Both views "medicalise" homosexuality and suggest it might be cured.

Although homosexual behaviour is known in all societies, the idea that the homosexual is a separate kind of person is relatively new and not a view held in all societies even now. In Britain we might distinguish between the actual sexual behaviour practised by many and the exclusively homosexual way of life which is much less common, at least at a public level.

What do sociologists do?

Sociology uses
different methods

Sociologists study human social behaviour using one or more accepted sociological methods. Sociology differs from other academic subjects which study people not only in its subject matter but also its methods. We need to look at HOW sociologists do research as well as WHAT they study.

The essential feature of the scientific approach is DOUBT. Scientists do not believe anything until evidence has been produced and they should be prepared to change their minds when new evidence is produced. Scientific methods usually involve the scientists in using their experience or inspiration to produce an educated guess that one thing causes another. This guess is called a HYPOTHESIS. The hypothesis is then tested by gathering evidence that will support it or disprove it. If a hypothesis is confirmed it becomes a THEORY or explanation.

Jane Wheelock (1990) conducted a study to test whether men did more housework if they became unemployed. Previous studies had not shown this to be the case. Wheelock conducted a survey, using interviews with married couples, and found that the key factor which encouraged men to do more housework was their wives being in full-time employment.

This illustrates the scientific approach.

1 Previously a sociologist had tested a hypothesis that: male unemployment (a cause) produced the effect of men doing more housework.
2 This was not confirmed.
3 An alternative cause, i.e. women being in full-time employment, was tested and confirmed for the population she surveyed.
4 Further studies might examine whether her findings only apply when men are unemployed.

SOCIOLOGICAL METHODS

These are discussed in a later chapter. At this stage they will be listed and explained in a simple fashion.

Experiments

Different sociological methods

The experiment is the most popular method in the natural sciences and in psychology. It is rarely used in sociology because it prefers to study people in a natural way rather than in a controlled way.

Surveys

Social surveys are probably the most popular method used in sociology. They study many people and collect information using interviews or questionnaires.

Observation

Observation and participant observation are ways of studying people actually going about their everyday lives rather than asking them questions about their behaviour.

SOCIOLOGY AND COMMONSENSE

Because sociology involves the study of ourselves it often appears to tell us what we already know. The difference between sociology and commonsense is that sociology can be shown to be wrong by research. Commonsense views can be challenged – we do not think the world is flat any more. However commonsense and traditional views are remarkably resistant to criticism because people want to believe them and they are often vague or even contradictory.

Proverbs are common sense sayings. They might sound wise but you can often choose one to support your views.
"Many hands make light work" means the opposite of "too many cooks spoil the broth".
"Look before you leap" is an alternative to "nothing ventured nothing gained".
Can you think of any contradictory proverbs?

There are a lot of commonsense views of the world discussed in this book covering a wide field, including what is natural for men and women, the effects of racial inequality, why children do well or not so well at school, and many other everyday issues.

Beware! The sociological evidence presented on such issues is not always what you expected or what you wanted to hear! The sociologist may not always be right and the ordinary observer of society may sometimes display a more sociological imagination. Consider these two views on family life in Newcastle.

An analysis of types, based on the mother

1 ....we have subdivided the problem families into three types ... These are: (1) the "friendly type", (2) the "sullen type", (3) the "vicious type".
  In the friendly type of problem family the mother is feckless and incompetent because of a defect, mainly of intelligence ...
  The sullen type of mother ... is furtive and suspicious.
  The vicious type is a moral defective, usually living with a husband or another man who is like unto her in this respect. Cunning and conceited ...

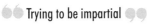 A personal historical record

2 Although you hear people talking about the good old days I can't remember much good about them. Things were very cheap but the money was very short. A labourer's money was about £1.50 a week . . . some of the boys were coming to school in their bare feet as their parents hadn't the money to buy them shoes. Poverty was certainly there. If you were out of work you had no income, there was no social security . . . you went to the Guardians . . . who enquired into your financial conditions. If you had no furniture to sell they may give you 25 pence.

The first extract is from a social survey published in 1954. The second is from an unpublished memoir of Charles Cuthbert Miller. He was remembering 1908 and writing this in 1985.

You will notice in the first that a problem family is explained by looking at the mother – do you think this is a full explanation?

In the second extract memory may play tricks, as the author acknowledges earlier, but nonetheless poverty is seen as a problem experienced by ordinary people who do their best to overcome it. Examine this passage later when you have looked at conflicting explanations of poverty. You might also comment on my use of a historical record of one man's point of view as sociological evidence.

Sociology and social policy

Some people confuse sociologists with social workers. Sociologists are usually more concerned with explaining the social world, whereas social workers have practical aims such as dealing with individual problems. Social workers and other professionals may use sociological knowledge to help them identify and explain social problems; e.g. they may draw on sociological knowledge about the extent and causes of poverty or the pattern of spread of sexually transmitted diseases.

On the other hand sociologists may study something because it is a social problem. This may be because it interests the sociologist or because someone is prepared to pay for the research to be done; e.g. football hooliganism and AIDS have both attracted large amounts of funding for research.

Should sociology be value free?

Some sociologists try to use scientific methods. Scientists try to be objective. This means that they try to forget their own personal attitudes and be detached from what they are studying. They hope to be politically and morally neutral.

Trying to be impartial

It has been argued that such neutrality, or value freedom as it is often called, is impossible. Sociologists often accuse each other or are accused by outsiders of being biased rather than objective. Usually it is when others do not like sociologists' findings that they accuse them of being biased. This is rather similar to the complaints made by politicians that the media are biased against a particular political party because they do not always support it uncritically.

Sociology in post-war Britain has been criticised from the political right for being too left wing and being biased against business and freedom and not recognising the benefits brought about by capitalism. It has also been criticised from the political left for not challenging the inequalities brought about by Capitalism. Feminists have attacked sociology for studying men from a male point of view and ignoring women.

2 > TOPICS AND SYLLABUSES

You should, of course, check the latest syllabus of your examination board or with your teacher. However Table 1.1 will give you a useful overview of the topic areas covered by the various syllabuses.

Chapter			SEG	ULEAC	MEG	NEAB	WJEC
1	Methods and Assessment		✓	✓	✓	✓	✓
2	Age	Childhood	✓	✓	✓	✓	✓
		Youth	✓	✓	✓	✓	✓
		Old Age	✓	✓	✓	✓	✓
3	Gender		✓	✓	✓	✓	✓
4	Race		✓	✓	✓	✓	✓
5	Class		✓	✓	✓	✓	✓
6	Poverty and Welfare		✓	✓	✓	✓	✓
7	Family		✓	✓	✓	✓	✓
8	Education		✓	✓	✓	✓	✓
9	Work		✓	✓	✓	✓	✓
10	Work, Leisure and Unemployment		✓	✓	✓	✓	✓
11	Population		✓	✓	✓	✓	✓
12	Urban and Rural Life		✓	✓	✓	✓	✓
13	Power and Politics		✓	✓	✓	✓	✓
14	Deviance and Social Control		✓	✓	✓	✓	✓
15	Religion and the Mass Media		✓	✓	✓		✓
16	Methods and Themes: Socialisation, Social Control and Social Change		✓	✓	✓	✓	✓

Table 1.1 Syllabus Coverage Chart

3 COURSEWORK

You will be accustomed to presenting teachers with work done in class or at home for them to mark. This gives the teacher the opportunity to check on your progress and to see if individual students are learning particular aspects of sociology. It also indicates to you how well you are doing. In addition written work can take the form of practice for the examination and will help you to develop problem solving and time management skills. So the moral of this introduction is "do your homework and do it on time!"

This section refers, not to written work in general but to the formal coursework which is assessed and contributes to the final examination mark for all examination boards. It was previously possible for adult students taking sociology in evening classes over a single year to take an alternative examination paper instead of coursework. This option may still exist in other subjects but not for sociology. For those of you doing sociology over perhaps as little as 30 evenings, organizing your time will be of crucial importance. This also applies to full-time students who may find themselves doing different subjects at school and having several pieces of coursework to complete and submit for the same deadline.

Private candidates are students who are not taking the course at school or college and enter the exam by contacting the exam boards directly. Private candidates need to be certain of the procedures and timing of coursework. They will possibly have to meet the moderator who marks their work for an interview to demonstrate their understanding of their work and show that they did it as, unlike other candidates, there is no teacher to confirm it is your own work.

WHY DO COURSEWORK?

The easy answer is because you have to. It is a requirement for GCSE Sociology. However there are a variety of benefits that you could and should gain from doing a successful piece of research.

1 You can get a significant number of marks before you enter the examination room.
2 You can be rewarded for skills apart from those tested in the final exams. The emphasis on memory and speed of thought and writing is lessened in coursework. You may feel calmer in the examination knowing that you have successfully completed some of the assessed work. You will take extra knowledge and understanding into the exam, particularly of sociological methods but also of the topic you have researched for your coursework.
3 You can spread your work-load more evenly throughout the year.

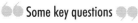 Benefits of coursework

4 You should acquire skills which will help you if you continue in your education or training or in employment. These include:
  i Time management.
  ii The ability to draft written work and then improve on it after advice or criticism.
  iii The ability to learn from difficulties or mistakes. This is the purpose of PILOT STUDIES at all levels of research.
  iv Research skills which can be applied in many different situations.
  v Working more independently and taking more responsibility for your learning than was usual in the days before GCSE. This will certainly help you in other future and higher education courses.

Make sure these worthwhile abilities are described on your records of achievement, reports, or references which can be brought to the attention of employers and admissions tutors when you apply for jobs or courses.

KEY QUESTIONS

There are certain key questions which need considering before commencing coursework. The answers can be found by consulting with teachers and referring to the syllabus and any coursework guidance notes that accompany it.

1. What marks are available for coursework?
2. How long should it be?
The following table will help answer these first two questions.

SUMMARY OF REQUIREMENTS UP TO 1995			
	NUMBER OF ASSIGNMENTS	MARKS ALLOCATED	RECOMMENDED LENGTH OF ENQUIRY
SEG	1	30%	1500–3500
NEAB	1	30%	1000–3000
LEAG	1	25%	2500
MEG	3	50%*	2000–3000
WJEC	1	40%	3000
(* 10% each for two assignments and 30% for enquiry)			
AFTER 1995 THE MAXIMUM NUMBER OF MARKS ALLOWED IS PLANNED TO BE 20%			

3. How are these marks allocated to the assessment of different abilities?
For example is the emphasis on knowledge, evaluation, presentation etc? Check with the mark-scheme used by your teacher.

Your own teachers mark your coursework and the standard of their marks is checked by the Examination boards. This usually involves a teacher from another school or college remarking a sample of the coursework from your centre to ensure there is a common standard for all candidates across the country. These people are called *moderators* and they send a report back to your teacher to confirm that their standards are correct or that they may need adjusting in some way in the future. The moderator can raise or lower the marks for your whole group. Normally there are no adjustments or they are fairly small.

Some key questions

4. What subjects may be chosen and do they need teacher and/or Board approval?
See below for suggestions of what topics to choose and what to avoid.

5. What methods may be chosen and do they need approval?

Suggestions for research are available with the syllabuses, in coursework guides and in examples of marked work published by the exam boards. Your research should employ an accepted method and be on an obviously sociological topic. Previous studies can be repeated. This chapter includes some suggestions and others are found throughout the book. The choice of method(s) is at least as important as the choice of topic.

6. What is the timetable for selection, planning, gaining approval and completion?

Teachers will have a deadline for submitting their marks to the Board. They cannot mark them all the night before this deadline! Many teachers will give you a schedule for doing the coursework, if not you will want to devise your own.

7. Is there a required or recommended format for the presentation of work?

See mark-scheme and notes on presentation below.

8. Who can help me?

Teachers can provide guidance, supervision and advice. So can parents and friends. However the study must be your own independent work. The boards keep a record of previous pieces of coursework and have discovered examples of cheating. You may, of course, repeat the same research as another student or sociologist but you must acknowledge that you have done this. There are coursework guides for GCSE and books which give advice on doing sociological research. Chapter 16 of this book will also help you on methods to follow.

CHOOSING A TOPIC

1 It must relate to the social structure of modern Britain. A comparative study where you compare modern Britain with the past or with another society is permissible, but is likely to be time consuming and risks being irrelevant. All boards require a direct link with the syllabus.

2 It must be sociological in approach. A child development study of a single child is NOT appropriate. Do not try to slightly change a piece of biology, geography or psychology. The best way to ensure this is to use recognised sociological methods in doing your research.

A survey is an appropriate method but the subject should be of sociological concern. It is not suitable just to survey a population's attitude to a particular person, event, product or activity. A survey of TV viewing would need to be looked at from a sociological view-point, such as the influence of family structure or position in the family on viewing habits.

Useful hints in choosing a topic

3 Most boards and teachers suggest that you choose a subject which relates to your own interests and experience, for example at school, at work or in the family.

4 The exam boards provide lists of suggested topics which indicate what is suitable and may inspire your choice.

5 Your research needs a specific research aim or a hypothesis. General titles such as "the family", "drugs", "leisure", etc. usually indicate a vague and unfocussed piece of work which is unlikely to do well. SEG has published a list of hundreds of actual titles used and their Chief Examiner for coursework has stressed that a title such as "Race and racial discrimination" is unlikely to be as convincing as "Racism in the criminal justice system: a case study" which was produced by a worker in a magistrates court who studied ethnicity and criminal sentences.

Choosing your subjects

Obviously your choice of topic will influence strongly your choice of subjects to include in your study. A study of peer group relationships in a college indicates that you will probably look at students, although workers would be acceptable. However

Decide who will be your subjects

you need to decide which particular students you will study. If you are going to use participant observation the question of access is important. If you are going to do a survey then you need to consider choosing a representative sample. Colleges will have a list of students which can be used as a sampling frame. Lists can usually be produced of people on different courses. You may be able to get total figures of the student population by age, ethnicity, gender and disability, but of course this information is confidential at the individual level. This could help you to choose relevant criteria for a quota sample (see ch 16).

Choosing a method

The uses and limitations of particular methods depends on your aims and the topic being studied.

Select your method (see also chapter 16)

- *Qualitative methods* may be better for in-depth studies of people's feelings; e.g. A. Oakley used *informal interviews* over a long period of time to discover women's experiences of maternity.
- *Quantitative methods* may be better suited to a survey of the behaviour of a large population; e.g. the National survey of sexual behaviour and attitudes used *structured interviews* to discover the average number of partners certain groups had.

  Practical problems also depend on you, the researcher. You must consider your time, money and individual characteristics.

- If you want to do a survey, time and money should limit the number of subjects you choose.
- If you want to do interviews, you need to have the confidence to approach people and the skills to get them to talk to you openly.
- If you want to do participant observation, you should consider whether your presence stops people behaving naturally. Covert participant observation depends on you being able to get into the group, avoid detection and record your observations accurately, without provoking suspicion.

Do it yourself!

Most projects are, at least in part, based on *primary research* rather than just secondary data. This is more fun for you; you will learn more and have more to write about when you are analysing and evaluating your own data.

SOURCES

As well as doing your own primary research you will want to refer to existing sources for a number of reasons.

- They may help you to formulate a research aim, by showing similar work in your chosen field.
- They may provide data to support or refute your hypothesis.
- You can compare your findings with existing work. Published statistics can provide a broad background to a small scale piece of research; e.g. your own research on gender and choice of school subjects could be compared with the national picture. (Examination boards publish national results broken down into subjects, grades and the gender of candidates.)

  Useful sources include:

- Text books.
- Sociology books based on original research. Some of these may be very difficult as they may be written for other sociologists. Others are accessible to a much wider audience. There is no need to read the whole book; you might just refer to descriptions of methods, or a summary of findings. The actual questions used in previous questionnaires can be "borrowed", if credit is given to the original author. They can then be used for similar or quite different purposes; e.g. questions given to factory workers about their experience of work could be given to housewives or professional workers.

Useful sources

- Sociology Journals are usually aimed at sociologists in universities but Sociology Review is aimed at A level students and some articles may give you good ideas.
- Electronic data sources include Newspapers on CD ROM which can be used to find relevant references very quickly and there are other data bases such as "textline" which may be useful. If these facilities are not available at your school or college then try a large local library.
- Government publications provide regular and very detailed statistical analyses of many relevant issues, such as population, employment, health, crime etc. Newspapers often report interesting bits of such reports and may whet your appetite for more detail.
- Your friendly librarian, if approached politely by teachers and students, can be a very useful resource telling you what is available and how to get it.

PRESENTATION

1 Follow the Board's guidelines and your teacher's advice. A Chief Examiner has emphasised that there are no extra marks for the heaviest-ever project! Stick to the recommended length (up to 3000 words for SEG up to 1995 and 1000–2500 in 1996).

Don't neglect presentation

2 Avoid an overlong introduction which just reviews what other sociologists have said about your topic. For example, a study of one specific aspect of current family life does not require a detailed history of the family in Britain nor a summary of everything written by Willmott and Young or anyone else.

3 You should:
   - Start with a table of contents.
   - Use separate chapters.
   - Use clear language.
   - Plan your lay-out and put things in a logical order, e.g. methods before findings.
   - Use a conclusion to indicate how successful you thought your research was and your conclusion should relate to the initial aim.
   - Finish with a list of sources used.

   Raw data such as transcripts of taped interviews or responses to questionnaires should not be in the main body of your report but in an appendix at the end.

4 There are few, if any, marks to be gained from presenting projects which look like professional publications that have been desk top published and elaborately bound. Spend your time and money more usefully! Projects can be typed but only by the candidate themselves. You should keep notes and raw data to demonstrate if necessary that typed or word processed work is your own.

5 From 1996, marks will be awarded for spelling, punctuation and grammar rather than presentation in general.

GETTING HIGH MARKS

Start with the mark scheme

Obtain your own copy of the mark scheme

Your teacher will mark your work. All teachers using the same Examination board will have the same mark scheme. This indicates what must be done to achieve high marks.

Aims

The aim or hypothesis should be clear and specific. You should ensure that the rest of the enquiry, i.e. the methods, content and evaluation, all relate to the aim. You should identify some questions or statements that develop the aim and which will be investigated in your research.

e.g. Aim: Investigate the degree of freedom enjoyed by children today.

Have a clear aim

You could pursue the influence of age, class, gender, ethnicity and whether children live in the town or country.

Methods

- You should have a *clear plan* of what you intend to do and how.
- You need to identify a *suitable method* or methods which will help you achieve your aim.
- You should be able to explain *why* you chose it and why alternatives were considered and rejected.
- You might include a *pilot study* to test the method itself and the actual questions you might ask.
- You should demonstrate that you have *collected suitable evidence.*

Explain your method

- You should *describe any difficulties* you encountered and whether you overcame them and, if so, how.
- You need to demonstrate that you can *use a method effectively* and understand the procedure, but you do not need to find a large representative sample to study. Twenty subjects completing a questionnaire or six subjects being interviewed will indicate whether you are developing the right skills.
- You could raise critical comments about your sample size and whether it is representative and gain credit for this kind of analysis.

Quality not quantity should be your aim.

Sources

- Sources should be used which are related to your aims. Both *primary* and *secondary* sources should be employed.
- Don't *just copy* from sources.
- Do attribute all sources.
- Don't just use sociology text books. Other sources show you can apply information to your research. TV, Radio, magazines, and even personal experience can be analysed in a sociological way.
- Teachers are a valuable "multi-media interactive resource"! If you use them carefully they will be able to give you detailed feedback on your ideas and work.

Analysis of findings

Look at what you have discovered and recorded and ask the questions:
WHAT, WHY, WHERE, HOW, WHO AND WHEN.

e.g. Why are children of a particular class allowed less freedom? What are the social implications of this? Will it influence their health, education or relationships within the family?

Do you think your findings are RELIABLE, VALID AND REPRESENTATIVE of a wider group of subjects.

Your presentation of results should help to show that you have thought about what you have found out. Graphs and bar charts are useful to indicate the relationship between factors and should not just repeat results in a different format. Do *use* any tables or data you have presented.

Evaluation

You should critically discuss your findings and the methods you used. Refer back to your aims when drawing conclusions.

AVOIDING AND OVERCOMING PROBLEMS

So far you might think that everything is bound to go smoothly. It won't. You will learn useful lessons from false starts and difficulties in getting data. Record these when you write up your project and show how you have learned from them.

You may wish to avoid major difficulties and this list may help.

- Do not be over ambitious and try to gather enormous amounts of data; even if you are successful it is not a wise use of your time.

Things to avoid

- Do not rely on other people's co-operation for the bulk of your material. You may find that interviews with MPs, Chief Constables and Directors of large companies are difficult or impossible to obtain.
- Do not write to others with vague requests for information on social problems like drugs, homelessness etc. Try to be specific and indicate what you want.
- Do not delay starting or working on your project whilst you hope someone replies to your request for information. Try to use sources which you know are open to you such as family or school.
- Do not choose participant observation as a method unless you are certain that you can get access to the group you wish to study. Real participation amongst work mates, friends or fellow students is easier.
- Do not break the basic ethical rules of social research. You should avoid deceiving subjects as to your intentions and respect their confidentiality. Your teacher should indicate the professional ethics of the sociologist and these are published by the British Sociological Association.

TYPES OF QUESTION

There may be some difference in the types of question set by the different exam boards. This table gives a broad idea. Of course you should become familiar with recent past exam papers of your own board.

	SEG	ULEAC	MEG	NEAB	WJEC
Full length essay	✔	✔	✔	✔	✔
"Mini-essay"	✔	✔	✔	✔	✔
Data response and/or stimulus questions	✔	✔	✔	✔	✔

 Types of question

IN ALL CASES BE GUIDED BY THE TIME ALLOCATED TO A QUESTION OR PART QUESTION.

- An *essay* with 30 minutes allowed could be up to two sides long.
- A *mini-essay* such as an 8 mark question out of 20 marks should be allocated about 14 minutes and could only realistically be a maximum of one side.
- A *data response* or *stimulus* question is not just trying to test your knowledge or memory but is attempting to test other skills. You must show you can *interpret* information given to you and can use it to answer questions.

INTERPRETING SOURCES OF DATA

Syllabuses and the questions based on them require the student to be able to interpret and critically discuss data in a variety of forms including:

1 short passages of text; e.g. extracts from sociology books or newspapers.
2 photographs, illustrations or cartoons.
3 graphs; bar graphs, line graphs, pictograms, etc.
4 tables of numbers.

You will want to practise interpreting all of these data sources which could appear in examination questions. If you have a particular weakness for numerical sources, practise more. Apart from questions in this book and in the Review Sheets you can use tables presented in newspapers which usually carry a commentary in the accompanying article. Real enthusiasts might try to interpret the tables in government statistical publications. These are generally much more complicated than required at GCSE but when simplified they provide useful information for coursework. They are often the source of more simple tables found in textbooks or newspapers.

SYLLABUSES, PAST PAPERS, MARKING SCHEMES

These are now all generally available from examination boards. They indicate the objectives of the syllabuses and the type of question used to assess these objectives and will give you an idea of the standard required.

WORDS USED IN EXAMINATION QUESTIONS:

You need to read through this section before you read the rest of the book. It will be most useful later when you attempt a question and are not sure what is required.

Identify
- One word or a short phrase will do. The answer may be in the sources presented in the question.

Identify and explain (e.g. 2 reasons for 4 marks)
- One mark for each reason and one for each explanation; usually one or two sentences in length for each explanation.

Identify and fully explain (e.g. one reason for 4 marks)
- A fuller explanation but focussed on only one reason. Three or four sentences making relevant and perhaps critical points.

"Explain" or "explain using examples" or "using the sources explain" (e.g. for 8 marks)

 **Be familiar with the words used in examinations**

■ Requires a mini-essay of up to a page. An organised list of points is required. Make sure you do give examples where requested to.

Describe and explain

■ Remember that explaining is more difficult but more important than just describing. Remember to refer your explanations back to the question.

Write an essay about . . . You may choose to include reference to any of the following, credit will be given for appropriate evidence.

■ Plan answer carefully. You do not need to use all the points given in the question. Evidence should be sociological, referring to studies or explanations. Also make sure your evidence is related to the question.

State an example.

■ One word or a short phrase.

Why

■ Give (sociological) reasons not just describe or list points.

Describe/Briefly describe

■ Straightforward description with examples.

Using examples show the difference

■ This requires you to *contrast* two things. Clearly state the differences rather than do two separate descriptions.

What is meant by the term . . . ? or **Explain the meaning of the term**

■ You need three or four sentences which explain rather than just describe a term. Examples will often help an explanation.

What explanations account for . . . ? (e.g. for 8 marks)

■ More than one explanation is required. Describe and explain, with perhaps 3 or 4 explanations. Again examples help.

How useful are . . .

■ This usually means "useful" to sociologists or government etc. Be critical; you might decide that an idea, explanation or method is useful up to a point. Discuss the strengths and weaknesses of ideas, methods etc.

What changes . . . What effects might follow such changes? (e.g. for 8 marks)

■ Remember to compare the time then and the time now. Also if it mentions "the last 30 years" then stay within the time period.

Using information from the extracts and your own knowledge explain . . .

■ These questions require you to interpret the sources to answer the question and also to apply knowledge you have brought to the examination.

EXAMINATION REVISION

Let past papers guide you. You must decide which subjects to cover and in what depth. Do not learn a minimum number of topics. You need a choice to avoid difficult or unpredictable questions. In addition questions may cover more than one topic and this is certainly the intention of many chief examiners.

Active revision

If you want to remember research evidence the best way to do so is not to repeatedly read through the same text book or set of notes but to try and USE THE INFORMATION IN AN ACTIVE WAY.

Make your revision active

It is probably best to practise real activities which you will have to do in the examination. If you start with a question and *a set period of time* to produce an answer, this can guide you as to how much you need to know and write.

If you want to do some initial reading on a subject, then the same principle applies; do not attempt to read long sections of books hoping that something relevant will appear and that you might remember it.

Instead:

1 start with a question
2 use a table of contents and an index to seek out potentially relevant material,
3 skim through it to ensure that it meets your needs

4 if it does, jot down relevant points whilst you are reading. A relevant point is one that helps you answer the question.

5 When you have found enough points and feel you can explain them adequately, you can stop.

6 Now write out your answer within the time set for that question.

This sort of active studying is more tiring than relaxing with your feet up reading through whole chapters but it will be much better in preparing you for the examination. Try the questions at the end of each chapter in this book *before* you look at the answers which follow.

DOING THE EXAMINATION

Hints in the exam room

1 Allocate your time in the examination according to the number of marks available for each question or part question. I have said this already but it is of crucial importance if you are going to make the best use of your knowledge and skills.

2 Use the items or extracts presented in the question; refer to them and also bring in other knowledge. Use a fluorescent marker to identify key passages on the Question paper so that you can refer to them quickly.

3 Where questions carry more than 1 or 2 marks PLAN your answer. This means deciding how many and which major points you are going to make and what evidence/examples you are going to mention.

4 Remember, you are doing sociology. Arguments will get more credit where you have used sociological terms and concepts and supported arguments with sociological evidence.

5 Answer the question. This may seem obvious but examiners always find large numbers of students who write everything they know about a topic, or answer a question they would have liked to see, or last year's question, rather than the one set.

6 Number questions and part questions clearly. Make sure you put your answer in the right place. If question (a) asks you to identify two agencies of socialisation for 2 marks and (b) asks you to explain the processes involved (for 5 marks), then do not waste your time putting explanations in question (a). You will not get any credit if you put the right answer in the wrong place.

Remember, the examiner is rarely looking for one particular "right answer" unless it is a simple interpretation of data in a question. Instead he or she is looking for a reasoned and relevant answer which demonstrates your knowledge and understanding of sociology.

CHAPTER 2

AGE

CHILDHOOD

YOUTH

OLD AGE

GETTING STARTED

This chapter concentrates on three stages in people's lives;

- CHILDHOOD
- YOUTH
- OLD AGE

Perhaps being "adult" is seen as normal whereas these other age groups are seen as problems in some way. A major theme throughout the chapter is to challenge many widely held assumptions about the influence of age on people's lives. Because ageing is seen as a natural process we tend to take certain characteristics of the various age groups for granted. Children are seen as innocent and helpless. Youth is associated with deviance. The old are seen as dependent.

Here are some useful definitions of terms you will come across as you study this chapter.

DEFINITIONS

CHILDHOOD is not biologically defined. It is the early stage of social life. Not all societies define childhood in the same way and some hardly recognise it at all.

YOUTH is a stage in life between childhood and adulthood. It may not be recognised but it is often seen as a social problem.

YOUTH CULTURE is a way of life common to all youth which develops as a response to the particular circumstances of their lives.

YOUTH SUB-CULTURES are groups of youth who have distinctive attitudes and patterns of behaviour. Often they are identified by dress. Sub-Cultures may be based on class, ethnicity or gender.

OLD AGE tends to be defined in terms of retirement from work and dependence.

MATURATION is the process of biological and perhaps psychological development.

AGE IS FREQUENTLY SEEN BY SOCIOLOGISTS AS A FORM OF STRATIFICATION, RATHER LIKE CLASS, RACE AND GENDER.

A CHECK LIST

When studying age groups you could compare their different experiences in terms of:

1 THE FAMILY

2 EDUCATION

3 WORK OR UNEMPLOYMENT

4 LEISURE AND SPENDING

5 PORTRAYAL IN THE MEDIA

ESSENTIAL PRINCIPLES

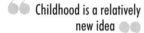

CHILDHOOD AS A SOCIAL CONSTRUCTION

Age, like race and gender, is generally seen by sociologists as a *social construction*. There are biological characteristics which distinguish age groups but the meaning given to them is socially defined. This means that ideas about age vary from time to time and from place to place.

This section refers to childhood but could equally be applied to the sociology of youth or the old.

P. Aires (1962) is notable for suggesting that:

1 Childhood is a relatively new invention.

2 Childhood did not exist in Europe during the Middle Ages.

❝ Childhood is a relatively new idea ❞

His history has been criticised but the idea that childhood is not a biological and psychological stage but rather is socially defined is still widely accepted. The recent history of childhood would need to consider:

1 The effects of the control of child labour.

2 The introduction of the age of sexual consent to deal with prostitution.

3 The introduction and extension of compulsory education.

4 The development of psychological ideas about child raising from Freud and others.

CHILDREN IN THE FAMILY

The role of children in the family has been influenced by culture and by history, i.e. it has varied from time to time and place to place.

1 The *normative view*, i.e. what the role of children *should* be, has changed from pre-industrial and early industrial Britain. Children were at that time seen as an *economic asset*, both as present and future *producers*. As such they contributed to family income and provided an insurance for the parents' future, especially important at a time where there were no old age pensions. Although this view of children is much less common today, the Low Pay Unit estimates that two million children under the age of 16 are currently working, and a recent survey showed that about 50% of 5th form students were doing part-time work.

2 In modern industrial society children have become the *centre of family life*. Sociologists identify the bringing up (socialisation) of children as one of the remaining essential functions of the family. The modern view of the family suggests not only more equality between husband and wife but also between parent and child.

3 Children have been described as a form of *conspicuous consumption*. They are a luxury and we talk of being able to *afford* to have (more) children. Children are a major aspect of the family seen as a unit of consumption, with children demanding many of the goods and services provided by modern capitalism. Leonard says children are seen as being there to be enjoyed by adults.

❝ Views of the role of children ❞

4 Marxists see the role of the modern family as *raising the future work force*. In this view children must be fed, clothed and taught to be obedient at no cost to employers.

THE NEW SOCIOLOGY OF CHILDHOOD

Children are people too

Modern approaches emphasize that children should not be dismissed as the passive recipients of socialisation but as people who make active choices about their own lives. Many sociologists say that in the past children were, like women, studied only as members of the family or as an influence on the leisure activities of adults.

Children are controlled by adults

Kitzinger (1990) argued that we should be concerned not just with the *abuse* by parents and others of power over children but also by the very existence and maintenance of that power. Hood-Williams (1990) has developed a similar view. Ideas which were previously used by feminists to describe the way in which men dominate women have now been applied to children. He talks of the family in terms of *age patriarchy*, seeing similarities between the social control of women and the control of the lives of children, who are to be obedient and are restricted in the way they dress and in matters such as where and when they are allowed to go out. For example, children are controlled in order to protect them from attack, just like women. Whereas in 1971, 81% of 7 and 8 year olds went unaccompanied to school, by 1993 this figure had fallen to only 9%.

 Adults dominating children!

Should teachers control children?

This view of the child as passive and in need of protection can be found in education where parents are encouraged by the New Right to exercise choice, because parents know best, not teachers. Children's choice is not considered so important by such groups. Children have also been used as a weapon by politicians in attacking "trendy" teachers. The Black Papers were published in the 1970s by right wing critics of progressive education. The view of children expressed in these papers was a traditional one:

> "Children are not naturally good. They need firm, tactful discipline from parents and teachers with clear standards. Too much freedom for children breeds selfishness, vandalism and personal unhappiness."

(Cox and Boyson, 1975, cited by S. Wagg in Sociology Review, Vol 1, No. 4)

TV is a bad influence

Similarly there is a debate over the effects of the mass media, with a strong emphasis on the need to protect children from corruption. The Right worries about sex and violence on TV, whereas feminists are concerned with gender stereotypes.

Children should speak for themselves

The new sociology of childhood recommends the use of sociological methods which will allow children to speak for themselves. This will change, not only the study of childhood, but also the way we see children.

This is similar to Oakley's argument that feminist research methods should let women speak for themselves.

CHILD ABUSE

The *rise* in child abuse statistics could be the result of one or more of the following:

1 More actual incidents caused by more *individual problems.*
2 More actual incidents caused by more *social problems.*
3 More cases *reported.*
4 *Changing definitions* of child abuse so that some kinds of behaviour are no longer tolerated.

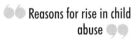 Reasons for rise in child abuse

Child abuse became a *social problem* in the 1960s. This does not mean that children were treated any better before this. What happened was that certain severe cases of child injury were publicly recognised as "baby battering", first in the USA and then in Britain. Previously people were unwilling to accept that such violence occurred within families. This was followed by a change in public opinion so that people became less tolerant of the ill treatment of children. Indeed the social definition of what is regarded as abuse or neglect has changed as society has begun to expect improvements in the general treatment of children. Later, during the 1980s, attention began to be focused on the sexual abuse of children. There were MORAL PANICS where sexual abuse was perceived to be an organised community activity rather than an individual form of deviance. The image of the child abuser changed from the evil stranger to the evil or sick family member, usually the father or step-father.

Critical thoughts:

1 There may be more actual abuse of children while at the same time we are becoming less tolerant of it.
2 There has not been the same public concern about child poverty as about the more sensational cases of abuse.
3 It may be that poverty, stress, alcohol and drug abuse are linked to child abuse in a complex way or that families with these problems are more likely to come to the attention of social workers than apparently respectable families. This is similar to the labelling theories of crime (see ch 14).

2 > YOUTH

❝❝ The idea of 'moral panics' ❞❞

Sociological studies of youth have tended to concentrate on rather small sections of the whole age group. In the 1960s and 1970s there was an emphasis on exotic and exciting groups of deviants, such as Teds, Mods, Rockers, Hippies, Skinheads and Punks. The Mass media shared this interest and there were a succession of what sociologists call *moral panics*, where youth was seen as presenting a major social problem. Both the media and sociologists were interested in the *styles* adopted by these youth sub cultures.

In the 1980s, sociologists shifted their attention to the problem of youth unemployment. This was often seen by the adult world as a problem presented by the young unemployed to the rest of society, rather than as a problem experienced by the unemployed themselves.

In the 1990s there is more emphasis on the lives of ordinary young people, i.e. neither the unemployed nor the deviant, particularly those neglected in previous studies, such as girls.

ORDINARY YOUTH

The existence of a youth culture depends on the idea that young people have different attitudes and values from the older generation. However many studies show that the more exotic sub cultures are exceptional and that most young people are little different in their concerns from their parents.

❝❝ Most young people are 'ordinary' ❞❞

C. Griffin wrote about "Typical Girls" who wanted to be homemakers. This confirmed the earlier work of S. Sharpe, who said that the major concern of schoolgirls were "Love, marriage, children, jobs and careers. More or less in that order." However Fuller's study of West Indian girls showed that they were also determined to find work which would ensure their later independence from men.

Sharpe reminded us that most young people live with their parents and get on with them. Typical boys seem more concerned with their future role as the breadwinner than with seeking to establish a distinctive form of lifestyle.

There seems, therefore, to have been an overemphasis in sociological studies on a small section of deviant youth, largely ignoring the fact that the majority are conforming young people. Studies concentrated on white, working class, urban youth and thus paid little attention to girls, ethnic minorities, or rural dwellers.

Girls

Although Margaret Mead wrote about girls growing up in Samoa in the 1920s, modern sociologists tended to dismiss them as either not participating in youth culture or perhaps as "hangers on" to male groups. Incidentally Mead's work was seen as interesting because of her description of the sexual freedom available for Samoan girls compared to American girls of that period. However a later study suggested that the Samoan girls had misled Mead about the extent of their sexual experiences.

Modern feminist writers began to write about girls in the 1980s. Initially they described little more than a "bedroom culture" influenced by romantic magazines where one or two girls became fans of media stars.

ETHNIC MINORITIES

Asian youth

Asian parents in this country are often seen as exercising rather strict control over their children and young people. However, where young people are the children of first generation immigrants they may be more independent because of their greater involvement in the wider society, e.g. through speaking English as a first language and being in school. To some extent Bhangra music, which is Punjabi in origin, has had a unifying effect on Asian youth who come from a variety of national and religious backgrounds.

Youth in ethnic minorities

Afro/Caribbean youth

S. Hall's study of the moral panic about mugging in the 1970s shows how the media, without substantial evidence, presented black youth as criminal.

Racial disadvantage may have led to the development of a variety of Afro/Caribbean youth sub cultures which have been imported from the Caribbean. Some young people may adopt, or at least admire, the "hustler" lifestyles of Rude Boys or Yardies. Racial prejudice may be countered by a desire to live separately from the dominant white culture and adopting the religious beliefs and lifestyle of the Rasta. Rastafarians identify with their African roots and their distinctive style is shown in language, hair, clothes, music and the smoking of ganja.

Gender and ethnicity

S. Sharpe in "Just Like a Girl" compared the life of Asian, West Indian and white girls in Ealing and showed that gender and ethnicity act together in shaping the experience of the young.

Remember that "ordinary youth" are more common than members of more visible and exotic groups although they may adopt some of the styles of the sub cultures.

A SINGLE YOUTH CULTURE?

Some sociologists argued that youth shared a common culture based on age, whatever their class or other characteristics. This culture was often seen as a rebellious one in opposition to the adult world.

The reasons suggested for the development of an age-based culture include the following:

Reasons for an Age-Based Culture

1 **Biological** changes associated with puberty, which are seen as influencing behaviour. Youth is neither childhood nor maturity.
2 **Psychological** developments which require children to prepare themselves for a life separate from parents.
3 The **affluent society** of the 1950s and 1960s which produced a new youth market for goods such as clothes and records. Youth earned adult wages but, being without adult financial responsibilities, had large disposable incomes.
4 The **social** position of youth between childhood and adulthood. This period has been extended as full-time education has postponed the time of entering the adult world of work, as has unemployment.

Following violent student unrest in Europe and the USA during the late 1960s, Marxist writers saw students as potential leaders of revolution. There appeared to be a youth culture based on opposition to the war in Vietnam and in favour of freedom from traditional rules, e.g. a permissive attitude to sexuality and drug use. There were characteristic styles in student music and clothes. We must consider, however, whether radical students were ever more than just one more youth sub culture, especially when students themselves represented only a small minority of the whole age group.

YOUTH SUB CULTURES

It has been argued that rather than a single youth culture including *all* of an age group, there are a variety of youth sub cultures which co-exist at any one time. These are not just the sensational or threatening ones which are described in the mass media but also include the lifestyles of so called "ordinary kids".

Youth sub-cultures

These sub cultures may be influenced by the family background of the youths. Teds, Mods, Rockers and Skinheads have all been associated with working class culture. In the USA delinquent gangs were described as exaggerating working class concerns with masculinity and toughness rather than rebelling against the adult world. The same view might be applied to football hooligans in this country. Young CND members were found to have come from middle class homes where parents shared their views. The Hippies are generally seen as being a middle class youth sub culture.

YOUTH UNEMPLOYMENT

The high rate of youth unemployment has been a major concern of governments. For example, in the UK in 1992 some 18.7% of males aged 16–19 were unemployed compared to 11.5% for all males. For females, some 13.8% aged 16–19 were unemployed compared to 7.2% for all females.

REASONS FOR THE HIGH RATE OF YOUTH UNEMPLOYMENT:

1. **The increased number of school leavers.** The bulge in the birth rate in the 1960s would explain increased competition for jobs from the late 1970s onwards. However the peak of the demographic upturn for school leavers in 1979 did not coincide with the highest levels of youth unemployment in 1982 and 1983.

2. **The increased number of married women seeking employment.** This also provided additional competition for school leavers.

Why youth unemployment is high

3. **High wages.** These were blamed by both economists and politicians, with high wages for job starters taking away any cost advantage in employing school leavers.

4. **New recruits.** These are more vulnerable to unemployment. First, employers respond to falling demand by not employing new staff rather than getting rid of existing workers. Second, there is a tradition of "last in first out" which is favoured by unions and by employers as a means of minimizing redundancy payments.

5. **Extra competition from subsidised labour.** Competition from other youth on training schemes in effect means a new supply of cheap workers lacking normal employment rights. This suggests that some employers may readily accept high labour turnover. Muncie (1984) argued that the Youth Opportunities Programme (YOP) actually encouraged the disappearance of permanent jobs for other young people.

6. **The absence of appropriate skills.** Skill shortages amongst young people has become a political and educational issue. Clarke and Willis (1984) see this as an attempt to blame unemployment on the unemployed themselves and on schools and colleges.

THE EFFECTS OF YOUTH UNEMPLOYMENT

The impact of unemployment on young people and their experience of alternatives to work, such as training schemes, has been widely documented. Youth cannot be regarded as a uniform group and any experience of young people will in turn be influenced by class, race, and gender.

Consequences of youth unemployment

1 Griffin (1985) suggested that girls were more likely to spend their time at home and to find it more difficult to enter the hidden economy than boys. The result of this was their being more likely to be involved in housework and perhaps to see pregnancy as an escape from unpaid domestic labour.

2 Troyna and Smith (1983) have shown the increased likelihood of unemployment amongst ethnic minority youth.

3 Wallace (1986) found that long periods of unemployment lowered the job aspirations of some young people who became willing to settle for any job. Boys retained their desires to be "breadwinners" and girls to be "homemakers".

4 C. Horton (1986) carried out interviews with young people and found that whilst they had a positive attitude to work and realistic aspirations they tended to regard the YTS as providing cheap labour rather than real jobs or useful training. Similar Government research suggested that the young were ill-informed about training schemes and that the problem lay more with the publicity rather than with the training itself.

5 Youth unemployment prevents the transition to adulthood marked by full-time work in "real jobs". The unemployed young and those still in school or training schemes are excluded from a consumerist society because of their "wagelessness".

6 The virtual disappearance of the youth labour market. Very few 16 year old school leavers go directly into work. This was normal in the 1960s.

7 The growth of 16 plus education in schools, VIth Form Colleges and FE Colleges.

8 The growth of a new industry providing training in competition with Colleges.

3 OLD AGE

CAUSES OF AN AGEING POPULATION

An ageing population means that the average age of the population rises, so that the proportion of old people in the total population rises. By the year 2021, nearly one in five of the population will be over 65 – compared to only one in ten in 1951. The following factors have played a part in this trend.

1 *Lower birth rates*
Birth rates have generally fallen this century although there have been baby booms (see chapter 11) This means a reduction in the number and proportion of young people.

2 *Longer life expectancy*
More people survive to old age than was previously the case and the old now tend to live longer. Even during this century, 25 years has been added to life expectancy because of improvements in living standards and to a lesser extent in health care.

3 *Immigration control*
Immigrants tend to be young and of child bearing age, and there is a tendency for some immigrants to have larger families in the first generation. However, compared to the 1950s and 1960s there is now virtually no immigration to the UK and this has taken away one of the factors producing a younger population. It is also the young who are most likely to emigrate.

Why the population is ageing

THE CONSEQUENCES OF AN AGEING POPULATION: THE SOCIAL POSITION OF OLD PEOPLE

Remember: the old are *not* an homogeneous group. They differ in terms of class, gender, ethnicity, health and other characteristics including AGE itself! Class, gender and ethnicity also influence access to resources such as housing, cars, health and general care. In other words the social position of the old is not fixed, it can vary over time and between societies.

Income

There are "two nations" of the elderly:

1 Those dependent on state pensions and benefits, which in the UK in 1993 were the lowest in the EC as a % of average wages.

2 Those with private pensions or savings. Usually this sub-group of the elderly have earned substantial amounts throughout their lives. These are less likely to be women, even though 2/3 of the elderly are women. Women live longer, but retire earlier, with correspondingly smaller occupational pensions even where they have access to these. In fact women dominate part-time employment and so have little access to occupational pensions.

Housing and care

In 1986 only 3% of the elderly were in residential care. During the 1980s there was a shift from state to private provision, which includes profit-making and charitable provision. A DOE study indicated that those elderly living in their own homes wished to stay there. The cost of supporting elderly claimants in residential care has risen from £10m in 1979 to £1,390m in 1990. The estimate for the end of 1992 was as high as £2,000. Old people's homes have been criticised in recent times for lack of privacy and even the physical abuse of residents. There has been a shift in government policy to encourage community care, frequently by unpaid informal carers. As many as 4m old people are cared for in this way, usually by a lone and ageing child.

Problems with an ageing population

Health

The old are often perceived as being unhealthy. They certainly do consume a large and growing proportion of NHS spending. However other age groups also cost more in terms of health care and it is Doctors who spend on the patient's behalf. Perhaps they over diagnose illness and over prescribe for treatments!

Retirement is often seen as a cause of ill health, although the linkage is two-way since it is more likely that the sick have to retire early. Retired old people in the USA are healthier than workers, but perhaps they are richer. Men leaving work may be more likely than women to lose their self esteem and to lose friends.

Dependency

Retirement, whether customary or compulsory, may make the old dependent on the working population. This has been seen as a major problem related to an ageing population. However there has been a tendency to reduce the working population in many ways, such as raising the legal and customary school leaving age, reducing working hours, increasing holidays and lowering retirement ages. So we cannot blame the shrinking working population and its having to support a growing number of old people on the old themselves. This shrinkage of the working population is in part a defensive measure on the part of governments to reduce the problem of unemployment. There are also substantial numbers of potential workers who are unemployed. Different government policies could bring these back into the active labour force.

The proportion of old people working is still falling, despite the fact that the old live longer and are probably more fit for work than in the past. Politicians, judges, doctors, artists and business leaders work when they are old, and there is certainly scope for other groups of elderly to work provided the demand for labour is sufficient and tax incentives exist.

Family life

The old may seem to be a burden on the young who care for them but the old may help the young by providing financial help for children and baby-sitting for grandchildren.

A COMPARISON BETWEEN THE OLD IN SIMPLE SOCIETIES AND MODERN BRITAIN

In simple, pre-industrial societies:

- The old have *high status*.
- They are the heads of family and kin groups.
- Their knowledge and skills do not become obsolete as technological change is slow.
- Knowledge comes from memory, tradition and wisdom.
- The old continue to contribute to valued activities.

In modern industrial societies, such as Britain:

- the old may have *low status*.
- The old tend not to head the family.
- Families are usually nuclear and kin live in separate households. The old frequently live alone, with their partners, with only one of their children or in institutions.
- The knowledge and skills of the old, and everyone else, becomes quickly outdated.
- Knowledge and skills come mainly from education and training rather than experience.
- There tends to be a formal, and often compulsory, retirement age which may force dependency onto the old. The Civil Service introduced compulsory retirement at 60 in 1859 because the workers' "bodily and mental vigour began to decline".

The old in previous times and now

(Critically review this rather stereotyped comparison in the light of the rest of this section on the old. It may be of interest to learn that in some Eskimo cultures the old were expected to wander from the tribe to die rather than be a burden on their kin.)

The beginning of this chapter suggested that age could be seen as a form of *stratification*. In Britain we tend to deal with various social problems associated with age such as child abuse, youth unemployment and retirement. We do not, however, tend to challenge the idea that it is acceptable that age should be a source of inequality.

" . . . and I have attacked this modern variant of the class system root and branch. It will not be possible for very much longer to propose this or that amelioration for the old, or the young, without taking up arms against the ageist society that industrialisation has produced. It was born in Britain and has spread everywhere, our most successful export."

(from M. Young *"Slaves Of Time"* in *New Statesman & Society,* 12.7.91)

As we have seen the State tells us when we have to begin school, when we will be tested at school, and when we can leave. There are laws defining when we can have sexual intercourse, marry, vote, drive, drink, retire, get a bus pass and many other activities.

EXAMINATION QUESTIONS

Q.1   Study ITEM A and ITEM B. Then answer the questions which follow.

ITEM A

A report reveals that parents are increasingly nagged by their children about what the family should buy.

More parents are also listening to their children, respecting their ideas, trying new products that the children suggest, and increasingly treating them as equals.

The report says that, in all social classes, children have the greatest effect on their parents' shopping from the age of five until about eleven or twelve. "At this stage children are old enough to be aware of products and of the power they can exert in determining which ones are bought . . . "

(Adapted from an article in *The Independent,* 1991)

ITEM B

GIRLS REJECT TRADITIONAL DRESS

Muslim girls in Bradford are telling their parents that wearing Western clothes, provided they are loose fitting and not too flashy, is perfectly in keeping with the Koran.

In the stricter Muslim families, where distrust of all things Western tends to be greatest, parents often prefer their daughters to wear the traditional shalwar-kameez.

More and more young Muslim women in Bradford are rejecting Pakistani dress in favour of baggy jeans and sweatshirts.

"We don't have to wear Pakistani dress as long as we are modestly dressed," Sajola Khohker, a university student, said.

(Adapted from an article in *The Independent,* 1991)

a)   Study ITEM A and state
     i) how children try to influence what their parents buy;
     ii) at what age the child's influence on the parents' shopping decreases.

(2 marks)

b)   Study ITEM B and state
     i) in which families do parents prefer their daughters to wear the shalwar-kameez;
     ii) which Western clothes do some Muslim girls say are in keeping with their religion.

(2 marks)

c) Ethnic background may influence the way parents expect their children to dress. Identify and explain two other ways in which ethnicity may influence a child's upbringing. *(4 marks)*

d) Identify and explain two ways in which the Government provides help and support for children in the United Kingdom. *(4 marks)*

e) Why have changes taken place in the relationship between parents and children during the twentieth century? *(8 marks)*

(SEG, June 1993)

Q.2 Study ITEM A and ITEM B. Then answer the questions which follow.

ITEM A

POPULATION

Expectation of life: by sex and age

	Males		Females	
	1906	1986	1906	1986
Expectation of life*	(Years)	(Years)	(Years)	(Years)
At birth	48.0	71.9	51.6	77.6
20 years	42.7	53.1	45.2	58.6
40 years	26.8	34.0	29.1	39.1
60 years	13.4	16.8	14.9	21.2
80 years	4.9	6.0	5.4	7.8

*The additional years which a person at a particular age could expect to live.

(From *Social Trends*)

ITEM B

Two statements by people who have retired:

"Your life's centred on the home. Instead of getting up to work you do what you want: dressmaking, decorating or gardening."

(Ex-manageress)

"When you retire it leaves a sudden gap in your life. One minute you're busy and the next you're on the shelf . . . In my job I met a lot of people, getting to know them. In retirement I miss this . . . "

(Ex-insurance man)

(From *Work and Retirement,* S. Parker, Allen & Unwin)

a) Study **ITEM A** and state
   i) how many years a male born in 1986 can expect to live;
   ii) the number of years by which the expectation of life of 40 year old females has increased between 1906 and 1986. *(2 marks)*

b) Study **ITEM B** and state
   i) what the ex-insurance man says he misses in retirement;
   ii) an advantage of retirement. *(2 marks)*

c) Identify and explain two reasons for the increase in the expectation of life in the United Kingdom during the twentieth century. *(4 marks)*

d) Identify and explain two ways in which the quality of life of a retired person may be influenced by his/her working life. *(4 marks)*

e) Explain the likely social, political and economic effects of the increase in the numbers of elderly people in the United Kingdom during the 1990s. *(8 marks)*

(SEG, June 1993)

Q.3 Study the extract below and then answer the questions which follow.

In every society, age is used as a basis for treating individuals differently. In western cultures, we limit certain activities, such as drinking alcohol, to those over a certain age. Becoming legally an adult depends on reaching a certain age.

In a large number of traditional societies, the moving from one age status to another is marked by various ceremonies, known as rites of passage. Moving from the status of a child to that of an adult is very important. It must be marked by traditional rites. These clearly announce the new status of individuals within their society. There are, of course, many examples of rites of passage to be found in modern industrial societies. We pass through various age-related status positions, such as youth, middle age and old age. At each point, we form bonds with others of a similar age. For example, teenagers form bonds with other teenagers and some young people join youth cultures.

In traditional societies, age is even more important. Among the Nuer people of East Africa, the status of any male depends entirely on the age set to which he belongs. Throughout his life, every Nuer man remains a member of the group of men with whom he was initiated into adulthood. He is always junior to those who became adult members of the society before him and senior to those who followed him.

The age set system is very important. It provides a way of sharing out authority and work. It gives both the young and old clearly defined roles, according to their age. The young men act together in defence of their tribe. Political decision-making is left to their elders, whose physical capabilities no longer allow them to take such an active part in society. It is also a way of providing status, because getting older is the main way of gaining status. In traditional societies, the elderly usually have a much higher status than do the elderly in modern industrial societies.

(Adapted from: D. Morris and P. Marsh, *Tribes,* 1988)

---

a) What is meant by the term culture? *(4 marks)*

b) Give one example of a rite of passage in any modern industrial society *(1 mark)*

c) Using evidence from your own experience and from studies you have read, explain whether or not there is a youth culture in modern industrial societies. *(7 marks)*

d) Name two ways that age sets are important in traditional societies, such as that of the Nuer people. *(2 marks)*

e) Explain why the elderly in traditional societies often have a higher status than elderly people in modern industrial societies. *(6 marks)*

f) The extract shows that people are treated differently because of their age. They can also be treated differently because of social class and ethnic backgrounds. Choose either social class or ethnic background and explain how it can affect a person's life chances. *(10 marks)*

The following is part of a question which deals with age and generation in a question mainly focused on another area of the syllabus.

Q.4 Identify and fully explain one reason why young people form sub-groups or sub-cultures. *(4 marks)*

ANSWERS TO EXAMINATION QUESTIONS

Q.1

a) i)   Nagging. (parent's answer)
      Making suggestions (children's answer)   ONLY ONE REQUIRED.

   ii) After 11 or 12

b) i)   The stricter Muslim families
  ii) Modest clothes which are loose fitting.

c) ■ Gender roles
     There is a greater distinction between the behaviour expected of boys and girls from several ethnic minorities than there is among the majority. There tends to be more restrictions placed on, say, Greek Cypriot or Asian girls than on the majority.

   ■ Religion
     Ethnicity may coincide with religion and children may be brought up with distinct beliefs and practices. Religious observance tends to be greater among ethnic minorities. The children of ethnic minorities learn dietary customs, which may be religious rules about what can be eaten and how it should be prepared.

> 66 Groups and social meaning are important 99

d) ■ Education is compulsory by law for those from 5–16.
     This helps children to learn appropriate behaviour so that they will fit into society. It also prepares children for work by teaching them general skills like reading and even specific skills like typing.

   ■ The Welfare State provides child benefit for all families with children. This is paid, usually to the mother, and helps them to provide food, clothing etc. for children. This universal benefit reaches children more effectively than benefits which have to be claimed and are means tested. The real value of child benefit has fallen since it was introduced.

e)   Families have become smaller. Only 4% of families in 1992 had three or more children. Parents have chosen to limit family size and developments in contraception and liberal abortion laws have made this easier. Parents are able to spend more time and money on fewer children.

       Childhood has become extended, because of raising the school leaving age and increased numbers in post-16 education. This means that children are dependent on parents for longer. The fear of road accidents and attacks on children has reduced children's independence. They are more likely to be supervised by parents than in the past.

       Children are gradually being seen as having rights. Parents are not allowed to abuse or neglect children. Childline is an example of outsiders campaigning for children's rights.

       Gender roles of both parents and children have become less distinct. A growth in the number of working mothers has been a major reason for this. Mothers may be less content to restrict their lives exclusively to child care. The children may be materially better off with working mothers and develop closer relationships with fathers who play a greater role in the home. On the other hand there have been fears about the lack of supervision exercised over children with working mothers. In the 1950s, and perhaps even now, this was used as an argument to keep women at home.

STUDENT'S ANSWER WITH EXAMINER'S COMMENTS

Q.2

a) i)   71.9 years.
   ii) 10 years

4/4 Good

b) i)   Meeting people and getting to know them.
   ii) You can do what you want: dress making, decorating or gardening.

Home or work would do

c) The increase has occurred because of better conditions at home and at work.

Should state comparison with 20th Century more clearly

In the 19th century people died because of their living conditions e.g. many children slept together in one small room and this spread disease.

There are more than 2 reasons identified – better to explain 2 reasons fully

Working conditions were poor. The working class worked very long hours for low pay. Trade unions and the law did not protect workers. People died of overwork and because of dangerous conditions in factories and mines.

Clearly explained, but could be fuller, 4/4

The National Health Service which was introduced in 1948 has increased life expectancy. It gives free health care so everyone can afford to see a doctor. There have been new drugs discovered which save lives.

Pay and security could be explained separately

d) Some people have well paid and secure jobs. They are able to save for their retirement and their jobs provide a pension. They are likely to have more possessions and better houses and probably paid their mortgages.

Low paid and insecure jobs may not give pensions. Some people are unemployed and unable to save or get a pension from their job and have to live on the State pension. Dangerous jobs may lead to ill health in old age e.g. coal miners.

Good comparison made, 4/4 just

e) ■ Social effects – are the increase in elderly people means that more old peoples homes and hospitals will have to be built to meet demand. More leisure activities will need to be provided for the old.
   ■ Political effects – as more voters are elderly Governments will pay more attention to pensions and benefits that the old receive.
   ■ Economic effects – many old people are quite well off they will want more health care, more leisure facilities and this will encourage the economy to grow. The Government might abolish state pensions and just give benefits to the poor.

Repeats 1st para. in places. Has a good range of points, but these are not spread through the social, political and economic effects, 5/8

The working population might have to pay more taxes to support and increased number of old people particularly for health care. This why they are encouraging care in the community.

Good awareness of current debates on ageing population

Overall the student shows a good knowledge of the issues involving age and the Welfare State. 17/20

OUTLINE ANSWERS

Q.3

a) Needs a definition, brief explanation and examples.
b) Could be religious (Christening, Bar mitzvah, wedding), educational (Degree awarding ceremony) work related (getting a gold watch on retirement).

c) You could present three points of view illustrated from personal experience and/or sociological studies. They need not be equally balanced.

1 There is a youth culture based on the emergence of youth as a distinct generation in the 20th century. Mention compulsory schooling, youth unemployment, youth as consumers, youth challenging adult rules etc.

2 There is no distinct youth culture just superficial differences based on fashion and spending habits.

3 There are a variety of youth sub cultures based on gender, class ethnicity, delinquency etc.

d) Refer to last paragraph in the extract. Name two from:
Sharing authority, sharing work, providing status.

e) Compare traditional with modern society using about three of these points:

- Compulsory retirement or taking an active part in society.
- The importance of being head of an extended family.
- Knowledge and skills become out of date or traditional skills are still important.
- The old are seen as, and are made, dependent in modern society. They are not respected and seen as wise.
  You could add a critical note that the elderly (particularly men) do hold positions of power in politics, business, the law etc.
  The old may be getting healthier and richer; this may change their status.

f) This question could be answered after reading the chapters on race and ethnicity or class.

If you choose race you could mention employment, housing, education, legal treatment, or risk of being a victim of crime. To develop these points you can refer to appropriate chapters.

If you choose class you could mention health, education, family life, occupational choice etc.

Q.4 Develop an explanation based on class, ethnicity or gender. Or look at youth as a generation caught between childhood and adulthood. (See chapter 16 for a fuller answer.)

REVIEW SHEET

In this, and the following Review Sheets, you can often check back to the text in the chapter to see if you have answered correctly.

List, and briefly explain, 3 different views of the role of children in the family.

1 _____

2 _____

3 _____

Outline 4 factors which might be involved in bringing about the observed rise in children being abused.

1 _____

2 _____

3 _____

4 _____

What reasons might explain the rise of youth cultures?

1 _____

2 _____

3 _____

4 _____

How might you explain a rise in youth unemployment?

1 _____

2 _____

3 _____

4 _____

5 _____

What factors might explain a rise in the proportion of old people in a country?

1 _____

2 _____

3 _____

What consequences might follow from an ageing population?

1 _____

2 _____

3 _____

Look again at Item A in Question 2. How many extra years could each of the following expect to live?

1 A male who is 20 years old _____

2 A male who is 60 years old _____

3 A female who is 40 years old _____

Using the same data, at what age would you expect each of the following to die?

1 A male who is now 40 years old _____

2 A female who is now 20 years old _____

3 A female who is now 60 years old _____

Comment on any differences you can observe from this table on male and female life expectancy

_____

_____

_____

Look carefully at the following Table.

Age and sex structure of the population

United Kingdom						Percentages and millions
	Under 16	% 16–39	40–64	65–79	80 and over	All ages (= 100%) (millions)
Mid-year estimates						
1951	–	–	31.6	9.5	1.4	50.3
1961	24.8	31.4	32.0	9.8	1.9	52.8
1971	25.6	31.3	29.9	10.9	2.3	55.9
1981	22.2	34.9	27.8	12.2	2.8	56.4
1991	20.3	35.2	28.7	12.0	3.7	57.6
Males	21.4	36.5	29.1	10.7	2.3	28.1
Females	19.3	34.0	28.3	13.3	5.1	29.5
Mid-year projections						
2001	021.3	32.6	30.5	11.4	4.2	59.2
2011	20.1	30.0	33.7	11.7	4.5	60.0
2021	19.5	30.5	31.9	13.6	4.5	60.7
Males	20.2	31.6	32.1	12.7	3.4	30.0
Females	18.7	29.5	31.6	14.5	5.7	30.7

(Social Trends, 1993)

Use the table (i.e. find statistics) to show the following.

1 An ageing population in the UK since 1951

_____

_____

2 Females live longer than males

_____

_____

3 A rising population for the UK over time

_____

_____

4 More females than males in the UK in 1991

_____

_____

5 More female than male elderly in 1991

_____

_____

6 More male than female youth in 1991

_____

_____

CHAPTER 3

GENDER

GENDER, SEX AND SEXUALITY

WOMEN AT WORK

HOUSEWORK

GETTING STARTED

Gender differences are obvious without studying sociology. However, sociology has, in the last 20 years or so, begun to examine more closely the relationship between men and women instead of seeing it as just a "natural" relationship that is biologically determined.

Sociology has tended to concentrate on gender inequality rather than gender differences. The feminist view that men oppress women has been increasingly accepted by sociologists. Class differences have been regarded for a long time as helping to explain the distribution of power and rewards in society. Feminists see gender differences as being at least as important as class differences in this respect. The sociology of gender is mostly the sociology of women and femininity although the study of masculinity is slowly developing.

The main areas of interest, and likely themes of examination questions, are:

- SEX, GENDER AND SEXUALITY
- HOUSEWORK
- WOMEN AT WORK.

Gender differences and particularly inequality must be examined throughout the syllabus, for example in the study of education, deviance, poverty and in particular the sociology of the family.

DEFINITIONS

SEX. This refers to the biological differences between male and female.

GENDER. This refers to the socially defined differences between men and women.

SEXUALITY. Refers to desires, needs and behaviour which are seen as specifically sexual in nature.

PATRIARCHY. The power relationship by which men dominate women.

STEREOTYPES. An over-simplified view that everyone in a particular group will conform to a particular (often inaccurate) pattern of behaviour.

1 > GENDER, SEX, AND SEXUALITY

" Natural differences! "

ESSENTIAL PRINCIPLES

These terms are defined at the beginning of this chapter. Sociologists are concerned with the relationship between gender, and sex and sexuality. This means they are interested in how biology influences social behaviour.

The main aspects of gender roles which appear to be influenced strongly by *biological* differences include aggressiveness, sexuality and of course motherhood. Nevertheless most sociologists now reject the view that gender roles are largely the result of biological differences between men and women. However the idea that differences between men and women are natural remains a powerful influence on the relationships between men and women. If behaviour is seen as "natural" then it is likely to be seen as *normal* and *desirable* and those who do not conform to expectations can expect disapproval. Furthermore, if gender differences are thought to be natural, then they could be regarded as unchangeable.

Some sociologists see gender differences as serving the interests of the whole society: e.g. the mother role ensures the effective upbringing of children. Feminists, however, see conventional gender roles as helping to maintain the domination of society by men. They see the roles as not just different but unequal.

Simple societies have been crudely portrayed as all presenting the same model of women caring for children at home whilst men go out to hunt, wage war or engage in some other aggressive activity. Even if this were an accurate view, and anthropology demonstrates that it is not, it has little relevance to modern industrial societies where most work requires little physical strength or aggression: e.g. teaching sociology is done equally well by men or women!

The history of the last two hundred years shows that being female did not spare peasant women from hard work in the fields or working class women from the 70-hour-week in factories and mines. Children have also only recently been seen as being frail and in need of protection.

War-time conscription of (unmarried) women reminded them that they were quite capable of performing most "masculine" work roles; e.g. the Queen trained as a motor mechanic. Although most women returned to more conventional roles at the end of the Second World War there are now virtually no roles which are denied to women on the grounds of biology alone. The Gulf War in 1991 saw a high proportion of women in the military units from Western nations and some served in front line roles.

LEARNING GENDER ROLES

Gender roles are learned from an early age.

" How gender roles are learned "

■ The family

In the *family* parents and other children act as role models to be copied. Parents also treat boys and girls differently. The details of upbringing depend in part upon class and ethnicity. Some cultures emphasise gender differences more, or at different ages, than do other cultures.

■ Peers

Children also learn from their *peers*. Feminist parents who deliberately blur gender division in the home are often surprised how quickly their children conform to conventional views of gender learned at playgroups and nurseries even before school.

■ Schools

Schools reinforce gender roles and create new ones, such as the suitability of some subjects and activities for boys or girls. Teachers and other pupils play an active part in this process. Reading schemes, text books and even examination questions have all been identified as reinforcing gender stereotypes.

■ The workplace

The workplace both reflects and reinforces traditional gender roles. Secretarial work has been described as "the business equivalent of housework". However relationships at work can also help to undermine pre-conceptions in situations where men and women work together or where women have leadership roles.

■ The mass media

The mass media of television, radio, newspapers, magazines, etc. both reinforce and challenge gender roles. Women in positions of power are available as role models for girls and many challenges to rigidly defined gender roles are publicised. Women writers have created a number of active heroic women who challenge the subordinate roles traditionally given to women. There has been interesting research on these challenges to women stereotypes in both Women's magazines and teenage romantic magazines, as well as analysis of the roles of women on TV.

■ Religious organisations

These have been seen as having very traditional views which help to continue the oppression of women. These views have been challenged, as have men's domination of important religious roles. Women clergy are found in some denominations of both Judaism and Christianity, although in both religions the opposition to women in such roles continues.

SEXUALITY

Both male and female sexuality are seen as being biologically influenced. However they are perceived rather differently:

"Male sexuality is seen as a force or natural energy that seeks release . . . It is a bit like a missile; once launched there is no stopping it – and launching is the arousal stage"

66 Male versus Female sexuality 99

While female sexuality is seen as:

" . . . Passive . . . submissive associated with motherhood and reproduction"

(S. Lees 1986)

However Lees also points out that sexuality is used to divide females into the virtuous and respectable and the impure and threatening. The former are potential wives, whereas although the latter can be used to gratify men, they are often regarded as worthy of contempt, not just by men but also by women.

If this sounds rather like a melodramatic Victorian novel, it is worth reading Lees in order to realise that she is actually writing about teenage girls in the 1980s. She shows how language such as "slag" and "slut" is used to describe not only girls who are sexually active but also those *said* by boys or other girls to be sexually active, or to describe girls who have not yet established themselves as "drags" who reject the boys attentions. The way to make female sexuality acceptable seems to be to link it with love and marriage. The choices then appear to be separation from boys or a regular boyfriend. If separation is chosen, then the girl can be described as a "drag" or "frigid". Girls tend to deny the accusations that they are "slags" but seem not to question the right of boys and other girls to make such judgements. On the other

66 Use of hostile language 99

hand there are no obvious words which can be used to disapprove of sexually active males or to approve of sexually active females.

The use of this hostile language acts as a form of social control. Girls must be careful, not just about their behaviour with boys but also about their dress, their friendships with boys and girls, and where they choose to go out.

The wider social effects of this view of women's sexuality documented by Lees involve the way it is used to control and oppress women. Rape, fear of rape and the use of hostile language can all be seen as limiting the freedom of women and encouraging them to seek the protection of marriage. Women are much more likely than men to avoid going out to certain places, especially at night, or to avoid using public transport.

It should be noted that in other cultures men may also take precautions to avoid sexual attacks by women. In this country, males in children's homes and prisons may fear sexual attacks from other males. There have also been recent police and press reports of sexual attacks on men in trains, but this does not seem to have led to cautious behaviour from men.

Some critics of modern feminism have argued that, by emphasising the risks of "date rape" and marital rape, they are portraying all men as potential rapists and perhaps reinforcing the old Victorian view that women are helpless.

MASCULINITY

Early feminist sociology protested that women had been neglected in traditional sociological research. They tended to be ignored all together or perhaps treated as a special case. Masculine behaviour was seen as normal and feminine behaviour a variation which needed explanation. Even talking about feminist sociology, where women research women's issues from a women's point of view, suggests that it is a special approach different from "normal" sociology. We do not talk about "masculinist" sociology – it is just sociology.

The study of men and masculinity is very underdeveloped. Masculinity may disadvantage men just as femininity disadvantages women. Certainly studying masculinity helps us to understand how men may oppress women. Men's aggression, sexuality and even violence is sometimes used to dominate women (and other men).

Masculinity has been used to explain the development of crime. Young men learn about being "sharp" and "hard" in sub-cultures (see ch 14). This masculine behaviour limits the activities of girls as well as boys. Friendship between the sexes is discouraged and feminine behaviour in boys is the subject of ridicule.

⁶⁶ Disadvantages of masculinity ⁹⁹

Men learn not to show emotion or weakness. This may make it difficult for them to develop relationships with families and may lead them to deny ill health and thus put off getting treatment. Women are more generally willing to discuss their bodies and to seek medical help.

Being called a "slag" indicates disapproval of female sexuality. Male sexuality is celebrated and is a way of demonstrating manhood. Disapproval is reserved for real or imagined homosexuality. The supposed association of homosexuality with femininity is used by some men to insult both women and homosexual men.

2 ▷ WOMEN AT WORK

GENDER AND EMPLOYMENT

In the past, most sociologists studied women as family members and men as workers. Early studies of married women workers saw work as interfering with the women's primary role in the family. Only later did feminists emphasise the other side of the coin, namely how family responsibilities disadvantaged women in the job market.

Men's roles in the family may also influence their choice of job and attitude to work. They are expected to be the main breadwinner and may be prepared to spend their lives in unsatisfying jobs in order to provide for their families. This instrumental attitude to work is described in Goldthorpe and Lockwood et al.'s study of "Affluent workers" in Luton (see chapters 5 and 9).

Women's employment as a social problem

In other times and cultures it has been regarded as absolutely normal that women work. But the employment of women has been seen as a "problem" throughout the twentieth century. The nature of the problem varies according to who is looking at it:

■ *Men* may see women as rivals who may force down their wages by being prepared to work for less or even to take "their" jobs.

⁶⁶ Seeing problems with female employment ⁹⁹

■ *Employers* may see married women as solving the problem of a shortage of labour, particularly where there is a pool of skilled and qualified women at home. Both teachers and nurses have been attracted back into the labour force by advertising campaigns and by more practical help, such as re-training, flexible hours and subsidised child care.

■ *Traditional thinkers* in Government and elsewhere have emphasised the need for women to be at home, caring for children, in order to minimise the risk of family breakdown, welfare dependence and juvenile delinquency.

TRENDS IN WOMEN'S EMPLOYMENT

1. More women work

The proportion of the labour force who are female workers has risen from 37% (1971) to 41% (1981) to 45% (1991). Women have increased their actual numbers as well as their proportion in the labour market, despite high male employment during the 1980s. The main increase has come from the employment of mothers.

2. Women work in different jobs from men

Recent trends in female work ●●

There is a gendered labour market. Women are concentrated in relatively few areas of employment and some jobs are overwhelmingly female, e.g. clerical, caring, cooking and cleaning. In 1985 (New Earnings Survey) 70% of full-time women workers were concentrated in just three types of employment. These were:

■ Clerical work (70% of these workers are women).
■ Education, Health and Welfare (again 70% are women).
■ Personal services (76% of whom are women).

3. Women are in lower levels of employment than men

As well as being found in different jobs, women tend to be concentrated in the lower levels of employment. For example, even the "feminine" professions such as teaching and nursing have disproportionate numbers of men in administrative and managerial roles. Again, in 1991 as many as 63% of bank employees were women, but (according to the Bankers union) only some 5% were managers. The banks own estimate is that 10% to 20% of women were managers – but even this would be a very small proportion compared to the overall employment of women in banks.

4. Women are more likely to be in ''middle-class'' jobs than men

67% of women, compared to 47% of men, are in non-manual occupations. They are, however, less likely to be in the highest ranking group of non-manual jobs, that is in those categorized as "managerial and professional".

5. Women have in recent times gained greater access to ''men's jobs'' and to higher levels of all jobs

Equal opportunities legislation has certainly not been an unqualified success and there remain many powerful and well-paid jobs where women are grossly under-represented or have yet to penetrate at all. However there are many signs of progress in women's struggle for equality. While full-time women earned, on average, only 64% of male hourly earnings in 1970, by 1993 this proportion had risen to 74%, though there is clearly scope for still greater equality.

6. Women and part-time work

Part-time work is largely undertaken in the UK by women. The proportions of employed men and women in part-time work are 3% and 39% respectively. Part-time work tends to be less well paid and less secure than full-time work. Although the figures are much less reliable, it appears that home working is also largely a female form of work done for male employers and often for very low pay. Both part-time work and home working fit in more easily with family responsibilities.

Women and the professions

Women tend to be found in the lower professions, such as nursing and teaching, whereas men tend to be found in the higher professions, such as the law, medicine, accountancy, architecture and engineering.

Within a given profession, men tend to rise higher than women. Male doctors are more often consultants and male lawyers more often Judges. Similarly, men disproportionately fill the managerial roles even in the traditionally "female" professions such as teaching.

Single or divorced women are often more successful in the professions than married women but married men do better than single men.

On the more positive side, increasing numbers of women are entering the professions and small numbers are reaching top positions.

Women and Trade Unions

One explanation of the disadvantages experienced in the labour market by women is the failure of the male dominated trade-union movement to defend their interests. In fact a case can be made that the unions have actively sought to exclude women from particular jobs and even from the work force in general. Women are less likely to be in unions than men and much less likely to be active members or leaders.

Ethnicity and employment

In 1990, the figures for being "economically active", i.e. working or being unemployed and seeking work, were:

"White women" 69%
"West Indian women" 73%
"Asian women" 58%

These simplified figures conceal significant differences *within* groups. For example within "Asian women" only 20% of "Pakistani/Bangladeshi" women are economically active, compared with higher figures for other sub-groups such as "Indian" and "African Asian".

Differences within ethnic groups

Further differences emerge if we compare the proportions of ethnic groups in part-time rather than full-time work. For example, only 15% of West Indian women, compared to 25% of white women, are in part-time work.

Recorded unemployment is higher among certain ethnic groups, such as West Indian women. This suggests not just the existence of racial disadvantage in gaining and retaining jobs but also a greater desire or need to be in full-time work on the part of West Indian women. It is only because they have registered as seeking work that they are included in the unemployment figures.

Differences between ethnic groups

On the other hand, Pakistani and Bangladeshi women of all ages are more likely than other ethnic groups to be regarded as economically *inactive* (not unemployed) because they are looking after the house and family. This applies to 42% of 16–24 year old Bangladeshi women compared to 12% of all 16–24 year olds. (Employment Gazette 1991)

West Indian and Guyanese women are most likely to be in managerial and professional jobs (31%) but are also most likely to be in manual jobs (37% compared to 32% for all women).

EXPLANATIONS FOR WOMEN'S INEQUALITY AT WORK

Women are a reserve army of labour

Marxists use this term to argue that women are available for work when required by employers but are not seen as being entitled to work. During war-time women were encouraged to perform a wide range of work roles but during peace-time recessions they have often been persuaded that they should be looking after their families.

A gendered labour market

Women do different jobs from men. They have been socialised to see some jobs as being more suitable for women. Schools may still encourage this view and, despite the law, discrimination against women continues. However if women do perform different jobs from men and if women's employment has risen while men's *unemployment* has risen, then it is difficult to see women as a reserve army of labour.

Home and family life

Why women face inequality at work

Women's responsibilities for child care and housework limits the types of jobs they can do. This applies mostly to wives and mothers but it can also affect the job chances of daughters who might be persuaded to leave school early and not to work in order to look after younger children or men in the family.

Family commitments often encourage women to take up part-time work. However it could be that this type of work is a desirable choice for some women.

Child care is difficult to find and expensive. Women are campaigning for tax relief on child care expenses and for subsidised or free child care to allow them to work. This might allow women who are trapped into benefit dependency to move into work.

3 > HOUSEWORK

Most students, particularly females, will be all-too-familiar with doing housework. However, if you are new to sociology you might be surprised at how much attention is paid to housework by sociologists. When A. Oakley published *The Sociology of Housework* in 1974, few people anticipated that it would become a central interest for many feminist writers.

66 Importance of housework 99

The importance of housework lies in its relationship with various roles within the family. For instance it indicates the nature of both marital and parent child roles. It also affects women's and men's lives outside the home, particularly at work.

Housework, seen as a separate activity conducted by non-employed married women at home, has a fairly recent history – it is not a "natural" activity for women. Oakley wrote that the housewife-role developed during the industrial revolution when children, and later mothers, were increasingly excluded from the factory by law and by the need to care for children. Housework has become women's main activity and it remains a largely feminine responsibility, regardless of ethnicity or class. However higher class women may employ other women to do this work for them.

The fact that women are *employed* to do housework and to care for children and others is a reminder that housework is *real* work. This is a central belief of feminist writers. Housework may be renamed "domestic labour" to make this point. Oakley recorded how her subjects described housework in similar terms to those used by factory workers when describing their jobs. Although it had the same features of being monotonous and unsatisfying it lacked the compensation of pay. Further, housework does not provide sick pay or pension and there are no paid holidays. In fact holidays may increase, rather than remove, a woman's responsibilities as she has to prepare to go and may even go on a self-catering (i.e. woman catering) holiday.

Oakley argued that labour-saving devices did not lighten the woman's burden but just raised the standards of cooking and cleaning demanded by her family. She also saw no reduction in the hours spent doing housework although working hours in paid employment have been reduced.

Some feminist writers have not only argued that housework is real work but also that women doing it are exploited by men. They describe the relationship between men and women in the same way that Marxists describe the exploitation of the working class by the Capitalists. Delphy wrote that men owned the domestic means of production (the house, washing machine and oven) and women operated the machines in the interests of men. Housework was real productive work where food was processed and served and clothes cleaned.

Men are seen as consuming more than their share of household production. In some traditional working class households, women served men food and waited for them to finish eating before sitting and eating what remained.

Society in general (or men, or the ruling class) benefits from the free care women provide for children, the old, the sick and those with disabilities. Any attempts to reduce spending on the Welfare State is likely to increase the burden on women as unpaid carers.

EXAMINATION QUESTIONS

Q.1 Read ITEM A and ITEM B. Then answer the questions which follow.

ITEM A

Sue Sharpe's study of a group of working class girls in London, "Just Like a Girl: How Girls Learn to be Women" (1976), showed that, for many girls, how they looked, dressed and related to boyfriends were more important to them than how they got on at school. They looked forward to leaving school and getting a job to earn money.

The education and class system acted against these particular girls because they were both female and working class. These girls had taken on a self-image that had very little to do with success in school. They had grown up with the view that love, marriage and having children were more important.

ITEM B

SCHOOL LEAVERS' QUALIFICATIONS, ENGLAND AND WALES

SET OF EXAMINATION RESULTS	1975/76		1985/86	
	Boys	Girls	Boys	Girls
2 or more "A" Level passes	16%	12%	14%	15%
5 or more GCE "O" Level (A–C Grades)	5%	7%	9%	11%
1–4 GCE "O" Level (A–C Grades)	25%	28%	25%	30%
No graded results	18%	17%	12%	6%

(Source: adapted from *Social Trends*, 1987)

a) According to ITEM A, how did the girls in Sue Sharpe's study see themselves and their future lives? *(2 marks)*

b) Study ITEM B and state:
   i) the percentage of girls who gained 2 or more "A" Level passes in 1975/76;
   ii) the percentage of girls who gained 1–4 GCE "O" Level (A–C Grades) in 1985/86. *(2 marks)*

c) Identify and explain two reasons why girls have achieved more academic success since Sue Sharpe's study was published. *(4 marks)*

d) Explain, with an example of each, the difference between "sex" and "gender". *(4 marks)*

e) Why are women less likely than men to become top managers? *(8 marks)*

(SEG, June 1989)

Q.2 Look at ITEM A and ITEM B. Then answer the questions which follow.

ITEM A

Source: *Best Magazine,* 16.2.1990

a) Study ITEM A and state two ways in which it seems to show traditional gender roles. *(2 marks)*

b) Study ITEM B. Identify and explain how science may have led to fewer gender role divisions in the kitchen. *(2 marks)*

c) Identify and explain two reasons why women are more likely to have part-time jobs than men. *(4 marks)*

d) Identify and explain two reasons why more women have found paid full-time employment outside the home in the United Kingdom during the last thirty years. *(4 marks)*

e) How has the increased number of married women in paid employment outside the home affected family life within the home during the last thirty years? *(8 marks)*

(SEG, June 1991)

Q.3 Socialisation, Culture and The Individual

"During the present century there have been widespread changes in social conditions and attitudes affecting both men and women".

(Social Trends, HMSO)

Can you think of a word which means "The Perfect Woman"?'

a) Using examples, explain what sociologists mean by GENDER. [4]
b) In what ways may education influence the development of female and male stereotypes? [7]
c) How have the roles of women and men changed during this century? Explain why this has happened. [9]

(MEG, June 1992)

Q.4 Study the extract below which refers to "conflicting demands" on women.

i) Name two of these conflicting demands. *(2 marks)*
ii) Explain how these demands can conflict. *(4 marks)*
iii) Explain why marriage for men might be seen as helpful to a career. *(4 marks)*

> The conflicting demands of home and career have a strong influence on the promotion prospects of women and are among the major factors which make them stop working. Marriage and children conflict with careers for many women. In contrast, marriage for men is generally seen as helpful to a career.

(NEAB, June 1991)

ANSWERS TO EXAMINATION QUESTIONS

Q.1

a) As girl friends and prospectives wives and mothers. They look forward to leaving school to get a job for money not a career.

b) (i) 12% (ii) 30%

c) Develop any two of these or other relevant points.
- National curriculum requires girls to continue taking maths and sciences. This leads to more success as these subjects are necessary for access to some higher education courses or jobs.
- Girls appear to do better at coursework and this was important in GCSE. (The marks for coursework are to be restricted it will be interesting to see how this affects girls' performance.)
- Teachers, parents and girls themselves have become more aware of equal opportunities.
- More successful female role models. Increased participation of women in the job market.
- Youth unemployment has encouraged more girls to stay on at school and go into FE and HE.

d)
- Sex describes biological differences e.g. women can have babies and men cannot.
- Gender describes culture differences between men and women (i.e. what society expects) e.g. women in the 1950s generally gave up work when they had children now they are less likely to do so. Men do not usually accept major responsibility for child care. (Choose your own examples.)

e) Explain and discuss 3 or 4 of the following or other relevant points:
- Discrimination. "Old boys" network. Stereotypical views of women's roles and managers' roles.
- Motherhood interrupts careers.
- Women are socialised to conform rather than lead.
- Lower aspirations. Different aspirations – able women may prefer the professions.
- It takes time for the new generation of well educated and ambitious women to reach the top.

Q.2

a) The girls are playing housewives whereas the boy is playing in a more physical and adventurous way.

b) Convenience pre-prepared foods have de-skilled cooking and made the preparation of meals quicker. Men are now able and willing to produce meals. Labour saving appliances like dishwashers reduce the time women must spend in the kitchen and may make men more willing to help.

c) Women may prefer part-time jobs as they can fit in with domestic responsibilities such as child care. Men tend not to be seen as having the primary responsibility for child care or housework and thus are available for full-time work.

Men are still expected to be the main breadwinner in a household and earn sufficient to support themselves and most of their family needs. Whereas women are still, often mistakenly, seen as secondary breadwinners who work for "extras".

(Men may do part-time work in addition to rather than instead of full-time jobs.)

d) Family breakdown or the fear of it has increased women's desire and need to be economically independent and be able to support herself and children. During the last 30 years the chances of marital breakdown have increased.

Attitudes have changed for both men and women so that women now expect work outside the home and it has become more acceptable to have children.

e) Paid employment improves women's "role bargaining" position in the home. They are likely to have a greater say in decisions. They also have a feeling of independence which if the marriage is faltering may encourage them to see separation as a solution. Women initiate most divorces and the divorce rate is rising.

Men are slowly beginning to participate more in domestic duties. There is little evidence of an equal division of labour. Studies showed that although unemployed men do not do more housework, if their wives are in full-time they do. Although neither husbands or wives may like such an arrangement.

Children tend to spare more time at home than in the past. Parents fear traffic and attacks on their children. If mothers are at home less or are busier when they are at home, children are likely to spend more time watching TV and playing video games.

Women working after they have had children prevents many families from falling into poverty and means others are much more prosperous than was the case in the past.

(You could also mention effects on the extended family, and on the parent-child relationship. Children may see less of mothers but more of fathers or other carers, such as grandparents.)

STUDENT'S ANSWER WITH EXAMINER'S COMMENTS

Q.3

Time allowed 30 minutes

a) Using examples, explain what sociologists mean by GENDER (4)

Gender is the term given to distinguish the female and male. A gender role is the role played by the male or female in society. Sociologists use the word gender instead of sex to define male and female.

Needs to distinguish gender from sex: needs example

2/4

b) In what ways may education influence the development of female and male stereotypes? (7)

Education influences the development of male and female stereotypes because it is where you first learn how to behave around other people.

Primary socialisation just helps to start the individual off. It is when they reach school that the real education of *living in society* is put into action. When you have to interact with other people and learn to get along with them.

When you are reading books and watching others you learn how to behave; you learn what women should do and you conform to what others do and what is expected of you.

Except for family and media

Good; you are judged by society's values, not family ones

Needs to mention formal and hidden curriculum

The answer concentrates on socialisation rather than gender stereotypes; 4/7

c) How have the roles of women and men changed during this century? Explain why this has happened. (9)

The roles of men and women have changed over this century. Instead of the women staying at home and cooking the dinner, having children and having to look after them, women have gone back to work in the offices and with the public.

The men in society have started to accept the fact that women are equal to them, women have made a stand and now even men stay at home and look after the children.

What has happened is that women and men have realised that they are the same and they can both do the same things and should have the same opportunities. Girls no longer do just what they are told they have realised they can do what they want.

More girls are staying on at school to obtain higher education and more are going for higher paid and higher status jobs. Many no longer wish to stay at home and they don't have to.

This answer describes how rather than explains why. A better answer might mention class differences both now and in the past. Could mention changes in the occupational structure and in demography. The answer is rather general and lacks depth. 4/9

Q.4

i) Home and career may make conflicting demands on women.

ii) Marriage and motherhood are roles which may dominate a woman's life. She will need maternity leave from work and continues to have responsibility for child care even if someone else shares the actual task. Care or sick children presents a particular problem as schools and child minders are unwilling to look after sick children.

Employers may want workers to work flexible (for the employer) hours which may interfere with child care. It may be necessary for a woman to move home and lose her job and interrupt her career development to follow her husband's career. She may have to forgo promotion herself if it requires moving and her husband and family wish to stay where they are.

iii) Wives may support their husbands' work by providing secretarial, reception and hostess services. Doctors' wives frequently provide telephone services and even assess patients' needs. Managers' wives may entertain clients and colleagues at home or accompany husbands eating out.

Farmers' wives and workers in other family businesses may play a major work role and are more committed and cheaper than employing others.

Marriage makes men appear more conventional and respectable. Footballers are encouraged to marry young to keep them out of trouble. Marriage suggests than men are not homosexual and removes a possible reason for discrimination. Wives provide men with emotional support that helps them to deal with work induced stress.

REVIEW SHEET

Explain the difference between sex and gender

_____

_____

List, and briefly explain, the factors which cause gender roles to be learned from an early age.

1 _____

2 _____

3 _____

4 _____

5 _____

What does Lees, in her study of teenage girls see as one of the uses of hostile language?

_____

_____

List two *disadvantages* of masculine behaviour.

1 _____

2 _____

How might the following groups see women's employment as a "problem"?

1 men   _____

2 employers   _____

3 traditionalists _____

List 3 trends in women's employment patterns in recent years.

1 _____

2 _____

3 _____

Briefly explain the *feminist* view of housework.

_____

_____

Look again at the table in Item B of Question 1, then answer these questions.

1 Find evidence from the table to show that girls have improved their performance over the 10 years.

_____

_____

_____

2 Find evidence from the table to help you compare the performance of boys with girls. What does this evidence suggest?

_____

_____

_____

Look carefully at the following table on part-time employment, then answer the following questions.

Reasons for taking a part-time job: by sex and marital status, Spring 1992

United Kingdom		Percentages and thousands		
		Females		
			Non-	All
	Males	Married	married	females
Reasons for taking part-time job (percentages)				
Student/still at school	32.8	0.4	31.1	7.1
ill or disabled	3.4	1.2	1.7	1.3
Could not find a full-time job	22.4	6.5	17.0	8.8
Did not want a full-time job	40.7	91.7	50.0	82.6
Part-time workers (= 100%) (thousands)	885	3,972	1,109	5,081

(Social Trends, 1993)

1 Use the figures in the table to compare female part-time employment with that of males.

_____

_____

_____

_____

2 Use the figures from the table to identify the main reason for females working part-time.

_____

_____

_____

_____

3 Using the figures from the table, do males or females have most difficulty in finding a job?

_____

_____

_____

_____

GETTING STARTED

Most sociological studies of race and ethnicity concentrate on inequality and conflict, and regard race as a social problem. There is, however, the possibility of discussing ethnic similarities and differences rather than just concentrating on the 'bad news'. This chapter will concentrate on inequality but if you are interested in *ethnic diversity* this is considered in the Family chapter (ch 7). You could also look at the relationship between ethnicity and religious belief and practice. Britain is a multi-cultural society with a variety of ethnic minorities. The size and geographical distribution of minorities is discussed in the population chapter (ch 11).

Some syllabuses treat race and ethnicity as a separate topic; others treat race and ethnicity as a form of inequality which exists in many aspects of social life and thus the topic is considered in different parts of the syllabus. In Britain the discussion of race relations is closely related to the issue of immigration. Immigration itself is discussed later, in the population chapter.

The main themes of questions typically set on this topic are:

■ DESCRIBING AND EXPLAINING ETHNIC DISADVANTAGE IN THE FIELDS OF HOUSING, EMPLOYMENT AND EDUCATION.
■ EXAMINING THE REPRESENTATION OF MINORITIES IN THE MEDIA.
■ COMPARING THE EXPERIENCE OF ETHNIC MINORITIES WITH OTHER DISADVANTAGED GROUPS SUCH AS WOMEN.

DEFINITIONS

RACE. This refers to real or perceived biological differences which are given a social meaning, e.g. skin colour.
ETHNICITY. This refers to a distinctive cultural identity accepted by the group themselves and/or attributed to them by others. It is often defined by religion and language as well as by place of origin.
RACISM. Racism usually refers to a hostile attitude or prejudice against an ethnic group. Marxists use the term to describe practices and social institutions as well as beliefs in inferiority.
RACIAL DISCRIMINATION. This is behaviour which treats ethnic minorities unfairly.

RELATED TOPICS include all those where there is evidence of disadvantage such as work, education, media, and deviance. Race and ethnicity are central issues in the study of development and stratification. Discussions of immigration need to include some consideration of race and vice versa.

Remember not to write about ethnic minorities as if they are a single group who all share the same experiences. Different ethnic groups have distinct lives and *within* any single ethnic group, age, gender and class may affect experiences.

ESSENTIAL PRINCIPLES

1 > RACE AND BIOLOGY

Humans are a single species. Biologists use the term *race* to describe a sub-group of a species of plants or animals with distinct characteristics. There are visible physical differences between human populations and these have been used to classify people into broad categories. These different races were still listed in some atlases and geography books in the 1980s. This crude division into usually three broad racial groups has little biological foundation and even less value to sociologists.

Societies give a social meaning to some real or imagined biological differences. In particular skin colour has been used as the basis for dividing populations and treating people unequally. In other chapters you can see how age and gender inequality is also often justified by referring to biological differences.

The modern science of genetics makes past scientific support for racial inequality seem ridiculous, if it were not for the tragic consequences of such misapplied "science". Skin colour is determined by fewer than 10 of the 50,000 genes which make up a human being, yet it has been seen as the basis for distinct "races".

In the nineteenth century, Darwin's theory of evolution was used to justify imperialism. Western colonial powers, like Britain and France, saw themselves as civilising (or destroying) "inferior" races. In 1906 the Bronx zoo in New York exhibited an African pygmy in the same cage as a chimpanzee; public protest was more concerned with the claim that men shared ancestors with apes than with the treatment of the pygmy. In the twentieth century, the doctrine of racial purity and superiority has led to the mass murder of Jews, Gypsies, Eastern Europeans, the disabled and others.

Scientists, themselves, shared and supported these odd views, some of which persist today. There is a continuing debate about the relative importance of genetic and environmental influences on intelligence. The debate often focuses on differences between groups who are seen as socially unequal, rather than on the differences between individuals each of whom inherits a unique set of genes.

💬💬 Little scientific support for race 💬💬

2 > ETHNICITY AND SOCIAL INEQUALITY

It is clear that the ideology of racial difference, however unsupported by scientific data, has real consequences for societies where racial inequality occurs. Conflict and inequality based on race or ethnicity can also occur when the signs of difference are much less visible than skin colour. Language, religion, nationality, tribe of origin and way of life can all be the basis of discrimination and hostility. For example, the distinctiveness of Gypsies is based on their travelling way of life, while Kurds have a different language from their neighbours.

The apartheid system in South Africa, which is slowly being dismantled, was based on alleged racial differences between a whole variety of ethnic groups. It was enforced not by biologists but by policemen using a system of passes and identity cards. The white population reserved for itself the positions of political power and the highest economic rewards.

Northern Ireland illustrates the way in which rewards can be distributed unequally on the basis of religion. Outsiders may not recognise who is Catholic or Protestant but employers and gunmen can. The signs include names and addresses, as well as church attendance and religious beliefs. In 1993 a government report on Northern Ireland indicated that Catholics were disadvantaged compared to Protestants in the fields of education, housing and above all jobs. Whereas Protestants have one of the lowest jobless rates in the UK, Catholics have by far the highest. Catholics are also underrepresented in higher status jobs. The position of men is worse than that of women. Protestant leaders however argue that the British government provides the Catholics with an unfair proportion of aid. All this despite the fact that Northern Ireland has had its own anti-discrimination laws for more than twenty years.

💬💬 Applications of racial ideologies 💬💬

3 > ETHNICITY AND EMPLOYMENT

1. A complicated picture

Race, age, gender and disability are all associated with differences and inequalities in employment and unemployment. Many writers have pointed out the difficulties of disentangling the web of disadvantage experienced by individuals who have not just one, but several of these characteristics.

Differences between and within ethnic groups

Westwood (1988) has pointed out that although sexual and racial oppression are different, the experience of *black women* in the labour market needs to be considered as distinct from men or white women. This observation is further complicated by the need to consider ethnic diversity *between* minority groups and the class differences *within* a minority.

Racial discrimination does not explain all disadvantages. It is not just white employers who exploit low paid workers; minority groups may also offer low paid and insecure work in poor conditions. Phizacklea's work on the fashion industry in East London indicates that the direct employers of female ethnic minority homeworkers are often male ethnic minority sub-contractors.

2. Patterns of employment

A wide range of survey data gathered since the 1960s shows a consistent pattern of disadvantage in the labour market for ethnic minorities. This data comes from a variety of sources. Some surveys have been conducted by sociologists with a particular interest in racial inequality; these include the influential PEP (1968) and PSI (1977 and 1984) studies. Other information has been gathered by looking at sub-samples of Government surveys. For the first time the 1991 census included questions which will allow researchers to identify the ethnic origin of households and thus of the labour force.

Types of disadvantage

The nature of the disadvantage compared to the white majority includes lower overall pay, lower pay for similar work, worse working conditions such as unpopular shifts, lower status work and higher rates of unemployment. This pattern of inequality is not, however, straightforward. As mentioned elsewhere, ethnicity cannot be studied in isolation. We must also consider the effects of age, gender, class, educational experience and whether the workers are immigrants or native born. There are also significant differences in the experiences of *different* ethnic groups.

Statistics which *aggregate* figures for different Asian minority groups conceal considerable differences. Those of Indian or East African origin are far more likely to be employed in middle class occupations than those of Pakistani and Bangladeshi origin who, in turn, are more likely to be unskilled manual workers or in low paid service work such as catering. These observations suggest that discrimination, though certainly a causal factor, is not the sole explanation for unequal patterns of employment.

There is a diversity *within,* as well as between ethnic groups. For example *gender* has a major influence on the socio-economic situation of the Afro-Caribbean group, with more than twice as many females as males in non-manual work. Educational background varies considerably within ethnic groups, just as it does in the population in general.

Geography can be important

The geographical distribution of ethnic minorities also influences their job prospects. Post-war immigration largely followed employment prospects. London and the South-East attracted more immigrants than other parts of the country and until recently unemployment was relatively low in these areas.

The recruitment of Asian males to the textile industries of Yorkshire and Lancashire led to large numbers of workers in low-paid, low-skilled employment. The decline of these industries also contributed to unemployment in these areas.

The *status* of different types of employment varies from time to time and from place to place. During the 1950s and early 1960s, employment in the British car industry was relatively well-paid and secure. Most of the semi-skilled work force was white; many car workers in Dagenham were Irish immigrants. In West Germany, by 1972 as many as 60% of Ford assembly-line workers were immigrant or "guest workers" and by 1975 the figure for black workers at Ford of Dagenham was similar.

The *public sector* has tended to employ a higher proportion from minorities than has the private sector. Therefore a reduction in jobs in Local Government, the Civil service and the NHS is likely to hurt ethnic minorities more than most. Local Government has not, however, always been a fair employer. In London the number of ethnic minority employees in Local Government was about the same proportion as found in the population as a whole. In Liverpool, despite an increase throughout the 1980s, the percentage of ethnic minority workers employed by the City in 1989 was only 1.6%, in a City where 7.6% of the population were from ethnic minorities. Some public sector occupations such as fireman were overwhelmingly white and of course male. D. Thomas (New society 1.11.1984) cites the figure of 50 black firemen out of a total of 6,951.

Ethnic minorities are by no means limited to low status occupations. There are large numbers of ethnic minority workers in the *professions*. For instance there are high proportions of Nurses and Doctors from ethnic minorities. Although there are increasing numbers of lawyers from ethnic minorities, there are very few QCs or judges. This also applies to women and the first black woman became a QC as recently as 1991. There is still evidence of discrimination in recruitment and promotion in both the health care and the Legal professions.

4 > ETHNICITY AND UNEMPLOYMENT

The issue of unemployment is discussed in chapter 10. However at this stage it is worth mentioning that unemployment rates have been, in general, higher for ethnic minorities than for the white majority. This is despite the fact that many immigrants from the Caribbean and the Indian sub-continent have settled in areas where there was a shortage of workers rather than a shortage of jobs.

Disadvantages in terms of unemployment

There is a considerable variation in the unemployment rates of different ethnic minorities. In the early 1990s those of Pakistani/Bangladeshi origin had nearly double the unemployment rate of those of Indian origin. This suggests that although racial discrimination undoubtedly exists, it is not the only explanation of different rates of unemployment. We should also look at the qualifications of the different groups; West-Indian/Guyanese women have higher educational qualifications than other ethnic minorities and even the white majority, but West Indian/Guyanese males do not.

5 > ETHNICITY AND THE LAW

We can examine the relationship between race and the law by looking at: OFFENDERS, VICTIMS and the LEGAL STRUCTURE.

1. "Offenders"

As we shall see in the chapter on deviance (ch 14) there is often a need to study those who have been dealt with by the law rather than simply those who break the law. Those who have been dealt with are alleged offenders who may be innocent or guilty, but may still be treated differently because of their ethnic origin.

If we compare offenders from ethnic minorities with the population in general we find that they are:

Problems for ethnic minorities

- more likely to be arrested
- more likely to be remanded in custody
- more likely to be given a prison sentence for the same crime and with the same criminal record than a member of the majority
- more likely to complain about police behaviour such as abuse and assault.

2. Victims

Members of black and Asian minorities are more likely to be victims of street crime than the white majority. Some, but not all, of these offences may be racially motivated. In the 1970s black youth were portrayed in the press as "muggers", when in fact the police statistics showed that they were disproportionately victims rather than offenders.

3. The legal structure

There are virtually no black or Asian judges and a relatively small number of non-white solicitors and barristers. Both the Law Society and the Bar Council have been shown to discriminate in their recruitment and training procedures. The number of black and Asian police officers has increased but is still less than half the number expected based on the proportion of the whole population who are from these minorities. There also exists a climate of mistrust between the police and courts on the one hand and ethnic minorities on the other.

6 > ETHNICITY AND HOUSING

Research in the 1960s suggested that housing conditions were poorer for members of the ethnic minorities than for the rest of the population. In a study in the Sparkbrook area of Birmingham, Rex and Moore found a pattern of disadvantage in both the private and council sectors. In trying to buy a home, incomes and savings were low and there was also evidence of discrimination by vendors, estate agents and mortgage lenders. In trying to rent from the council there was the problem of long waiting lists and also evidence suggesting the allocation of ethnic minorities to less desirable properties. In response to these problems, immigrants tended to buy shared houses in cheaper, run-down areas and borrowed at high rates of interest. Minorities are often blamed for the conditions of the run-down areas they live in and may also experience harassment from neighbours if they live in areas where the population is largely white. Some Local Authorities have tried to prevent racial harassment of their tenants by other tenants.

 Housing disadvantages

More recent studies have indicated improved housing conditions for second generation immigrants, particularly those who have moved up the class ladder. In addition, racial discrimination in the area of housing has been illegal since 1968. Of course minorities often choose to live together.

7 > EXPLANATIONS OF RACIAL INEQUALITY

BIOLOGICAL EXPLANATIONS

The idea that whole populations are brighter or stronger than others has no scientific basis. *Individuals* are certainly advantaged or disadvantaged in particular activities by their genetic inheritance, but the distribution of genes between different *ethnic groups* in Britain gives no clues as to which ethnic groups are best suited to particular positions or roles. Biology has been misused to give a "scientific" justification for inequality.

PSYCHOLOGICAL EXPLANATIONS

Explanations of racial inequality

These focus on the prejudices of individuals and groups against outsiders. Experiments show that individuals will discriminate against those seen as *different* even if this is at a cost to the person discriminating and if the differences were artificially created for the purpose of the experiment. In real life, an employer who does not employ the best person or a pub-owner who turns away customers because of their colour, will suffer a loss, yet on occasions such actions still occur.

Psychologists trying to explain the behaviour of those who committed barbaric acts in concentration camps in the second world war have come up with conflicting results. Adorno argued that the individuals had a particular type of "Authoritarian personality" formed in childhood, whereas Milgram claimed that in certain situations most people will be obedient to authority and commit cruel and murderous acts if someone else gives the orders. Thus for Adorno the solution lies with the individual personality, but for Milgram the solution lies in changing the situations the individuals find themselves in.

SOCIALISATION

Racial prejudice is not directly measurable but a number of surveys have tried to measure the extent of *hostile attitudes* in this country. Some have simply asked people if they are racially prejudiced and others have asked people whether they agree or disagree with a list of tolerant or prejudiced statements.

If certain sections of the population are prejudiced then we might explain this by looking at the process of socialisation. Children may learn the intolerant (or tolerant) attitudes of parents within the family. Within schools, racism may be learned in the playground but also in the classroom. Reading books for younger children have been criticised for producing racist stereotypes. Some have been re-edited and some removed from the shelves. Text books too have been criticised. Geography text books were still reproducing spurious racial classifications in the 1980s and portraying stereotypical views of the third world. Immigrants are portrayed as a problem rather than as an asset and economic and social history may be very one sided.

Religious institutions may reinforce or challenge racism. Separate churches and separate schooling for Catholics and Protestants in N. Ireland has fuelled distrust and conflict. Political conflict in the former Yugoslavia has been reinforced by the mistrust of other religions. On the other hand, religious groups have actively challenged racism in South Africa, the USA and Britain.

The role of the mass media in creating, reinforcing or even challenging racist stereotypes is discussed in ch. 15.

ECONOMIC

Economic explanations of racial inequality are often based on Marxist theories of class.

There are two main parts to this approach:

1 Racist beliefs help to maintain Capitalism. This might occur in a number of ways. The economic exploitation of those from different backgrounds, first in the countries colonised by the British and later as immigrants here, has sometimes been justified by pointing to their supposed inferiority. Racial minorities can also be blamed for the inevitable problems that Marxists see emerging in capitalist society, such as unemployment, poverty, housing shortage and crime. Racism portrays a country divided by colour not class. The working class does not then see itself as a united group and is less likely to resist oppression by capitalism itself, in the view of many Marxists.

2 Immigrants and ethnic minorities may form a reserve army of labour. In other words they are available for work when required but are not seen as entitled to a job. Some European countries who did not give migrant workers the right to be citizens or residents can then "export" their unemployment. In Britain, immigrants have citizenship rights but are still more likely to be unemployed. This argument has also been applied to married women workers (see chapter 3).

POWER

Sociologists influenced by Weber have suggested that racial inequality is the result of minorities having less *power* and therefore being disadvantaged in the "markets", not only for jobs but also for education and housing. This lack of power comes in part from discrimination but also from the non-participation of minorities in organisations like political parties and pressure groups which influence decision making. This lack of power and the alleged concentration of minorities at the bottom of the class structure led some writers to talk of a black *underclass* in Britain but particularly in the USA.

EXAMINATION QUESTIONS

Q.1

a) What is meant by the term "migration"?   *(2)*

b) Explain why people have migrated to Britain.
    How has British society gained from this migration?   *(9)*

c) Using examples, show the difference between prejudice and discrimination.   *(4)*

d) Show how prejudice and discrimination might affect the life chances of ethnic
    minority groups.   *(10)*

(Total 25)

(NEAB, June 1991)

Q.2   Read ITEM A and ITEM B. Then answer the questions which follow.

ITEM A

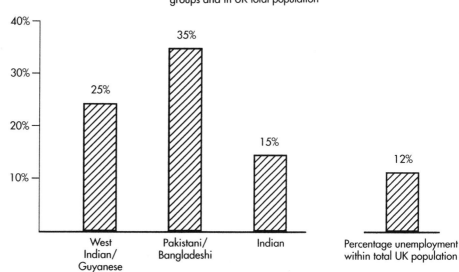

Source: adapted from *Labour Force Survey 1984,* HMSO

ITEM B

Often minority ethnic groups do not have equal employment opportunities. West
Indians are more likely to be found in manual than in white-collar jobs. Asians
are less likely than Whites to be found in white-collar jobs although there are
relatively more Asians than West Indians in these positions. Asians also tend to
have high rates of self-employment but these are usually in small businesses.

a) Study ITEM A and state:
   i) which of the minority ethnic groups shown have the greatest level of unemployment;
   ii) which of the minority ethnic groups shown has the least unemployment.

   (2)

b) According to ITEM B,
   i) in which type of employment are West Indians more likely to be found;
   ii) in which type of self-employment are Asians likely to be found? *(2)*

c) Identify and explain **two** factors, other than those given in ITEM B, for minority ethnic groups not having equal employment opportunities. *(4)*

d) Identify and explain **two** ways, other than employment opportunities, in which minority ethnic groups may experience disadvantages. *(4)*

e) How do sociologists attempt to explain racial discrimination? *(8)*

(SEG, June 1990)

Q.3 Read ITEMS A and B. Then answer the questions which follow.

ITEM A

Serious illness by social class   Fatal accidents at work by social class

Fig 4.2

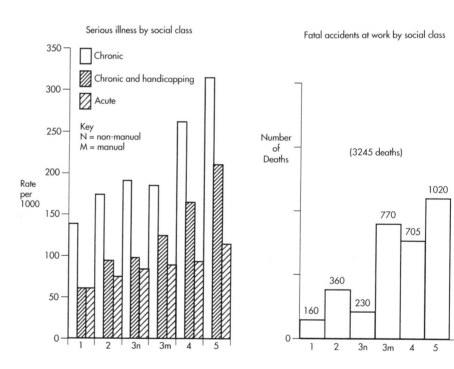

Key
n = non-manual
m = manual

Source adapted from 'Social Class & Health Inequalities', M. BLAXTER in *Equalities and Inequalities in Health*, C. O. CARTER AND J. PEEL (Academic Press, 1976)

Source: adapted from *Occupational Mortality*: 1970–2 (HMSO, 1978)

ITEM B

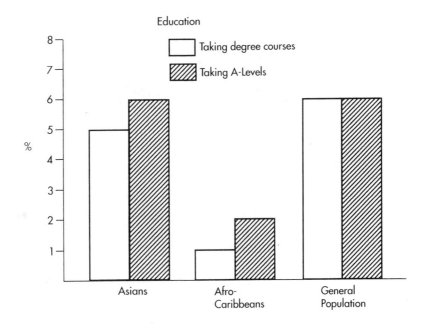

a) Look at ITEM A. What rate per 1000 of Social Class 3n suffer chronic and handicapping illness? *(1)*

b) Look at ITEM A. Which social class has the fewest fatal accidents at work? *(1)*

c) Look at ITEM B.
   i) Which group had the highest percentage taking A levels? *(1)*
   ii) What percentage of Afro-Caribbeans were taking degree courses? *(1)*

d) Identify and explain two ways in which social class might affect a person's life chances. *(4)*

e) Identify and explain two reasons why some of the elderly continue in employment beyond retirement age. *(4)*

f) Identify and fully explain **one** social consequence of the unequal status in the workplace of most women in relation to men. *(4)*

g) "There are many opportunities for members of ethnic minority groups to achieve a high standard of education and high status jobs in Britain today." Identify and fully explain **one** way in which this view can be either supported or rejected. *(4)*

(SEG, June 1991)

Q.4

Social Stratification and Inequality

['Alex' appears in the *Dail*

a) Private education is mentioned in the Source. Using examples, explain what is meant by a Public School. *(4)*
b) In what ways may the school a person attends influence the opportunities he/she has later in life? *(7)*
c) CLASS is one basis for inequality in modern Britain. Choose **ONE OTHER** basis for social inequality and explain how it occurs and the effect it may have on individuals *(9)*

(MEG, June 1993)

ANSWERS TO EXAMINATION QUESTIONS

Q.1
a) Migration refers to the movement of individuals or groups from one place to another with the intention to settle there. This may be within a country or from one country to another.

b) (There are clearly two parts to this question but no indication of the distribution of marks between the two. Aim to produce answers of more or less equal length. Only a selection of the following points would be necessary.)

Immigration to Britain can be explained by looking at "push" factors which encourage people to leave their country of origin and "pull" factors which make settling in Britain attractive.

At the turn of the century Jews fled from Russia to many countries to avoid persecution. Most went to the USA but many came to Britain and most Jews in Britain are of Eastern European origin. In the 1930s Jews tried to escape from Nazi Germany but immigration control limited the number who were allowed to settle in Britain (and most other countries).

Asians fled from discrimination in East Africa (Kenya, Uganda and Tanzania) to Britain in the early 1970s. Most held British passports. In order to restrict immigration the Government changed the law so that British passport holders were not necessarily entitled to settle here.

Economic opportunities have attracted Irish immigrants to Britain for hundreds of years. Ireland has suffered from mass emigration to the USA and Britain because of famine and limited employment opportunities.

During the 1950s and early 1960s economic growth and full employment attracted numerous Commonwealth immigrants to Britain particularly from the Caribbean and the Indian Sub-continent. Active recruiting campaigns were conducted in the West Indies by the NHS, British Rail and London transport.

Changes in the law have removed the right of Commonwealth citizens to settle in Britain.

Britain has benefited from immigration in a variety of ways. People who emigrate from their country of birth are often the most enterprising, ambitious and sometimes the best qualified. Many immigrants have created new businesses which have provided employment and increased our national wealth. Immigrants from all over the world have frequently chosen the clothing industry to start new businesses and catering and shops are often chosen by immigrants as businesses.

Immigrants with professional qualifications have played a vital part in maintaining public services. Since the 1950s there have been large numbers of Doctors and Nurses in the NHS from the Indian sub-continent, the Caribbean, West Africa, Malaysia and Ireland.

The cultural life of the country has been enriched by the art, music and literature of immigrants. Sometimes the ethnic roots of culture are obvious as with popular music from the Caribbean. On other occasions it is not so visible, for example the contribution of Jews to the early development of film and TV in this country. Entertainment and sports are fields where immigrants have excelled; their achievements have become a source of national pride. An obvious contribution to the life of the consumer has been the opening of different restaurants and the arrival in the shops of a variety of new food products.

c) Prejudice is an attitude, which is usually hostile, towards a group of people. It exists in people's minds and therefore cannot be directly observed. Prejudice may or may not lead to discrimination. An example of racial prejudice is thinking that people are inferior in ability or morality because of their race.

Discrimination is behaviour and can be observed. It involves treating people differently. Racial discrimination usually means treating people unfairly because of their race or ethnic origin. For example, denying people equal opportunities to get a job. There is however the possibility of positive discrimination to help people overcome the disadvantages of discrimination against them.

d) In the field of employment the prejudices of some employers has led them to discriminate against minorities when recruiting or promoting staff. Figures also indicate that minorities are more likely to be made redundant. Thus the life chances of minorities are worsened by their being less likely to get good jobs and being more likely to be unemployed.

Employers may also discriminate because they are concerned about the prejudices of others such as other employees or customers. Before it was made illegal some large shops refused to allow non-white immigrants to serve food in case it upset customers. Despite being illegal, research and individual cases indicate discrimination in employment persists.

In the Education system research indicates the underachievement of some ethnic minority groups. Discrimination is unlikely to be the sole cause of this as some minorities achieve more than the majority. Discrimination may occur in relationships between pupils and between teachers and pupils. Teachers may have low expectations of some minority groups and accept low standards. They may expect deviant behaviour from some groups and be more likely to treat them harshly.

Prejudice and discrimination may disadvantage minorities in the housing markets although discrimination is illegal. Landlords may refuse to let to non-whites or charge more rent. Mortgage lenders may be less willing to provide funds for buying houses and councils may allocate less attractive homes to minorities.

Racial harassment and violence may threaten the sense of security or even the lives of members or minorities. It is widely perceived by minorities and others that the law provides less protection to them and the relations between some ethnic minority communities and the police are poor. Discrimination and prejudice have been identified in research.

Q.2

a) (i) Pakistani/Bangladeshi

   (ii) Indian

b) (i) Manual jobs

   (ii) Usually in small businesses

c) You should explain two from this list or other suitable factors. Discrimination, lacking contacts, not living in areas where there are job opportunities, not having desired educational qualifications (note that many ethnic minority groups tend to be more not less qualified), limited aspirations etc.

d) Explain two from this list or other suitable points.

   Housing, education, treatment by the police and law, experience of violence.

e) Develop at least two explanations. They must be sociological NOT psychological or commonsense. Economic (Marxist) explanations blaming capitalism; socialisation from media, school etc., Britain's imperial history, lack of power held by minorities, fear or resentment of immigrants when there is competition for jobs and houses. Politicians exploiting racial tensions to gain support.

Q.3

a) 100 per 1000

b) Class 1

c) i) Asians (same as general population)

   ii) 1% (much higher now and higher for women than men)

d) Explain how class affects any two from: health, unemployment, housing, educational achievement, access to political power etc.

e) Develop and explain why they WANT to, because of enjoying the job or wanting to maintain social contacts etc. Some people want to avoid spending more time with their partners – think of the marital tensions in TV comedies such as "One foot in the grave" (or "Till death us do part" for older readers).

   And why they HAVE to, because of high living expenses, low or no pension etc.

f) Develop one of the following:

   ■ Seen by society in general and by individual husbands and wives as a secondary breadwinner.

   ■ Made dependent on men.

   ■ Worse promotion chances.

   ■ Less likely to be trained.

   ■ Sexual harassment.

   ■ Family poverty for single parent families etc.

   (For (e), (f) and (g) you can use more than one point if it is part of the explanation for your main point. e.g. lower pay is in part a result of worse promotion chances.)

g) You could support the view by examining various developments which have widened educational opportunities for ethnic minorities or encouraged them to take advantage of existing opportunities. Or you could discuss legal changes which have outlawed discrimination.

STUDENT'S ANSWER WITH EXAMINER'S COMMENTS

(NB The first two parts of the question refer to education and inequality. This question is taken from a MEG paper and is under the heading of "Social stratification and inequality".)

Q.4

a) Private education is mentioned in the source. Using examples, explain what is meant by a Public School. *(4)*

Understanding OK. Develop points a little further, with examples. 3/4

> A Public School is one you have to pay to go to. It is for rich people and sometimes for clever children ("boffins"). It is private and not run by the council.

b) In what ways may the school a person attends influence the opportunities he/she has later in life? *(7)*

Some relevant points but more evidence needed to support arguments. Don't restrict argument to private schools only. 3/7

> Children from public schools and Grammar schools get better qualifications and therefore get better paid and more important jobs. The old boy network means that people are chosen because of the posh school they went to not because they could do the job best.

c) CLASS is one basis for inequality in modern Britain. Choose ONE OTHER basis for social inequality and explain how it occurs and the effect it may have on individuals. *(9)*

Could indicate that assault and discrimination are illegal, but still occur.

Good. Refers to evidence and shows knowledge of research.

Sensible comparison.

Could also discuss housing, job choice, political behaviour, etc. 6/9

> Racial inequality means people are treated badly because of their colour. They may be bullied at school and violently attacked in the street. They are not allowed in places.
>
> Black people are more likely to be unemployed than white people and they are not always allowed to do top jobs. Some sociologists showed that people do discriminate against black and Asian people by pretending to apply for jobs and finding that even when people have the same qualifications white workers are chosen.
>
> In N. Ireland the basis for inequality is religion. This is like racial inequality.
>
> Inequality may affect individuals and make them angry and they might riot or they may just get on with their lives and try to ignore inequality.

Overall the most convincing parts of the answer are when the student uses sociological evidence and ideas. 12/20

NB The Review Sheet for this chapter is found at the end of Chapter 5, and covers inequalities related to both ethnic background and class.

THE CLASS SYSTEM AND OTHER FORMS OF INEQUALITY

OCCUPATION AND CLASS
CASTE SYSTEM
ESTATE OR FEUDAL SYSTEM
MARXIST THEORY OF CLASS
CHANGES IN CLASS STRUCTURE
SOCIAL MOBILITY
DISTRIBUTION OF INCOME AND WEALTH

GETTING STARTED

This chapter is mainly concerned with the examination of class inequality in Modern Britain. The three previous chapters have dealt with other forms of social inequality which may influence people's life chances, namely age, gender and race. In addition to class there is also a brief consideration of other forms of economically based inequality, such as caste and the feudal system.

It should be noted that age, gender and race may all influence people's access to economic rewards. The system of slavery found in the British Empire until its abolition in the early 19th century and in the USA later in that century was based on racial differences. The most common occupation for female slaves in the USA was domestic service. In this case the servants' low social position was based on class, race and gender.

The main themes in questions set on this topic include:
- THE USEFULNESS OF DIFFERENT OCCUPATIONAL CLASSIFICATIONS.
- THE RELATIONSHIP BETWEEN CLASS AND LIFE CHANCES.
- THE DIFFERENCE BETWEEN CLASS AND OTHER FORMS OF STRATIFICATION.
- DIFFERENT EXPLANATIONS OF CLASS INEQUALITY.
- THE CAUSES AND CONSEQUENCES OF SOCIAL MOBILITY.
- THE DISTRIBUTION OF WEALTH AND INCOME.

The influence of class can be seen throughout society and thus throughout the different topics in this book.

DEFINITIONS

CLASS. Class is a type of stratification based on economic inequalities. There are different definitions of class which may emphasise occupation, ownership, income or even people's view of themselves.

SOCIAL MOBILITY. This refers to the movement of individuals or groups up or down the class structure.

STRATIFICATION. Ways in which society can be sub-divided into different types or groups; usually involves ranking.

EMBOURGEOISEMENT. The process of the working class becoming middle class.

POWER. A broader idea than class, also including status and party (i.e. organisational strength).

MERITOCRACY. A system in which ability, not inherited position, determines who gets to the top.

ESSENTIAL PRINCIPLES

THE REGISTRAR GENERAL'S CLASSIFICATION

This has been used since 1911 for official statistics and is frequently used by sociologists as it is generally accepted, despite the criticisms below. It was updated for the 1991 census. The grading was based on the *status* of the jobs, which in turn is often related to the skills and qualifications required for entry into those jobs. The

---

Social Class based on Occupation 1991
Registrar General's classification

I	PROFESSIONAL, ETC
II	MANAGERIAL AND TECHNICAL
III (N)	SKILLED NON-MANUAL
III (M)	SKILLED MANUAL
IV	PARTLY SKILLED
V	UNSKILLED

---

66 A widely used occupational classification 99

Department of Employment uses the new Standard Occupational Classification which has nine categories of jobs and deals more effectively with women's jobs than did earlier classifications.

MARSHALL'S (1988) SIMPLIFICATION OF GOLDTHORPE (1983)

SERVICE CLASS	1.	Higher prof., admin and owners
	2.	Lower prof., admin and managers
INTERMEDIATE CLASS	3.	Routine clerical, sales and service
	4.	Owners of small firms, self-employed
	5.	Lower technicians and foremen.
WORKING CLASS	6.	Skilled manual
	7.	Semi-skilled and unskilled manual.

---

66 An alternative classification 99

Alternative schemes of class structure related to occupation have been devised because some sociologists find them more useful. A popular one was used in the Oxford Mobility Studies. It is based on differences in *pay and working conditions*.

66 Rise of the service sector 99

The numbers in each group have changed because of changes in the occupational structure. Generally there has been a consistent increase in the non-manual jobs compared with the manual ones, and in particular there has been a growth in professional occupations. Table 5.1 below indicates the broad rise in service sector occupations at the expense of the more traditional industrial and agricultural sectors in the advanced economies. Since 1960, the share of total production coming from the agricultural sector has declined from 6% to 2.2%, that coming from the industrial sector has declined from 41% to 32.7% whereas the service sector has increased its share of total output from 53% to 65.1%. This is what is often meant by the phrase "the rise of the service economies". The decline in the contribution of industry in general, and manufacturing in particular, is what is meant by the term "de-industrialisation".

	1960	1980	1985	1990
Agriculture	6.0	3.1	2.6	2.2
Industry	41.0	36.5	34.2	32.7
(manufacturing)	(30.4)	(24.7)	(23.2)	(22.4)
Services	53.0	60.4	63.2	65.1

Sources: OECD (1992) Economic Outlook: Historical Statistics 1960–1990.

Table 5.1 Percentage shares of total output (National Income) contributed by various sectors: the advanced industrial market economies.

CRITICAL VIEWS OF CLASSIFICATIONS BASED ON OCCUPATION

Sociologists have pointed out a number of problems with using occupations as a measure of class. Some of these problems apply to particular classifications and some to the whole idea of jobs indicating class.

66 Criticisms of using occupations as the basis for class 99

1 Marxists point out the absence of the rich, i.e. the owners of the means of production.
2 The poor and the unemployed are excluded.
3 Women often appear to be in higher class occupations than men. However "women's jobs" are frequently in the lower levels of each grouping. Women often earn less than men in the same groups or even earn less than some men in groups below them. Also the promotion prospects of many women are considerably inferior to that of men in the same, or lower, class of occupational group.
4 The division between non-manual and manual jobs has often been used to distinguish the middle class from the working class. However this is not very useful when applied to women, as many personal service jobs are low paid, low status and low-skilled yet are defined as non-manual, and therefore "middle class"!
5 Wives and children are classified by the male head of family. This may be inappropriate in cross-class families, particularly where women have higher level jobs than men.
6 It has been argued that all women are "proletarianised" (i.e. are exploited, like the working class) by their experience within the family, and that this is not reflected in occupational classifications.
7 The ranking of occupations is largely based on status, yet there may be disagreements about the relative positions of jobs. A particular job could, of course, change its ranking over a period of time and this may not be reflected in the official classification.
8 In some schemes the ranking depends on judging the skills used in a job. However there are problems in evaluating skills; e.g. skills are sometimes judged according to who has them. In particular, women's skilled jobs are sometimes ranked lower than men's precisely because it is women who do the jobs. The idea of ranking jobs is almost inevitably subjective, whether it is done by the Registrar General's staff or by a survey of public opinion (e.g. the Hall-Jones scale).
9 Self-assigned class may explain behaviour, such as voting, better than the position a person occupies in an occupational scale.

Positive points

1 Occupation is a good predictor of life expectancy, infant mortality and many other indicators of health.
2 Parents' occupation predicts reasonably accurately the educational achievement of children, particularly where both parents' class is considered.

Does it matter if the classifications are inadequate?

The validity and reliability of sociological studies and of Government statistics are threatened if the occupational groupings are unsuitable. For example, social mobility studies measure movement up and down the classifications, therefore we must be confident which occupations are higher and which lower if the findings of such studies are to have any meaning.

2 > THE CASTE SYSTEM

Although class is accepted as the most common form of stratification in industrialised societies, there are other forms of inequality. *Caste* is one of the least open systems of stratification. A person's position is determined at birth and generally fixed for life. The most important example of a caste system is found in India. Relationships are regulated by Hindu religious beliefs and there is the idea that lower castes could pollute higher castes by contact, so there is a complex set of rules and taboos which limit social contacts, such as eating, touching and speaking.

There are four major castes (VARNA) in India and a host of local sub-divisions (JATIS). There is also a substantial part of the population who are outside, i.e. below, the caste system. These outcasts are the "untouchables". Caste will largely determine occupations and marriage.

The caste system still has a major influence on the lives of Hindus but has been undermined by industrialisation and Government policy, both of which have opened up education and jobs to lower castes. It has also declined amongst Indians who have emigrated to other countries.

3 > THE ESTATE OR FEUDAL SYSTEM

Feudalism existed before industrialisation in many societies where the economy was based on agricultural production. The three *Estates* were NOBILITY, CHURCH and COMMONERS. Each had rights and duties, although most of the rights were enjoyed by the King and the nobles. People were born into families of high or low status with the majority being landless agricultural labourers or serfs. The top of the ladder was the King and the land owning nobility. There was a small possibility of upward mobility through the Church or, for a very few, by being recruited to the nobility because of services to the King.

The remnants of this system exist in Britain today through the continued existence of a Monarch and Lords. Feudalism persists in a more influential form in parts of Latin America where poor peasants work for large landowners.

The end of the feudal system was brought about by two major influences:

1 The rise of a powerful commercial and industrial class (what Marx called the Bourgeoisie).
2 The spread of ideas about the rights of man (it was usually man and not woman) and equality. There were, for example, revolutions in France and the USA.

THE IMPORTANCE OF SOCIAL CLASS

Occupation of the head of household is frequently used as the measure of a family's social class. This still predicts the family members' life chances in a number of ways:

1   Life expectancy.
2   Infant mortality.
3   Health.
4   Number of teeth.
5   Smoking.
6   Suicide rates.
7   Working conditions.
8   Housing conditions.
9   Educational achievement.
10   Divorce rates.

4 MARXIST THEORY OF CLASS

GCSE does not require an understanding of sociological theories. (Enthusiasts must wait for A level!) However it is worth knowing the basic Marxist theory of class because it has influenced sociological thinking about class, whether or not you agree or disagree with Marxist views.

Karl Marx (1818–1883) was born and educated in Germany but lived and worked in London. He wrote critically about the effects of early capitalism on the lives of the working class. Britain, which was the first Capitalist society, was the richest country in the world but the condition of the industrial workers was even worse than it had been when they worked on the land.

Marx saw the economy as the foundation upon which the rest of society, such as the family, church and political system, was built. These institutions existed, in his view, to protect the rich and to oppress the workers.

He said that there were only two important classes. These were:

Two key classes for Marx

■ THE BOURGEOISIE, or capitalists, who owned the means of production, such as factories and mines.
■ THE PROLETARIAT, or working class, who were the wage labourers who worked in the factories.

Thus he defines class only in terms of OWNERSHIP; not, for example, by occupation or income. There are then only TWO CLASSES in Marx's view. Marx predicted that the working class would continue to be exploited by the owners and become poorer until they became CLASS CONSCIOUS (i.e. realise that they were exploited and that they were strong enough to resist). They would then overthrow the owners in a revolution.

Capitalism would be succeeded by a classless communist society. It would be classless because there would be no private ownership of the means of production.

Marxist sociologists have applied these ideas to many areas of the subject. They have explained the absence of a revolution by pointing out that the workers have not become class conscious because they are kept FALSELY CONSCIOUS by various institutions, such as the family, school, church and the media.

Criticisms of Marx

1 Class is not the only form of inequality. People are ranked by Caste, status, political power, age, race and gender.
2 Ownership is not the only way to define class. There are significant differences in wages between people at the top and bottom of the occupational ladder and it is difficult to see them as belonging to the same classes as Marx would. To Marx they would be members of the proletariat, whether rich or poor, because they worked for others rather than owned the means of production.
3 Ownership of the means of production is spread fairly widely in modern industrial societies. Some industries are still publicly owned, e.g. the Post Office. However the Government's privatisation policy has increased the number of shareholders who are owners of businesses. The savings and pension contributions of individuals are also invested in shares in these institutions which means that individuals may be owners and yet have little control over how the businesses actually operate. Ownership of the means of production when share ownership is widespread is clearly different from the situation when Marx was alive.

Problems with the view of Marx

4 There are more than two classes. There are middle classes and many divisions in the working class itself.
5 The working class is getting richer not poorer.
6 Communism in practice has not followed Marx's predictions. There were no communist revolutions in industrialised Capitalist countries. Russia, China and Cuba were largely agricultural economies when they had their revolutions. The Russian army brought communism to Eastern Europe, not a worker inspired revolution. Further, gross inequalities continued to exist in communist societies. In fact Communism in Eastern Europe and the old USSR collapsed after 1989.

MAX WEBER (1864–1920)

Weber was a major critic of Marx. Many current sociological debates about class are influenced by the views of Marx and Weber. Weber said that social inequality was based on differences in POWER not just class.

A group's power was based on:

- CLASS
- STATUS
- PARTY

Weber's broader view of power

CLASS was not just defined by ownership but also by MARKET SITUATION. This means the ability to command rewards in the job market, which depends on skills and bargaining power. Weber argued that there was a growing middle class and his followers have argued that there are in fact a number of middle and working classes. This contradicts the Marxist view of only two classes based on ownership.

STATUS is the honour or prestige attached to a particular group. It may not always coincide with class. Rich members of ethnic minorities may be of a high class but in a racist society have low status.

PARTY refers to groups who are organised in order to gain power. Political parties, professional associations and Trade Unions are examples of power through organisation.

---

5 > CHANGES IN THE CLASS STRUCTURE

The following factors are seen by many as leading to changes in the class structure.

1 Embourgeoisement
2 A Fragmented Working Class
3 The Underclass
4 Proletarianisation
5 A Fragmented Middle Class.

EMBOURGEOISEMENT

The 1950s saw changes in the lives of the working class. Full employment provided a feeling of security, while higher wages opened up new opportunities to own consumer goods, such as televisions, cars and travel abroad. The Welfare State appeared able to deal with ill health, old age and the little unemployment which remained. The 1944 Education Act had provided free secondary education for all.

Although economic growth during the 1950s was higher in many European countries than in the UK, and even more so in the USA, there was a feeling of optimism about the economic future. The Conservative party won three consecutive elections with increased majorities and the 1959 election campaign slogan was "You've never had it so good". These changes led some sociologists to claim that "we were all middle class now". The process of the working class becoming middle class was called *embourgeoisement.*

Becoming middle class

A famous study of workers in Luton by Goldthorpe, Lockwood et al. argued that the working class had not become middle class. They might earn incomes similar to the middle class but their attitudes and social behaviour remained distinct. They did, however, argue that there was now a *new working class* which had given up traditional values. This new working class was home-centred, with families cutting themselves off from neighbours and from extended families. The workers saw their jobs as a means to earn cash and were not unduly concerned that they might be unsatisfying, e.g. repetitive assembly-line jobs at Vauxhall. They wanted high pay to spend on family and home.

This new working class of the 1950s sounds very like the descriptions of working class Conservative voters of the 1990s. They were renamed "Essex man" or described in almost sociological terms as C2s. (C2 is the equivalent in the Registrar General's Classification of a III (M) i.e. a skilled manual worker.)

The effects of changes in the class structure on voting behaviour is discussed in the politics chapter and the *Old and New working classes* are described further there (ch 13).

A FRAGMENTED WORKING CLASS

Instead of the working class disappearing and everyone being middle class, there is a view that the working class has become fragmented or divided into a variety of sub-groups. This presents a problem for Marxists who see a *united* working class as necessary to resist the exploitation found in Capitalist society. Divisions within the working class could be based on age, gender or ethnicity. These are discussed in separate chapters.

There could also be divisions based on income, skill, qualifications, job security, working conditions etc. The distinction between the old and new working classes also considers home ownership and whether workers are employed in the private or public sectors.

The divided working class is not a new idea. In the 1960s Rose described an "ideal type" of working class which only included 25% of manual workers. They were in unions, tenants, left school at the minimum age and thought of themselves as working class.

IS THERE AN UNDERCLASS?

The concept of an UNDERCLASS has been popularised by Politicians and journalists who have borrowed the term from sociology and tended to use it in a sensational way when discussing poverty, crime and morality. Sociologists see an underclass as a distinct group of people who are trapped beneath the working class. As the rest of us get better off, the underclass have been left behind and the gap is widening.

The term has been used in a variety of ways:

1 Americans have used it to describe the inner city poor who are often black or Spanish speaking.

2 Although it was used by some British sociologists to describe ethnic minorities in the 1960s, it is more frequently used to describe those who live on run-down council housing estates where unemployment is high.

66 The so-called 'underclass' 99

3 Right wing writers define the underclass in moral terms and see their inferior culture as the cause of poverty. Young males are seen as unwilling to work and drifting into crime, and family life is seen as breaking down with increased numbers of welfare-dependent single mothers.

4 Left wing writers see the underclass as trapped in low-paid insecure work with little hope of upward social mobility. Their worsening position is the result of unemployment, unequal distribution of income and the failure of the Welfare State.

Critics of the underclass view argue that they are not a distinct group with a different culture who are separated from the rest of society. They say that people drift in and out of poverty because of unemployment or the family life cycle. For example, few would see the old, who make up a substantial proportion of the poor, as being criminal or idle.

PROLETARIANISATION OF THE MIDDLE CLASS

Marxists have argued that, rather than us all becoming middle class, the middle class is being depressed into the working class. They call this the proletarianisation of the white collar (i.e. office) workers.

66 Growth of the white-collar workers 99

The reasons for proletarianisation includes the worsening pay and working conditions of office workers as compared to factory workers. The de-skilling of office work has been identified as an important cause of its reduced status, as has the increased proportion of women doing office work.

In the 1950s, Lockwood argued that office workers were still better off than factory workers, particularly because they enjoyed job security. This security may now have gone for many white collar workers, particularly those in local government and banking, but there are still advantages in terms of pay, promotion chances and working conditions. During the early 1990s, non-manual workers earned, on average about £80 a week more than manual workers. The gap for men was wider, that for women more narrow, than this figure.

A FRAGMENTED MIDDLE CLASS

Before the war the middle class was a small minority of about a quarter of the population. They enjoyed considerable advantages over the working class. Changes in the occupational structure and the expansion of education has not only increased the size of the middle class but encouraged the development of inequality within the ranks of non-manual workers.

The middle classes vary according to their class origins (i.e. from which class their parents come) and this affects the life chances of their children. The children of the upper middle classes have a more secure future than the children of routine clerical workers, for example.

IS BRITAIN BECOMING A CLASSLESS SOCIETY?

Prime Minister John Major spoke of his vision of a classless society during the 1992 election campaign. If we wish to evaluate the chances of this occurring we could look at:

- Changes in the distribution of wealth.
- The effects of taxation on redistributing income.
- Changes in benefits.
- Changes in the education system.
- The relationship between health and class.
- Changes in the way people feel about class which might be reflected in voting, leisure activities and other spending.

These issues are discussed in the next section of this chapter and in the Poverty chapter (ch 6). The latest figures are available in official statistics, e.g. Social Trends.

💬💬 A classless society! 💬💬

---

6 ▷ SOCIAL MOBILITY

WHAT IS SOCIAL MOBILITY?

Social mobility is movement up or down the class structure by individuals or groups.
Sociologists are interested in different kinds of mobility:

💬💬 Types of social mobility 💬💬

- **Intra-generational mobility.** This describes the movement within an individual's working life. For example, manual workers may become non-manual workers or routine office workers may be promoted to managers.
- **Inter-generational mobility.** This compares the classes of parents and children. Most studies have compared the jobs of fathers and sons.
- **Stratum mobility.** This refers to the movement of a group of people. For example, the social position of routine office workers compared to other workers has fallen over the last 50 years (see the note on proletarianisation). More dramatically, the dismantling of apartheid in South Africa has changed the legal position, political power and status of the various non-European groups.

WHAT ARE THE CAUSES OF SOCIAL MOBILITY?

1 **Changes in the occupational structure.** These have created more room in the middle classes. There are fewer manual jobs in factories, ship yards, docks, coal mines and on the railways, so the working classes have shrunk. There are more service and office jobs, so the middle classes have expanded. There has been a significant growth in professional workers, as demand for the services of the traditional professions such as law and medicine has increased and also as new professions in health, social services and business (e.g. personnel managers) have developed.

💬💬 Causes of social mobility 💬💬

2 **Educational reforms.** These have created more opportunity for people to move up the social ladder as they gain higher level jobs which require educational qualifications. The proportion of people going into higher education has nearly trebled in the last 15 years. Previously the introduction of secondary education for all in 1944, and the subsequent development of comprehensive schools, encouraged a higher degree of social mobility.

3 **Lower birth rates.** A fall in the birth rate, especially in the middle classes, has increased the need for recruitment from the children of the working classes to fill middle class jobs. Similar opportunities have arisen for women and ethnic minority

workers who were previously disadvantaged in the job market. They have become more sought after by employers as the number of school and college leavers has fallen.

4 **Changing recruitment practices.** Equal opportunities law and new recruitment policies have opened up some jobs so that colour, gender and disability may be less of an obstacle to getting on.

5 **Marriage.** This has been a way for women to be socially mobile. Women tend to marry men of the same social class or higher. Youth and beauty have been assets for women wishing to marry richer men.

THE EFFECTS OF SOCIAL MOBILITY

Sociologists have compared *closed societies* with *open societies*. In a closed society children tend to retain the social position of their parents, e.g. in the Caste system. In an open society there is more equality of opportunity and a higher rate of social mobility. Rates of inter-generational mobility are in fact broadly similar in most modern industrial societies.

Impact of social mobility

Class conflict is reduced where people think that their chances of being upwardly mobile are reasonable. Where people think they have little or no chance of individual advancement, e.g. getting promoted, then they are more likely to look for a collective improvement in pay and conditions through trade union activities.

The benefit to society as a whole of high levels of social mobility is that it should ensure that the most able people fill the most important positions. The term *meritocracy* has been given to societies where the most able reach the top, rather than those whose families have always been in important jobs.

Downward social mobility has not received the same attention from sociologists and in any case has been less pronounced because of the causes described above. The loss of money and status by aristocrats, the rich, show business personalities and politicians is often described in Sunday newspapers for our entertainment. Divorce, ill health and disability can all cause downward mobility for families.

THE EXTENT OF SOCIAL MOBILITY

The Oxford Mobility Study investigated the effects of post-war economic growth and educational reform on mobility. In 1972 they found a more open society than earlier studies, e.g. only 25% of the top class had fathers from this class. However the life chances of those at the top remained much better than those at the bottom. The major cause of increased mobility was identified as the expansion of the Service Class (see earlier) owing to technological change, rather than increased open competition to get to the top.

Updates of the study found that the opportunities for manual workers' sons to get into the Service Class had improved, from 1 in 4 to 1 in 3. However the arrival of high levels of unemployment increased the risk of moving down for manual workers. Women remained less likely to be upwardly mobile than men.

PROBLEMS WITH STUDYING SOCIAL MOBILITY

1 Comparing the father's final position with a possible *temporary* one for the son, who might move up, or even down, later on.

2 Relying on possible unreliable records for fathers' occupations.

3 The ranking of jobs may change, e.g. routine office work has probably dropped in status.

4 Studies have used different occupational categories. This means that they cannot be safely compared with each other. The classification schemes themselves have been criticised.

Problems with social mobility

5 Studying only two generations conceals the possibility of the sons of downwardly mobile fathers returning to their original class. This is illustrated by Jackson and Marsden's finding that working class boys in grammar schools often had mothers with middle class origins.

6 The classification of women is problematic. Heath found that women are more often downwardly mobile and are often excluded from both skilled manual work and top jobs.

7 Studies often neglect both the unemployed and the rich owners of wealth. In fact the Service Class used in the Oxford studies is so large that it does not distinguish those with really top jobs. Critics suggest that there is still a small elite at the top, recruited from men who went to public schools and Oxford or Cambridge.

7> **THE DISTRIBUTION OF INCOME AND WEALTH**

Income is usually earned from working, and is received in the form of wages or salary. But it can be unearned, as when it is received as a gift or as a return on capital (e.g. interest on a building society account).

During the 1980s the distribution of income has become more unequal. The rich have got richer and the poor have got poorer, both relative to the rich and, in some cases, poorer in real terms.

If you imagine the total of all incomes as the national cake then the rich are getting a bigger slice (of a bigger cake) and the poor a smaller slice.
- The top 20% earned 34% of total income in 1979 and 40% in 1989.
- The bottom 20% earned 10% of total income in 1979 and 7% in 1989.

❝❝ Income inequality ❞❞

In general the wages going to manual workers (the working classes) have risen more slowly, if at all, than the incomes of non-manual workers (the middle classes). Although the tax and benefits system does redistribute income from richer to poor, since 1979 the overall changes in the taxation and benefits system have not helped to re-distribute income in this direction, in fact quite the opposite as shown above.

Who is low paid?

Low pay is a major cause of poverty (see chapter 6). Women and/or ethnic minority workers are more likely to be low paid than white males, and this is discussed in the previous two chapters. People with disabilities are particularly disadvantaged in the job market and are more likely to be unemployed and low paid than any other group.

Gender and income

Women's average pay remains considerably lower than men's pay (see ch 3). The gap has narrowed in the last twenty years but is still larger than elsewhere in Europe. The figure for women's average earnings compared to men is 72%. Some of the difference is due to men working longer hours and also earning overtime, but the average hourly rate for women is only 74% of that for men. Both these figures are the highest ever recorded for women. (Figures from 1993 New Earnings Survey.)

Problems with earnings surveys

- They tend to measure *individual's earnings,* when our standard of living normally depends on *household income* and *household expenditure.* For example, a household with two working adults and no dependent children is probably better off than one where one earner has a dependent adult partner and children.
- The Earnings surveys tend to count wages and salaries and disregard income from rent, dividends, interest and private pensions. This means that the income of the better off is underestimated.

❝❝ Problems with earnings surveys ❞❞

- Benefits are also not counted as earnings and this underestimates the income of the poor.
- Income gained from self employment tends not to be counted, yet this represents a significant source of income.
- Earnings from the "black economy" and crime are not recorded. Some studies have estimated the black economy (i.e. income received but not declared for tax) as high as 8% of total National Income.

THE DISTRIBUTION OF WEALTH

Wealth is cash or other assets, such as land, which are owned by individuals or groups. The major forms of wealth held in the UK apart from cash and land are businesses, shares in companies, stocks etc. These are generally referred to as *disposable wealth* as they can be sold and the money spent as you wish.

Private homes and the rights to retirement pensions are referred to as *non-disposable wealth.* They may be of considerable value, but individuals are unable to sell them in the case of pensions and are used on a daily basis in the case of houses. An increase in the value of houses does not particularly help those who must stay in the housing market. The table below shows the effects of including housing and pension rights in calculations of wealth. If pensions were *included,* wealth is less unevenly distributed, with the top 1% owing 11% of wealth and the bottom 50% owning 16% of wealth.

●●Wealth inequality●●

Wealth is much more unevenly distributed than income. This is still the case even if non-disposable wealth is considered, but much less so. Various business magazines and newspapers publish a list of Britain's wealthiest. They include show business figures, owners of private companies, people who have sold private companies or floated them on the stock exchange. There is a high proportion of entertainers and sports persons among the wealthiest people of Afro-Caribbean origin. There are still a considerable number of landed aristocrats who have inherited wealth with their titles; the Queen is easily the richest of these. Her wealth and income remain secret despite her agreement in 1992 to pay income tax. She will pay on a voluntary basis so that the Inland Revenue will not have access to her accounts.

Table 5.2

Percentage of wealth owned by the richest:	1971	1976	1990 (1)	1990 (2)	1990 (3)
1%	31%	21%	18%	11%	27%
10%	65%	50%	51%	37%	63%
50%	97%	92%	90%	84%	92%
The poorest 50% owned	3%	8%	10%	16%	8%

(Source: Social Trends 1988 and 1993)

(1) includes houses
(2) includes pension rights
(3) excludes houses

You do not need to know the figures but you should be able to interpret the table, answer questions about it and explain the findings.

EXAMINATION QUESTIONS

Q.1 Study ITEM A and ITEM B. Then answer the questions which follow.

ITEM A

A SURVEY OF BRITISH ATTITUDES TO SOCIAL POLICY

People were asked whether the Government had a duty to reduce the income gap between rich and poor or to provide a decent standard of living for the unemployed. Between a fifth and a quarter of the people who were surveyed said that the Government did not have such a duty.

Opinions were divided on what kind of benefits the state should provide. The salaried middle classes were willing to increase taxes to pay for improvements in education. They were unenthusiastic about working-class benefits, such as providing housing for people who could not afford to buy a house. On the other hand, the majority of manual workers supported such benefits.

(Adapted from an article in *The Independent,* 1991)

ITEM B

DISTRIBUTION OF HOUSEHOLD INCOME
percentage of all household income
received by groups of households

Proportion of all Households	1979	1987
Top fifth of Households	34.3%	39.1%
Next to top fifth of Households	23%	22.2%
Middle fifth of Households	18.2%	16.9%
Bottom fifth of Households	14.4%	12.9%
Next to bottom Fifth of Households	10.1%	8.9%

(Adapted from *Social Trends*)

a) Study **ITEM A** and state
   i)   the proportion of people surveyed who said that the Government did not have a duty to reduce the income gap between rich and poor;
   ii) the purpose for which the salaried middle classes were willing to increase taxes. *(2)*

b) Study **ITEM B** and state
   i)   the percentage of all household income received by the middle fifth of households in 1987;
   ii) which fifth of households increased its percentage of all household income between 1979 and 1987. *(2)*
c) Identify two examples of wealth and explain how they can produce income for the owners. *(4)*
d) Identify and explain two policies by which a government might reduce the income gap between rich and poor. *(4)*
e) What explanations might sociologists give for the changes in the distribution of income in the United Kingdom since 1979? *(8)*

(SEG, June 1993)

Q.2 Study ITEM A and ITEM B. Then answer the questions which follow.

ITEM A

Some sociologists have suggested that since the 1960s we have seen a division within the working class. On the one hand are affluent manual workers who own their own homes, buy expensive consumer goods and go on expensive holidays. On the other hand are manual workers who are less well off, who live on Council estates and who consume more basic items. The affluent workers may well vote Conservative, whereas the less well off are still more likely to vote Labour. It is as if the two groups of manual workers belong to quite different social classes.

ITEM B

Beliefs about the most important difference between social classes in Britain, 1984, by occupational group.

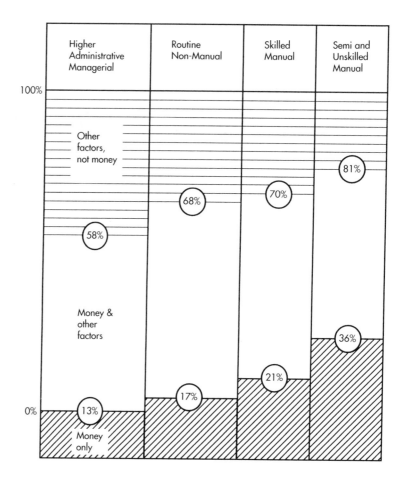

Source: adapted from a Table in paper by N BRITTEN, *BJS 1984*

a) Study ITEM A and state:
   i) where the less well off workers are more likely to live;
   ii) what the two groups of workers have in common. *(2)*
b) Study ITEM B and state:
   i) the group which was most likely to see "money and other factors" as the most important difference between social classes;
   ii) the percentage of skilled manual workers who saw "other factors, not money" as the most important difference between classes. *(2)*
c) Identify and explain two ways in which the working conditions of non-manual workers are likely to be better than those of manual workers. *(4)*
d) Identify and explain any two forms of social stratification. *(4)*
e) What factors, other than earnings, do sociologists consider before placing people in different social classes? *(8)*

(SEG, June 1992)

Q.3

a) What is meant by the term "social mobility"? (2)

b) Explain how people become socially mobile.
   What effects has social mobility had on British society? (9)

c) Using examples, show the difference between class and status. (4)

d) Show how social class position might affect a person's life chances. (10)

(Total 25)

(NEAB, June 1992)

Q.4

Study **ITEM A** and **ITEM B.** Then answer the questions which follow.

ITEM A

Some major surveys used in "Social Trends"

Name of survey	How often survey is conducted	Who is questioned	Area covered	Response rate (percentages)
Census of Population	Every 10 years	Household Head	United Kingdom	100
British Social Attitudes Survey	Every year	Adult in Household	Great Britain	67
British Crime Survey	Occasionally	Adult in Household	England & Wales	77
General Household Survey	All the time	All adults in Household	Great Britain	84

(Adapted from *Social Trends*)

ITEM B

COUNTING UNEMPLOYED PEOPLE

The International Labour Organisation calculates that the true level of female unemployment is 1.1 million, which is 53,000 higher than the British government's figure. The International Labour Organisation's figure includes people who are not receiving benefit. These people are excluded from the British government's figure.

(Adapted from *The Independent,* 1991)

a) Study **ITEM A** and state
   i) which survey has the lowest response rate;
   ii) which survey does **not** cover Scotland. *(2)*

b) Study **ITEM B** and state
   i) which women classified by the International Labour Organisation as unemployed are excluded from the British government's figure;
   ii) how many women were unemployed according to the International Labour Organisation. *(2)*

c) Identify **two** secondary sources which may be useful to researchers studying poverty and explain why they may be useful. *(4)*

d) Identify and explain **two** advantages a researcher may gain by undertaking a pilot study. *(4)*

e) Why should sociologists be careful when using official statistics in their own studies? *(8)*

(SEG, June 1993)

ANSWERS TO EXAMINATION QUESTIONS

Q.1

a) i) Between a fifth and a quarter.

   ii) Improvements in education.
   (Education gets the mark but best to be sure!)

b) i) 16.9%.

   ii) The top (fifth of households).

c) Owning a house is wealth which can produce income if it is rented to someone else.

   Savings in a Building Society produce income in the form of interest.

   Note:

   Wealth is OWNED by people. It could be valuables, land, savings etc. (I own most of my family home, the rest is mortgaged, and the right to a teacher's pension when I retire; neither produce any income.)

   Income is money, which is earned by working or by "using" your wealth. It may be rent, interest or dividends on shares.

d) 1 Any progressive tax will take more from the rich than the poor whether it is on income or wealth. e.g. Income tax or capital gains tax.

   2 Intervention in the labour market e.g. minimum wages or increased power for Trade Unions would raise wages for lower paid workers.

   Alternatives include:

   3 Paying low paid public sector workers more.

   4 Benefits which favour the poor.

e) (At least two explanations should be discussed. Choosing three or even four might require less detailed analysis.)

   The Governments since 1979 have reduced the standard rate of income tax which affects most tax payers. They have also cut considerably the higher tax rates and this has left more income in the pockets of the highest paid.

   At the same time the government has made it more difficult to claim some benefits such as unemployment benefit, which is no longer available for those under 18. The real value of some benefits, such as child benefit, has also been reduced by inflation.

   There has been an increase in the number of people who are poor because they are dependent on benefits. The reasons for this include high levels of unemployment and the increase in single parent families because of more family breakdown.

   High levels of unemployment and trade unions weakened by declining membership and changes in the law have allowed many employers to pay low wages. This has widened the gap between rich and poor.

Q.2

a) i) On council estates

   ii) They are manual workers

b) i) Routine non-manual workers. (68 – 17 = 51)
   (subtract "money only" figure from the other figure in the same column which represents "money and other factors" and "money only")

   ii) 30% (100 – 70 = 30)

c) Possible answers to be explained include:

   Shorter hours worked, longer holidays, pension entitlement, paid sick leave, lower risk of accident or hazardous substances, more control over work.

d) Class, caste, race, gender, slavery, feudalism etc.

   The explanation should include basis for membership of groups and the type of inequality experienced.

   e.g. Class is based on economic differences. Marx said it was based on ownership of the means of production; other writers use occupation to distinguish classes.

   Class influences people's access to rewards in society such as health and income.

e)   Explain and discuss at least two and preferably 3 or 4 of the following.
         Objective factors: occupation, education, housing, family background etc.
         Subjective factors: what class people think they are, class consciousness,
     political values etc.

Q.3
a)   Movement up or down the class structure by individuals or groups. You could
     briefly mention inter-generational and intra-generational mobility.
b)   People become mobile through education, unemployment, employment and
     promotion, marriage, divorce, ill health etc. Remember movement can be down
     as well as up. Changes in the occupational structure and/or the birth rates of
     different classes create the space for upward mobility.
         The effects include getting the best people into the most important jobs,
     reducing class conflict, dividing families if only some members are mobile.
c)   Class is objective and based on economic differences. Status is subjective and
     based on honour or prestige. They may or may not coincide. Explain and
     illustrate.
d)   Explain and discuss the effects of class on 3 or 4 of the following: Health,
     education, family life, employment and promotion, housing, political power, etc.

STUDENT'S ANSWER WITH EXAMINER'S COMMENTS

Q.4
1   Time allowed 35 minutes.

a)   Study ITEM A and state:
     i)   how many women achieved social mobility;   *(1)*
          | Marrying up or marrying down. |

 Good 2/2

     ii) on what basis the social class of a child is defined   *(1)*
          | The occupation of the father defines the class of the child. |

b)   Study ITEM B and state:
     i)   what percentage of the sons of lower middle class fathers were middle class in
          1983;   *(1)*
          | 34.2% of the sons of lower middle class fathers were middle class in 1983. |
     ii) what class the sons of working class fathers were most likely to be in 1983.
                                                                                 (1)

Good 2/2

          | They were most likely to be working class. |

Relevant point.

Could be expressed more
clearly; no explanation. 3/4

c)   Identify and explain two ways in which the class structure of Britain has changed
     since 1945.   *(4)*
     | The class structure has changed since 1945 because of better education for all.
     This has closed the gap between the classes as the middle class and working
     class are educated together in comprehensives.
         Working class and white collar jobs have become the same status. |

Relate this point to
mobility.

Relevant, but no
explanation. 2/4

d)   Identify and explain two difficulties faced by sociologists when they come to
     measure social mobility.   *(4)*
     | Sociologists don't always agree what class a job is. People in the same job earn
     different amounts.
         What happens if the wife is the main breadwinner? |

e)   The children of professional workers are more likely than the children of semi-
     skilled or unskilled manual workers to achieve a professional position. Explain
     why this is so.   *(8)*

66 Some relevant points. Could mention how people choose jobs and if class background helps to get them. 5/8 99

Children of professional workers are more likely to achieve a professional position because they have better life chances. Middle class families provide a good start in life, not a silver spoon! but help.

Parents help with education by giving encouragement and help. They are more likely to have a private education. Professional parents will show their children the importance of education and will encourage them to go to university. Parents will be role models who he can follow into the professions. His peer group often go into professions too.

66 Overall, shows reasonable knowledge of the subject. Material could be applied more effectively to the questions actually set. 14/20 99

REVIEW SHEET

This Review Sheet covers both ethnic and class inequalities (i.e. chs. 4 and 5)

■ All humans are members of a single _____

■ Every individual inherits a unique set of _____

■ Look back to the chart shown under ITEM A of Question 2 in Chapter 4.
   1 Use the figures in the chart to show that the ethnic minorities are disadvantaged compared to the rest of the UK population (in terms of unemployment).

      _____

      _____

   2 List some factors which might account for the disadvantage you have noted.

      _____

      _____

■ Look back to the charts shown under Item A of Question 3 in Chapter 4.
   1 Which social class had the highest rate of acute illness?_____

   2 What was that rate (approximately)?_____

   3 Use the chart on serious illness to demonstrate the disadvantage of class 1 compared to class 5

      _____

      _____

   4 Use the chart showing fatal accidents at work to demonstrate the disadvantage of class 1 compared to class 5.

      _____

      _____

■ Look back to the chart shown under Item B of Question 3 in Chapter 4. Use the chart to demonstrate the disadvantage of Afro-Caribbeans in educational opportunity compared to the general population.

      _____

      _____

■ List some of the problems involved with using *occupations* as a measure of class.
   1 _____
   2 _____
   3 _____
   4 _____

■ Name, and briefly describe, the two classes which Karl Marx identified.
   1 _____

      _____

   2 _____

      _____

■ Explain what is meant by "embourgeoisement".

      _____

      _____

■ Briefly describe the following
1 Intra-generational mobility

_____

2 Inter-generational mobility

_____

3 Stratum mobility

_____

■ List some of the factors which have brought about greater social mobility.

1 _____

2 _____

3 _____

4 _____

■ Look back to the chart shown under Item B of Question 2 in Chapter 5.
1 Use the figures in the chart to compare the view of the Semi and Unskilled Manual worker on "money only" to that of the Higher Administrative Manual worker.

_____

_____

2 Use the figures to compare the attitudes to work of the different occupational groups.

_____

_____

Great Britain

	Age group (percentages)				
	0–15	16–29	30–44	45–59	60 and over
Ethnic group					
West Indian or Guyanese	24	30	19	19	9
Indian	29	25	25	14	6
Pakistani	44	23	20	11	3
Bangladeshi	46	26	15	11	3
Chinese	25	28	29	13	5
African	31	28	28	10	2
Arab	23	30	33	9	5
Mixed	54	24	13	6	3
Other	27	27	31	10	4
All ethnic minority groups	34	26	22	13	5
White	19	21	21	17	21
Not stated	36	22	16	11	15
All ethnic groups[1]	20	22	21	17	20

[1] Including White and Not Stated.

(Social Trends 1993)

■ Use the figures in the table above to compare:
1 the age distribution of the ethnic minority groups as a whole with that of the whole population (all ethnic groups)

_____

_____

2 the age distribution between the different ethnic minority groups

_____

_____

POVERTY AND WELFARE

DEFINING AND MEASURING POVERTY

EXPLANATIONS OF POVERTY

WELFARE STATE

VOLUNTARY ORGANISATIONS

GETTING STARTED

In this chapter we look at the definition and measurement of poverty. We see that some of the definitions of poverty involve falling below some *absolute* standard of living, whereas others involve looking at the *relative* standard of living of different individuals and groups in the society. After trying to find facts and figures to measure changes in poverty, we look at some of the explanations behind increasing levels of poverty. We then look at the role and operation of the welfare state, before concluding with an account of the role of the Voluntary Organisations.

The main themes in questions set on this topic area include:

■ THE PROBLEMS OF DEFINING POVERTY.
■ THE PROBLEMS OF MEASURING POVERTY.
■ WHO ARE THE POOR?
■ ASSESSING DIFFERENT EXPLANATIONS OF POVERTY.
■ HOW EFFECTIVE IS THE WELFARE STATE?
■ ROLE OF THE VOLUNTARY ORGANISATIONS.

DEFINITIONS

ABSOLUTE POVERTY. This means lacking the basic necessities of life. Health and even life is threatened.

RELATIVE POVERTY. This exists when people earn so much less than average pay that they are unable to participate in ordinary living patterns.

SUBJECTIVE POVERTY. This is the feeling of being left out of every day life because of a lack of money.

THE CULTURE OF POVERTY. The set of values, norms and behaviour patterns which distinguish the poor from the rest of society.

THE WELFARE STATE. Government intervention in society to deal with social problems and provide social services. The main services are health, education, social security (including unemployment benefits) and housing.

RELATED TOPICS INCLUDE:

■ Stratification
■ Family
■ Work and Unemployment
■ Underdevelopment
■ Urbanisation.

ESSENTIAL PRINCIPLES

Defining poverty is a political as well as a sociological problem.

ABSOLUTE POVERTY

1 **THE PROBLEMS OF DEFINING AND MEASURING POVERTY**

Rowntree tried to define poverty in a scientific way by calculating an *absolute poverty line* based on the *minimum income* necessary to maintain a healthy life. This method involves selecting a "shopping basket" of necessities such as food, clothing and housing and calculating the family income required to buy it. He distinguished *primary poverty* caused by low income from *secondary poverty* caused by spending unwisely.

66 Cycle of poverty 99

Rowntree also discovered THE CYCLE OF POVERTY which demonstrated how people could move in and out of poverty during their life-time as their income and commitments changed. A typical pattern would show that couples were best off before they had children and then when their children were employed but still living at home. They would be worst off when they had dependent children and when they had retired. Single people are generally worse off than the married at all stages.

THE PROBLEMS with this method include:
1   Deciding what is a necessity is difficult. There is no fixed list; e.g. in rural areas and others not served by public transport, you might need a car to work and to shop. Even the necessary intake of food to maintain good health depends on occupation or age.

66 Problems with measuring absolute poverty 99

2   Assuming that the poor, even if they have the minimum income have the opportunity and understanding to spend as wisely as the experts recommend. Otherwise the "minimum" level of income may still fail to maintain good health (i.e. secondary poverty will exist).
3   Basic needs change. Longer life expectancy and smaller families means that people now have to make greater provision for their old age.

RELATIVE POVERTY

The *relative poverty line* is calculated by listing not just what is required for subsistence, but in addition what is needed to take part in everyday life. Townsend produced his own list of items which he said were necessities. In 1954 this included newspapers but not contraceptives. His revised 1979 list had 12 items covering diet, social activities and housing.

66 'Relative Poverty' 99

MACK and LANSLEY (1985) did a sample survey asking the public which of a list of 35 items were necessary for a minimum acceptable standard of living, not just survival or subsistence. They calculated the number of the poor and the depth of their poverty by identifying those who lacked a number of the 26 items that most of the subjects in the survey said were necessities in terms of today's lifestyles. They found, using this measure, that 22% of the population were on the margins of poverty and 5% in intense poverty. The most necessary 4 items of the 26 items described were housing, heating, the sole use of indoor toilet and bath, and freedom from damp. The least necessary of the 26 were cigarettes and a car.

THE PROBLEMS with this method include:

1   Ensuring that those who lack items do so through lack of means rather than by choice. For example, dietary needs such as eating a joint of meat once a week, eating meat or fish every other day, eating two hot meals a day and children eating three meals a day, are all included in the 26 items.
2   Being aware that what is seen as a need may change, so that lists must be updated regularly. When the government first paid additional payments to the poor for exceptional needs they allowed claims for one corset (wife only) and one waistcoat (householders only). In 1968 Coates and Silburn found that 22% of residents on Nottingham housing estates were "in poverty" and 90% had TV but only 10% had refrigerators.

Problems with measuring
relative poverty

Another way of calculating relative poverty is to look at changes in the distribution of income and wealth in the country.

■ Townsend (1991) used the government's own figures and claimed that from 1979–1989 the income of the poorest 20% had fallen by 4.6% while the income of the richest 20% had risen by 40%.

■ Piachaud (1991) calculated that the income of a married claimant of unemployment benefit had fallen from 35% of average earnings in 1979 to 27% in 1990.

■ J. Williams (1992) showed how the proportion of individuals with below half *average income* had increased from 10% of the population in 1979 to 20% in 1990. This is one of the ways in which the government has defined the poor, although it does not state an official poverty line. In a practical sense, the level of income support also indicates the government's view on a poverty line, since those with income levels below the figure specified are entitled to a cash supplement to make up the difference.

Who are the poor?

The social groups who are most vulnerable to poverty vary from time to time and place to place. Frank Field, a Labour MP and writer on poverty issues, claimed that there is an "underclass" of the long term unemployed, single parent families and the elderly who have been made and kept poor by the Government's economic and social policies since 1979. Other politicians and sociologists have used the term "underclass" to describe poor people who "behave badly". This might be measured by illegitimacy, crime or the unwillingness to work. Thus the problem of poverty becomes, in this view, a problem for the non-poor who feel the need to control the poor as much as to take measures to reduce their poverty.

The underclass again

The Rowntree studies

Rowntree pioneered social survey research with a study of absolute poverty in York in 1899, which was followed by similar studies in 1936 and 1950. In 1899 the main causes of poverty were low wages, large families or the death of the chief wage earner. In 1936 the main causes were low wages and unemployment, and by 1950 old age and sickness were the only significant causes. It appeared that economic growth and the Welfare State were leading to the elimination of poverty, except for a residual group who would require higher benefits.

Abel Smith and Townsend rediscover poverty (1960)

In 1960 they found that, once again, low wages and large families had caused an increase in relative poverty. They also argued that the extent of relative poverty had doubled, so that 14% of the population were now classed as poor, and these were as likely to be children as the old. Unemployment at this time was very low, with around $\frac{1}{2}$ m people living in families where the father was unemployed.

THE GROWTH OF RELATIVE POVERTY IN THE 1980s

Table 6.1 below shows a large growth (about 60%) in the number of people qualifying for income support between 1978 and 1991. Almost 5 million people received this cash benefit in 1991.

Poverty on the march!

	1978 (Feb.) ('000s)	1991 (Nov.) ('000s)
Pensioners	1,735	1,504
Unemployed	678	1,513
Sick and disabled	222	} 1,806
Others	382	
Total	3,017	4,823

Source: CSO

Table 6.1 Number receiving income support (previously supplementary benefit)

We can see that the poor in the 1990s remain a familiar list:
- the unemployed and their families.
- the low paid and their families.
- pensioners.
- the disabled and their families.

The same picture can be seen from the figures for *households* in Table 6.2. This shows the *percentage* of various household groups whose income is *less than half* that of *average* UK income. For example, in 1989 as many as 69% of all the households which had at least one person (head or spouse) unemployed earned less than half average UK income. Again, in 1989 as many as 40% of all households with at least one person (head or spouse) over 60 years had less than half average UK income. Being unemployed, old, in part-time work (i.e. usually low paid), was likely to bring you into relative poverty.

	1979	1981	1987	1988/9
Couple, both in full-time work	1	2	4	4
Couple, one in full-time work, one in part-time	2	3	5	5
Couple, one in full-time work, one not working	6	8	15	15
Single, in full-time work	2	1	3	4
One or more in part-time work	15	23	21	26
Head or spouse aged 60 or more	20	14	21	40
Head or spouse unemployed	58	52	67	69
Others	35	34	50	58
All economic types (%)	9	11	19	22
All economic types (m)	5.0	6.2	10.5	12.0

Source: Department of Social Security (1992)

Table 6.2 Percentage of each group whose income is below 50% of average UK income, 1979–1988/9

2 EXPLANATIONS OF POVERTY

The first three explanations suggest that poverty is not just a lack of money and that it may be caused, or perpetuated, by the poor themselves. The later explanations concentrate on social causes and tend to emphasise inequality as a major cause of poverty.

BLAME IT ON THE POOR!

Poverty has been seen as the deserved result of weakness or wickedness. In Victorian Britain the poor were criticised for having large families and for spending their money unwisely, particularly on alcohol. The tabloid press still tell us about "scroungers" who neither need nor deserve benefits. Those in rich countries often regard Third World poverty in these terms.

THE SOLUTION was seen as encouraging the poor to behave better, through schools and churches. Missionaries did not only travel all over the world, they also ventured into the "uncivilised" inner cities.

THE UNFORTUNATE POOR

Is poverty the fault of the poor?

After the Second World War it was widely thought that the problem of poverty was disappearing for the following reasons:

- The expansion of the Welfare State.
- Economic growth bringing higher wages.
- Full employment.

The few who were still recognised as poor were seen as special individual cases, such as the old, sick or disabled.

THE SOLUTION was seen as improved benefits for all, or at least for the needy.

By the 1960s poverty had been rediscovered among the low paid. Since the 1980s full employment is no longer seen as a realistic political aim.

THE CULTURE OF POVERTY

Some explanations suggest that poverty is not just a lack of money but also that *the poor are different* from the rest of society. The poor are seen as sharing a distinctive set of attitudes and behaviours. They are said to feel helpless, dependent, inferior and live for today rather than plan for the future. This distinctive culture has been associated with the idea that there is a poor UNDERCLASS. In the USA it has been used to explain the disproportionate number of the poor who are members of minority groups.

There are different views on the relationship between this culture and living in poverty. The alternatives include:

❝ Poverty culture ❞

1   (an inferior) CULTURE causes POVERTY
2   POVERTY causes (an inferior) CULTURE which maintains POVERTY
3   POVERTY causes (a positive adaptive) CULTURE which helps the poor survive.
This third viewpoints does not blame poverty on the poor.

THE SOLUTION would be to change the culture rather than give the poor higher benefits. In the USA there were educational initiatives in the 1960s "war on poverty" which tried to help children escape from the cycle of poverty, where low income limits educational success.

SITUATIONAL CONSTRAINTS

Critics of the cultural explanations claim that economic conditions limit the opportunities of the poor. Low pay, high unemployment and racial disadvantage all prevent the poor improving their position.

THE SOLUTION would require increasing opportunities for people to acquire adequate paid jobs. Racial discrimination could be tackled and improved childcare made available for single parents.

THE FAILURE OF THE WELFARE STATE

If the aim of the Welfare State is to redistribute incomes from the rich to the poor, it has had only limited success. The level of benefits is seen as inadequate and some of the poor are not even entitled to benefits.

❝ Are others to blame for poverty? ❞

THE SOLUTION would be to ensure benefit levels are adequate, either by raising them for all or TARGETING them on the very poor.

Some NEW RIGHT sociologists claim that poverty is perpetuated by making the poor dependent on benefits.

THE SOLUTION would be to ensure that benefits do not exceed possible earnings and to make people work for benefits. This is called "WORKFARE".

THE POWERLESSNESS OF THE POOR

The poor may be weak, not just because of their lack of money but also because they lack the *political power* which comes through organisations such as political parties, pressure groups or Trade Unions. Vulnerable groups may include the old, the young, women, ethnic minorities, immigrants, the sick and people with disabilities.

THE SOLUTION would be for the poor, perhaps with the help of others, to acquire more power.

MARXIST VIEW

Poverty is seen as the inevitable result of inequality resulting from the exploitation of the working class in Capitalist societies. The poor and the unemployed have a "useful" warning effect on those in the working class who are in work and relatively well paid.

THE SOLUTION would be the end of exploitation and the redistribution of income following the revolutionary overthrow of Capitalism.

WOMEN AND POVERTY

Feminists have argued that women are particularly vulnerable to poverty. They often work part-time and tend to do "women's jobs" which are frequently low paid. Marriage and motherhood may make women dependent on men or, in many cases, on the State.

THE SOLUTION is for women to have equal opportunities to find well paid work. More equality in marriage, better child care facilities and more flexible working hours would help to achieve this.

An alternative to the feminist account of women's poverty comes from New Right sociologists who have spoken of single mothers being "married to the State" and would like to discourage single parenthood.

3 THE WELFARE STATE

WHAT IS THE WELFARE STATE?

In the Welfare State the government uses its power to modify market forces by:

1 Ensuring a minimum family income, whether people work or not.
2 Tackling the effects of problems such as sickness, retirement and unemployment.
3 Offering good social services to all, irrespective of class, race or gender.

There were early attempts to provide for the disadvantaged, such as through the workhouses for the poor (described in Oliver Twist) and through Old Age Pensions introduced in 1908. However the Welfare State in the UK is generally seen as dating from the Beveridge Report of 1942 which laid down the principles and from the various Post-War Acts which came into force in 1948 and put some of these principles into practice.

Beveridge wrote that the State should battle with the "five giant evils" which included physical want itself and 4 other evils which contributed to physical want.

The 5 giant evils he named were:

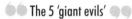 The 5 'giant evils'

■ POVERTY
■ DISEASE
■ SQUALOR
■ IGNORANCE
■ IDLENESS

Most current social policy and administration can be seen as aimed at dealing with one or more of these evils. Conventionally the Welfare State includes Social Security, the NHS, Housing aid, Education and Personal Social Services provided by social workers. Left wing sociologists would also wish to include policy towards tax allowances, occupational pensions and sick pay and all government economic policy affecting employment and wages as part of Welfare Policy. At present many of these policies seem to benefit the well-off in addition to the poor.

VIEWS ON THE ROLE OF THE WELFARE STATE

Many see the main issue for the Welfare State as being the extent to which the Welfare State reduces inequality and in particular redistributes resources between the rich and poor. There are different political viewpoints on this:

1 Reformist social policy suggests that the Welfare State has been, or is potentially, the solution to poverty by providing a safety-net for those temporarily or permanently unable to support themselves.

Views on the Welfare State

2 Marxists see the Welfare State as either an illusion which fails to redistribute income or as a successful safety valve to dampen down protest and maintain false consciousness.

3 The New Right sees the Welfare State as perpetuating poverty by keeping the poor dependent and removing the incentives to improve their situation.

WHAT IS INEQUALITY?

When we considered stratification (ch 5) it was suggested that inequality could be measured using three dimensions:

1 The distribution of rewards, e.g. income, wealth and power.
2 Opportunity, i.e. access to rewarded positions. (life chances)
3 Subjective measures, e.g. the experience of deprivation.

We now consider how different parts of the Welfare State might help to reduce these different forms of inequality.

Taxation

Progressive and regressive taxes

- Progressive taxes redistribute income, e.g. different rates of income tax with the richer paying a higher proportion of their incomes in tax
- Neutral taxes affect people equally by taking the same proportion of the incomes of rich and poor.
- Regressive taxes favour the better off by taking a smaller proportion of their incomes, e.g. a ceiling on National Insurance contributions for all earnings over a particular level.
- Direct taxes are charged on income and are usually progressive, e.g. income tax.
- Indirect taxes are charged on spending and are usually regressive, e.g. VAT on buying certain goods and services means that both rich and poor pay the same absolute amount of tax.

Since 1979 the overall burden of tax has increased slightly but has shifted considerably from direct to indirect taxes. The rich have benefited, particularly from a lowering of direct rates of tax. All governments tend to increase taxation. Wealth is not effectively taxed and the distribution of wealth is much more unequal than the distribution of income.

Benefits

1 Many benefits have increased in value, but not relative to earnings. The UK spends less on social security than other EC countries but more than the USA. It is, nevertheless, now the biggest item of public expenditure whereas in the past it was exceeded by defence and education.

2 Tax allowances on private health, education and housing spending all favour the better off. Other sources of private welfare, such as occupational pensions and sick pay, are also tax allowable for employers.

Role of benefits

3 The poor may not take up benefits because of ignorance or pride. There may be administrative problems in claiming benefits for some of the most needy, for example the homeless.

4 Some groups have ceased to be eligible for particular benefits. For example, entitlement to unemployment benefit has been removed from under-18s and full-time students can no longer claim housing benefits or maintenance benefits during holiday periods.

5 Some benefits are *targeted* on those who can demonstrate need, usually through a means test of income and assets, e.g. Family credit. Other benefits are *universal*, e.g. child benefit, old age pensions, access to the NHS. Expenditure on roads and subsidies for rail fares and the opera are on items used more by the better off.

6 There is a *poverty and unemployment trap* where people dependent on benefits would be worse off if they worked. To escape from the trap, people need to be able to get work which is not low paid. Increasing numbers of both the employed and self employed earn less than benefits. This is not generally because benefits are generous but because of rules about who is eligible, e.g. home owners in work get neither housing benefit (which is restricted to tenants) nor help with repayments (which is restricted to the unemployed).

Conclusions

1 Even before 1979, Townsend claimed that: "The richest 20% of the population gained nearly 4 times as much from the social services as the poorest 20% . . . particularly via education and housing benefit."

2 Westergaard and Resler argue that any redistributive effect is WITHIN rather than BETWEEN the classes. The healthy, working, better paid lower-classes pay for the sick, the unemployed and dependent lower classes. The family life-cycle influences whether you pay or receive. For example, families with dependent children or the retired are more likely to receive benefits than families without dependent children.

3 *Residual models of poverty* suggest that the poor are special cases and support selective help through means tested benefits. Politicians refer to this as targeting benefits. *Structural models of poverty* see poverty as the result of inequality and a major redistribution of rewards or see revolution as an outcome which might otherwise follow.

4 Gans suggested that welfare professionals are some of the major beneficiaries of the welfare state through their salaries.

5 The problems of quantifying the number of the poor and their condition remains, partly because of disagreement over definitions. The real income of the poor has risen since the Second World War (not every year) but they are relatively worse off compared to average earnings.

4 VOLUNTARY ORGANISATIONS

Voluntary organisations are non-profit making and are not controlled by the State. They are often charities and although many workers are unpaid they may employ paid staff. They may replace, supplement or even oppose the State. Although not set up by the State they can be very powerful. The National Society for the Prevention of Cruelty to Children (NSPCC) exercises similar powers to social workers in protecting neglected or abused children.

Before the Welfare State, most health and social services were provided by voluntary organisations. The State gradually took over responsibility for provision, particularly after 1945. Recently, Conservative governments have encouraged the expansion of voluntary and private provision, e.g. for the care of the old or the sick in the community, partly to reduce public spending and partly because of their disapproval of a large state sector and conviction that the private sector is more "efficient".

The main activities of voluntary organisations are:

1 To provide services; e.g. Dr. Barnados and Women's Aid provide housing and care.
2 To act as pressure groups to influence government and publicise social problems; (e.g. SHELTER campaigns for the homeless, MIND for the mentally ill and the Child Poverty Action Group (CPAG) for poor children.
3 To spread information and advice; e.g. The Citizens Advice Bureaux.

The ADVANTAGES of voluntary organisations over State provision include:

 **Benefits of being voluntary**

1 They act as the nation's conscience; speaking for the forgotten and the underprivileged.
2 Sometimes it may seem necessary to criticise the State. This is more easily done by independent voluntary organisations.
3 They can focus on small specific groups, such as those with particular diseases and disabilities, e.g. SANE and The Spastics Society.
4 Being small and independent they can respond quickly and flexibly to new or changing social conditions. New ideas can be tried on a small scale, e.g. new therapies for those with disabilities.
5 People may prefer to be helped by voluntary organisations rather than accept State help which may carry a social stigma.
6 Voluntary organisations may encourage self-help rather than dependency.

The DISADVANTAGES associated with voluntary organisations include:

Problems of being voluntary

1 They may encourage the Government to shed provision which should be universal.
2 They may disguise structural problems like poverty and homelessness by dealing with symptoms rather than causes.
3 Staff may not be properly trained.
4 Volunteers may threaten the employment of paid workers.

EXAMINATION QUESTIONS

Q.1 Study ITEM A and ITEM B. Then answer the questions which follow.

ITEM A

In "Poverty in the UK" (1979) Peter Townsend attempted to discover how commonly people in the United Kingdom experienced poverty. A sample of the population was given questionnaires which sought information, not just about their income, but, for example, about the kind of food they ate, the kind of conditions in which they lived, the kind of leisure activities in which they participated.

For Townsend, being in poverty means not having sufficient income to buy the kind of food, live in the kind of conditions, participate in the kind of leisure activities, which are all generally accepted as part of the average standard of living in their society. The poor thus suffer relative deprivation. They cannot afford to buy what others typically buy, do what others typically do.

ITEM B

SPENDING PATTERNS

	Family on state benefit	All households
housing repairs	£0.82	£5.89
fuel	£11.46	£12.26
food	£30.50	£45.20
alcohol	£2.47	£8.69
tobacco	£6.59	£4.95
clothing and footwear	£3.55	£16.64
durable household goods	£3.13	£19.56
other goods	£5.69	£16.53
transport	£4.40	£30.46
services	£4.78	£25.04
miscellaneous	£0.45	£1.47

(Source: *New Society*, 6.3.87, J Bradshaw and J Morgan)

a)   Study **ITEM A** and state:

i)   the meaning of "relative deprivation";
ii)   the main sociological method used by P. Townsend in his study of poverty.
(2)

b)   Study **ITEM B** and state:

i)   the item in the table on which the "family on state benefit" spends most money;
ii)   the **two** items in the table on which the spending of "all households" was greater than the spending of "families on state benefit" by more than £20.
(2)

c)   Identify **two** separate groups in our society who are likely to be living in poverty
     and explain why this is so.   *(4)*
d)   Identify and explain two ways in which the Welfare State has tried to help those in
     poverty.   *(4)*
e)   In what ways have sociologists explained the continuation of poverty in spite of
     the existence of the Welfare State?   *(8)*

(SEG, June 1992)

Q.2   Study ITEM A and ITEM B. Then answer the questions which follow.

ITEM A

In 1983 "Breadline Britain", a survey carried out for London Weekend
Television, looked at 'relative poverty' as 'the minimum standard of living laid
down in society'. The survey found that:

6 million people could not afford some necessary item of clothing;

3.5 million people could not afford carpets and washing machines;

3 million people could not afford to heat the living areas of their homes.

"Breadline Britain" stated that 7.5 million people (or 13% of the population) were
living in poverty.

ITEM B

PERCENTAGE OF PEOPLE WHO DESCRIBED EACH OF THE FOLLOWING
ITEMS AS NECESSARY

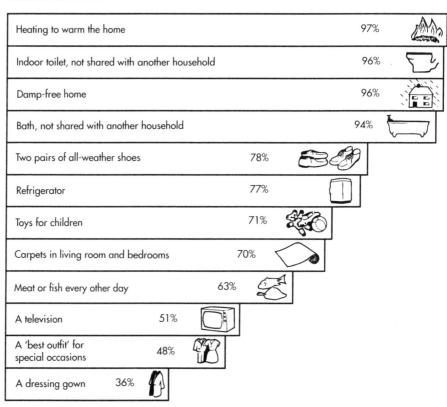

Heating to warm the home	97%
Indoor toilet, not shared with another household	96%
Damp-free home	96%
Bath, not shared with another household	94%
Two pairs of all-weather shoes	78%
Refrigerator	77%
Toys for children	71%
Carpets in living room and bedrooms	70%
Meat or fish every other day	63%
A television	51%
A 'best outfit' for special occasions	48%
A dressing gown	36%

Sources: adapted from *Poor Britain*, J MACK and S LANSLEY (Allen & Unwin) 1985

a)   Study **ITEM A** and state:
     i)   the number of people who could not afford carpets and washing machines;
     ii) the percentage of the population who were living in poverty.   *(2)*
b)   Study **ITEM B** and state:
     i)   the percentage of people who considered a television as necessary;

    ii)   which of the following was considered most necessary – a television, a refrigerator, a dressing gown.   *(2)*

c)   Briefly state **three** reasons why women are more likely to be living in poverty than men.   *(3)*

d)   Identify and explain any **two** ways in which the welfare state or voluntary groups may help people in need.   *(4)*

e)   What may be seen as the main causes of poverty in the United Kingdom over the last ten years?   *(9)*

(SEG, June 1992)

Q.3   Social Stratification and Inequality

"Deprived kids are far more likely to die"
Britain is STILL a country where the rich live longer and the poor die sooner. And the gap has grown. Poverty is a killer, while the wealthy are able to buy health, the survey concludes:

"Social inequalities increased during the 1980's. And so has the health gap between rich and poor."

Today all the major and minor killers – notably lung cancer and coronary heart disease – hit the poor hardest.

(From an article on a survey by the Association of Community Health Councils for England and Wales, *Daily Mirror* 2/1/91)

The largest will in Britain was published yesterday. The 6th Marquess of Cholmondeley, the former Lord Great Chamberlain, who died last March aged 70, left estate valued at £118,221,349.

(*Daily Telegraph,* 11/12/90)

PEOPLE living in deprived parts of the Edinburgh area are twice as likely to die prematurely as those who live in more affluent communities a report revealed yesterday.

A strong link between poverty and early death has been established by the Lothian Regional Council.

(*The Scotsman,* 12/4/90)

JOHN MAJOR says that he wants to see a classless society, which sounds fine, noble and desirable in theory.

But in practice if it were achievable – which it isn't – it would be terribly boring.

I don't want a classless society any more than I want one where every one is so lovely natured there's no scandalous gossip and nobody to look down on.

In a classless society I couldn't have climbed up a notch or two, egged on by my mother who used to hiss in my ear, "Talk posh" if ever we met one of her friends from the golf club.

---

a)   Briefly describe TWO definitions of poverty.   *(4)*

b)   Why do working class people have a lower life expectancy and worse health on average than middle or upper class people?   *(7)*

c)   Why do large differences in wealth continue in Britain?   *(9)*

(MEG June 1992)

ANSWERS TO EXAMINATION QUESTIONS

Q.1

a) i)   Poor in comparison with the average standard of living. You can use the words from the item such as "generally accepted", "average", "typically".

    ii)   A sample survey using a questionnaire. (see second sentence)

b) i)   Food

    ii)   Transport and services.

        (Subtract figure in "state benefits" column from the "all households" column.)

c)   Select two suitable groups and explain why they are poor to get both marks. You could choose the unemployed, the retired, the disabled, single parent families etc.

    An explanation can be brief e.g.:

    Single parent families may be poor because women's wages may be insufficient to pay for child care. Thus mothers may be forced into dependency on state benefits.

d)   Again you must offer explanations of your points. e.g. Free health care means the poor can use the NHS when they are sick without being afraid they could not afford treatment.

    Any benefits could be explained. You could also use education or housing but make sure you can explain how they help the poor.

e)   Discuss three or four explanations of poverty such as: The Culture of Dependency created by too high benefits, benefits which may not reach the poor and may be too low, low wages, rising unemployment etc.

    You will be more likely to gain high marks if you show you are familiar with sociological theories of poverty such as the culture of poverty, Marxist views, the poor lacking power, poverty being functional for society if not the poor and feminist perspectives which explain the poverty of women and single parent families. You do not need all or most of these but two would provide a good answer.

Q.2

a) i)   3.5 million

    ii)   13%

b) i)   51%

    ii) A refrigerator

c)   ■ More likely to be single parents.

    ■ More likely to work part-time.

    ■ Lower pay.

    You should place each reason in a complete sentence and then explain why it is so. e.g. women are more likely to work part-time because it can fit in with family responsibilities.

d)   Explain any two from: free health care, providing housing and/or housing benefit, benefits for the unemployed, disabled etc. Voluntary groups provide facilities, raise money, campaign for improved rights and facilities etc.

e)   Explain and discuss three or four of the following:

    Unemployment, family breakdown, reduced benefits, fall in the value of houses, shift from direct to indirect taxes, the development of a culture of dependency, etc.

    Remember the question asks you to focus on the last 10 years. Discussions of, for example, Rowntree's studies will not be relevant.

STUDENT'S ANSWER WITH EXAMINER'S COMMENTS

Q.3

a) Briefly describe TWO definitions of poverty   *(4)*

> Two definitions of poverty are:
>
> Poverty – when you can't afford things for yourself or family, when you can't afford to go out or buy treats.
>
> Absolute poverty – when you can't afford anything, when you can't pay bills and when you are in financial problems.

Some idea, but not clearly explained. 2/4

b) Why do working class people have a lower life expectancy and worse health on average than middle or upper class people?   *(7)*

> Working class people have a lower life expectancy than middle or upper class people because they have not had a good education, so therefore they can't get a good job which means they are stuck with the dangerous jobs e.g. miner, builder. So they could have an accident at work and die. Whereas middle and upper class people normally have office or clerical jobs and the risk of death is very low.
>
> Working class people's health is worse on average than middle and upper class people because they might live in housing which is damp and this is bad for your health. They might not have money to buy good healthy food and be picky about what they eat so they might have fatty and sugary food which could lead to heart attacks, high cholesterol.
>
> When one of the family gets ill or needs treatment they might not be able to afford the medicine or whatever is needed so whatever illness they have would probably get worse which all boils down to poverty.

Quite good. Identifies jobs and gives some explanation.

Some good points here – housing and diet considered.

NHS is largely free, especially for the poor.

Quite Good. 5/7

c) Why do large differences in wealth continue in Britain?   *(9)*

> Large differences in wealth continue in Britain because when children are born into a family it can be very hard for them to be socially mobile.
>
> If you are working class it is unlikely that you can afford to go to a posh boarding school, so you might not get a really good education which means that when you go for a high class job you won't get it because your qualifications are not good enough. This means you will be stuck with a working class job that does not pay a lot of money.
>
> Whereas if you were middle or upper class you would get the best of education which means you would get the best jobs because you were well qualified and get paid a bigger salary.
>
> The contrast is that middle class children mostly get middle class jobs and better money than working class children who get working class jobs. This is why there are still large differences in wealth because the rich get richer and the poor stay poor.

Sees the relationship between family, education and wealth. Considers social mobility.

Income not wealth is being considered here. 4/9

11/20. Overall some reasonable points, particularly in part (b).

REVIEW SHEET

Explain the difference between absolute and relative poverty.

_____

_____

List some of the problems involved in calculating an absolute poverty line.

1 _____

2 _____

3 _____

List some of the problems involved in measuring relative poverty.

1 _____

2 _____

Look back to Table 6.2. Use the figures on income distribution in this table to show:

1 that the unemployed are disadvantaged _____

_____

2 that the elderly are disadvantaged _____

_____

3 that those in part-time work are disadvantaged _____

_____

Briefly refer to some of the factors which might be involved in bringing about poverty.

1 _____

2 _____

3 _____

4 _____

List the five "giant evils" identified by Beveridge when founding the Welfare State.

1 _____ 3 _____ 5 _____

2 _____ 4 _____

Consider the views of the following groups towards the Welfare State.

1 Reformists   _____

2 Marxists   _____

3 New Right   _____

Explain the following:

1 Progressive taxes _____

2 Regressive taxes   _____

3 Targeting   _____

4 Universal benefit _____

Briefly identify some of the advantages of voluntary organisations compared with State provision of welfare services.

1 _____

2 _____

3 _____

Briefly identify some of the disadvantages of voluntary organisations compared with State provision of welfare services

1 _____

2 _____

3 _____

Look again at the table in Item B of Question 1. Use the figures in the Table to show how a family on State benefit is disadvantaged in terms of:

1 Spending on clothing and footwear

_____

2 Spending on food

_____

3 Spending on durable household goods

_____

Look again at Item B in Question 2. Use the figures to compare the importance of a television, a refrigerator and heating to the typical family

_____

_____

Look at the table alongside.

1 What percentage of total income (after tax) is received by the bottom 10% of income receivers? _____

2 How does this compare with the top 10% of income receivers?

_____

3 If there was perfect equality, how much should the bottom 10% of income earners receive out of total income? _____

4 Use the figures in the table to show that there is inequality in terms of the income distribution. _____

_____

_____

5 How would you expect this distribution of income *after* tax to compare with the distribution of income *before* tax? _____

_____

_____

Income receivers	1989 % of income
Bottom 10%	2.8
Bottom 20%	6.5
Bottom 30%	10.9
Bottom 40%	17.4
Bottom 50%	25.5
Bottom 60%	35.2
Bottom 70%	46.7
Bottom 80%	60.1
Bottom 90%	75.9
Bottom 100%	100.0

Percentage shares of income after tax in the UK

GETTING STARTED

The family has always been an important topic in sociology. The family was originally seen as a basic social arrangement which was beneficial for individual family members and for the stability of the wider society. However, since the rise of feminism there has been a shift in emphasis to a more critical point of view. It is no longer taken for granted that families are necessarily good for individuals or for society.

The main themes on which questions are often set on this topic:

- TYPES OF FAMILIES AND FUNCTIONS OF THE FAMILY.
- ROLES OF PARENTS AND CHILDREN.
- DIVORCE AND THE DECLINE OF THE FAMILY.
- CHANGES IN FAMILY LIFE IN MODERN BRITAIN (INCLUDING ETHNIC DIVERSITY).
- ALTERNATIVES TO THE (CONVENTIONAL) FAMILY.

RELATED TOPICS:

- Age.
- Gender.
- Population.
- Socialisation and Culture.
- Poverty and the Welfare State.

DEFINITIONS

FAMILY. There are sociological disputes about defining the family. The main characteristics are living together, economic cooperation, reproduction and socialisation of children. The family often, but not always, coincides with the household.

HOUSEHOLD. A group of people who live together under one roof and share certain aspects of their lives, such as eating together. The household is often the unit of study in social surveys such as the census.

NUCLEAR FAMILY. Consists of parents and their immature children. G. P. Murdock claimed that the nuclear family was *universal*.

EXTENDED FAMILY. Includes the additions to the nuclear family of other kin. They may be a third generation or the families of adult brothers or sisters.

KINSHIP. Kin are a larger family group where relationships are based on "blood" (perhaps we ought to say genes nowadays) or marriage. In many societies some relationships are seen as more important than others in defining rules of inheritance of property or incest.

- PATRILINEAL KIN are traced through fathers.
- MATRILINEAL KIN are traced through mothers.

INCEST TABOO. This is a rule which forbids sexual relationships or marriage within a kinship group. The number of forbidden partners varies enormously. For Sikhs it is anyone of thousands bearing the kin name, whereas English law only prohibits sexual relations or marriage between very close family, such as parents, children, brothers and sisters. First cousin marriage is allowed.

SOCIALISATION. The process by which the values and accepted patterns of behaviour in a society are learnt.

CHAPTER 7

THE FAMILY

FAMILY TYPES AND FUNCTIONS

FAMILY ROLES

FEMINIST CRITICISM

DIVORCE

ETHNIC DIVERSITY

ALTERNATIVES TO FAMILY

ESSENTIAL PRINCIPLES

1 > FAMILY TYPES AND FAMILY FUNCTIONS

The list of definitions at the start of this chapter considers different types of families. When sociologists talk about the *functions* of the family they mean the ways in which the family satisfies certain basic needs which all societies have. Lists of the functions vary but this is a typical list:

1 Sexual, reproductive and legitimising function.
2 Socialisation and social control function.
3 Economic or maintenance functions.
4 Companionship functions.

1 SEXUAL, REPRODUCTIVE AND LEGITIMISING FUNCTIONS

Families provide the basis for rules controlling sexual behaviour. These may vary between societies and change over time. These rules are often supported by religious beliefs. We expect married couples to have a sexual relationship and there are rules against incest which prohibit relationships between other family members. Sexual relationships outside of marriage are more or less disapproved of by different groups. (You might consider the possible consequences of a society where there were no rules about sexual behaviour.)

> ❝ Some typical family functions across different societies ❞

In most societies the family provides the location for having and caring for babies. Any alternative to the family would have to deal with this task as well as with the other functions listed here.

The minimum legitimising function is the providing of a father for a child. This means that some man accepts the responsibility for child care. In the past, illegitimacy has meant that the child may lack certain legal rights and carry some kind of social stigma.

2 SOCIALISATION AND SOCIAL CONTROL FUNCTIONS

As we have seen, members of society have to learn the values and accept patterns of behaviour of that society. The family is the primary agent of this process, which is called socialisation. Parents have authority over children and there are usually ties of love and affection which encourage conformity.

3 ECONOMIC OR MAINTENANCE FUNCTIONS

In pre-industrial and early industrial societies, families are usually units of economic production. However, in modern industrial societies there tends to be a separation of home and work, although the family is still linked by economic cooperation. Those who have paid employment accept responsibility to provide for dependent members. The family can be seen to be a unit of economic consumption. Many products from cars to cornflakes come in family sizes.

4 COMPANIONSHIP FUNCTIONS

As families have become more home-centred and the nuclear family more isolated from kin and friends and neighbours, there has been an increased emphasis on the affection and warmth provided within the family.

2 > FAMILY ROLES

We have seen that *roles* are expected patterns of behaviour associated with a particular social position. Most discussion of family roles has focused on marital (conjugal) roles but questions may require consideration of parent-child roles or the roles of the old. Roles are learned through socialisation.

The "March of progress" view suggested by Willmott and Young suggests that the family has evolved through three stages to meet the needs of a changing society and that a fourth stage was emerging in the 1970s.

The four stages were:

1 THE PRE-INDUSTRIAL NUCLEAR FAMILY
2 THE TRADITIONAL WORKING CLASS EXTENDED FAMILY
3 THE MODERN SYMMETRICAL FAMILY
4 THE MIDDLE CLASS STAGE IV FAMILY.

STAGE 1. PRE-INDUSTRIAL NUCLEAR FAMILY

Stages in the development of the family

In pre-industrial society and in the early days of the industrial revolution, men, women and children all worked together in the home. In fact Oakley said that the housewife role did not develop until factories led to the separation of home and work.

STAGE 2. TRADITIONAL EXTENDED FAMILY

BOTT (1957) distinguished *segregated conjugal roles* where the lives of couples were largely separate from *joint conjugal roles* where the couple shared more activities in the home. She said that more separate lives were associated with a close-knit social network, where the couple were close to extended family and neighbours. Whereas the more equal joint roles were associated with a loose-knit social network, where the couple were isolated from family and neighbours. Other writers have described such families as *privatised, isolated* or *homecentred*. Social networks were found mainly to be influenced by geographical mobility and housing, rather than by class in Bott's study.

Roles in the extended family

Tunstall (1962) writing about fishermen, Dennis, Henriques and Slaughter writing about coal miners (1956), and Willmott and Young writing about the London Eastenders (1950s and 1960s), all described the persistence of segregated roles in traditional working class communities. Thus class, occupation, housing, family structure and geographical mobility are all related to roles.

PARSONS concentrated on the modern isolated nuclear family in the USA and saw men and women as making equal but different contributions. Based on social psychological studies of small groups he claimed that:

Roles in the isolated nuclear family

1 Men had *instrumental roles* (e.g. working outside the home)
2 Women had *expressive roles* (providing companionship inside the home)
3 Parents had *leader roles*
4 Children had *follower roles*.

He noted that in the USA there was little difference between the roles of sons and daughters. (Asian children in this country might disagree.) This left the family with two basic functions:

1 Stabilisation of the adult personality.
2 The socialisation of children.

STAGE 3. MODERN SYMMETRICAL FAMILY

The symmetrical family

According to Willmott and Young, modern industrial societies are best suited by the nuclear family and by a tendency to more equality in marriage. Willmott and Young called this "The Symmetrical Family" (1973). Marriage was seen as emphasising companionship and love and the couple as being more home-centred. They said that there was now more equality in the relationship, but they tended to discuss the division of labour in the home in their study rather than any inequalities in power.

STAGE 4. MIDDLE CLASS (STAGE 4) FAMILY

This was seen by Willmott and Young as the family of the future. (As this was written some 20 years ago you are in a position to check their prediction. What do you think?) This type of family was to be found amongst the upper middle classes of managers and professionals. It was less home-centred than the stage 3 family, with both husband and wife having interesting jobs and pursuing their own leisure activities outside the home.

3 ▶ FEMINIST CRITICISM

Following A. Oakley in 1974, many feminists have argued against the existence of a more equal symmetrical family. They have argued that inequality can be shown by looking at:

1 The division of labour in the home.
2 Decision making in the family.
3 Domestic violence.

1. The division of labour

Men do not share housework. They may "help" but still leave women with the primary responsibility for child care and housework. Rapaport found that even in dual career families, where both husband and wife had professional jobs, the wife's work pattern had to conform to the family needs. (See housework, ch. 3)

2. Decision making

Edgell found that even in middle class families, both "very important" and "important" decisions were made by men alone or by husbands and wives jointly. However women decided on food, clothes and interior decoration.

Criticising the more equal symmetrical family

Men have a greater say in "important" family decisions because they are more often seen as the main breadwinner, and this is supported by the benefit and tax systems. Men benefit more from family spending whereas wives make sacrifices. Men's personal spending is less scrutinised by their spouses and they feel less inhibited about spending on themselves.

3. Violence

Dobash and Dobash argued that violence against wives has largely been seen as normal by our society and has rarely been challenged by the courts, the media or the police. The abuse of children can also be seen as evidence of the inequality between parent and child.

CRITICISM OF THE FEMINIST VIEW

1 Women may maintain power by controlling the home, child rearing and contacts with relatives.

A counter-criticism of feminists

2 Women, as well as men, remain in favour of marriage and the family.
3 Housework may be creative and satisfying, particularly child rearing and home improvements. Housework is not supervised and the woman is relatively free to choose her pattern of working.

HOUSEWORK AND UNEMPLOYMENT

J. Wheelock has presented new evidence which rejects the commonly held view that male unemployment does not alter the domestic division of labour. In a study of couples in NE England she found that the domestic division of labour *was* influenced by the joint effects of *male unemployment* and *women's working* hours. Wives in full-time paid work spent less time on housework and their husbands did more. Often the attitudes in these families lagged behind their actual behaviour with both women and men being unhappy with the change in roles. It seems that women's lack of time forces men to do more housework.

---

4 ▶ DIVORCE AND FAMILY DISORGANISATION

Family disorganisation is the term used to describe the breakup of the family unit for a variety of reasons including divorce. W. Goode wrote that families were disorganised when:

1 The family did not fulfil its functions.
2 The members did not perform their roles property.

(At this stage remind yourself of the functions of the family and the roles of wife, mother, husband and father.)

Causes and effects of family disorganisation include:

1 Death, disability and serious illness of one or both partners.
2 Illegitimacy.

3 Divorce, separation, desertion, annulment or continuation of an "empty shell marriage". (When partners live in the same household but there is little or nothing left of the marriage.)

Causes and effects of family disorganisation

4 Conflict between members, including abuse or neglect of children or parent.
5 Disruption caused from outside by unemployment, war, imprisonment or persecution.

For each of these cases consider how role or functional failure is likely to occur. e.g. illegitimacy suggests the failure of the father role and a possible undermining of the economic maintenance function.

CRITICAL THOUGHTS

Goode is assuming that the conventional family is a good thing and that variations are likely to result in problems. Despite the problems which might follow from divorce, for many people it is primarily a solution to a problem rather than a cause of one. However, divorce is seen as a threat to the future of the family because of religious attitudes which see the marriage as a holy and indissoluble union and romantic notions that marriage is based on everlasting love.

DIVORCE IN BRITAIN

Since 1960 there has been a massive 600% increase in the divorce rate in Britain which has had a considerable influence on the state of the family and the make up of households. By 1987 the UK tied with Denmark as the EC country with the highest divorce rate. Over 1 in 3 marriages in the 1990s currently end in divorce.

CAUSES OF A RISING DIVORCE RATE

A. Oakley suggested that conflict in the family arose because:

1 Marriage does not meet women's high expectations because their responsibility for childcare and housework makes them economically dependent on men, being without money they can regard as their own.

Why divorce is rising

2 Men rely on wives to ease their anger and frustrations, whereas women have no one to turn to.
This might be a greater problem in nuclear rather than extended families.
3 Women are economically and physically less powerful than men. This may make them feel a lack of control over their lives or even experience violence.
4 Men control women's sexuality and fertility as women are expected to "please" their husbands and bear them children. When Oakley wrote this in 1982 there was no legal recognition of rape within marriage. This has slowly changed in the 1990s.

RECENT CHANGES IN VIEWS TOWARDS MARRIAGE AND DIVORCE

1 *Legal changes* have made divorce simpler and cheaper. Women now have improved rights to property. However easy divorce laws are not necessarily related to high rates of divorce. Even when Americans had to seek divorces in other countries or in other States in the USA they had the highest divorce rate in the Western world, whereas Norway has a low divorce rate despite very liberal divorce laws.

Changing views towards marriage and divorce

2 *Higher expectations* of marriage now exist, particularly from women, and there is more emphasis on the companionship function. Nuclear families with few children make the relationship between husband and wife more important.
3 *Increased employment* opportunities for mothers and the availability of *Welfare benefits* give women the possibility of being economically independent from husbands.
4 There has been a change in *moral values* which has made divorce more acceptable. This can be associated with the declining influence of religious values. In 1992 the separation and potential divorce of the Prince and Princess of Wales was not thought by the Prime Minister to present constitutional problems for the future King and head of the Church of England. In the USA, divorce rates are higher for non-church goers and for inter-faith marriages.
5 Young marriage based on romantic love has been associated in the past with higher divorce rates but this was before the popularity of *co-habitation* as a preparation or replacement for marriage.

EFFECTS OF A RISING DIVORCE RATE

Impacts of rising divorce rates

- Need to house more households
- Rise in single parent families
- Increased risk of poverty for families affected; financial strain of supporting (where this occurs) more than one family group
- Remarriage increases risks of future divorce for persons involved. The *children* of the remarried are also more likely to divorce when they marry
- Positive benefits of escape from unhappiness or violence.

5 > ETHNIC DIVERSITY

Britain is a multi-cultural society. Many sociologists have written descriptions of the family life of various minorities. Surprisingly many of these studies seem to confirm popular stereotypes, such as father-dominated extended families. Of course the family life of minorities is likely to be as varied as that of the majority, being influenced by class, religion and generation as well as by individual factors.

WHY DO ETHNIC MINORITIES HAVE DISTINCTIVE PATTERNS OF FAMILY LIFE?

1. Economic influences

A past history of slavery is claimed to have encouraged the development of female led Afro-Caribbean families. Modern difficulties of immigrants finding employment and housing may have encouraged the persistence of extended family ties.

2. Cultural influences

Why ethnic differences occur in the patterns of family life.

Traditions are more likely to be kept up when the minority maintains a distinct language and religion.

3. Discrimination and disadvantage

It may be that racism encourages minorities to maintain their distinctive culture, whereas tolerance encourages assimilation. The family has been described by Westwood and Bhachu (1988) as a source of strength and resistance against racism.

SOUTH-ASIAN FAMILIES

People originating from the Indian Sub-continent form one of the largest collections of ethnic minorities in Britain, with over 1.4 million persons. This "Asian" population may have some common characteristics but may also be divided in various ways such as religion, country or region of origin, caste, class and language.

Common features of South-Asian families

J. E. Goldthorpe (1987) reviewed several studies of Asians from different religious and national origins living in various parts of Britain and identified the following common features:

The typical South-Asian family.

1. Men exercise authority over women.
2. Parents exercise authority over children.
3. The old exercise authority over the young.
4. Marriages are arranged between kin groups.
5. The sexes are segregated, girls are chaperoned and the idea of family honour is strong.
6. Families are extended, often living in large multi-generational households and supporting each other in getting jobs and housing.

Some of these studies were done in the 1970s and may be out of date now. Westwood and Bhachu (1988) described Asian families as having larger *households:*

ASIAN	average size 4.6	73% include children
WEST INDIAN	average size 3.4	57% include children
WHITE	average size 2.3	31% include children

Muslim, Bangladeshi and Pakistani families are more likely to be larger than white families but are not more likely to be extended. Sikh and East African Asian households are more likely to contain three generations. Overall only 21% of Asian households are extended families but of course family ties can be maintained by living close by or through visits and the telephone.

Differences between South-Asian groups

1 Muslims in Pakistan favour cousin marriages.
2 Hindus and Sikhs marry outside Kinship groups but inside caste groups.
3 Divorce is relatively easy for Muslims but impossible for Hindus.
  (Consider why the divorce rate is lower for ethnic minorities than for the majority in Britain.)

AFRO-CARIBBEAN FAMILIES

The framework for discussing Afro-Caribbean life in Britain has been strongly influenced by the study of black family life in the USA. There is a general assumption that black British families are more likely to be female headed single-parent families than white families and that this is a "bad" thing. In particular such families have been blamed for causing poverty and crime.

	1971	1984	1988
ALL FAMILIES	8%	12%	16%
AFRO-CARIBBEAN FAMILIES	29%	31%	43%

Table 7.1   % of female headed single-parent families

The explanations for more Afro-American mother-led families include:

💬💬 Reasons for the mother-led Afro-Caribbean family 💬💬

1 African patterns of family before slavery.
2 The separation of men from women and children during slavery.
3 The disadvantages experienced by men in getting secure employment after slavery.
4 The culture of poverty.
5 The system of paying welfare benefits to households without males may encourage the family to break up.

(Consider if any of these explanations could apply to the experience of black families in Britain. It's worth bearing in mind that in the USA, but not in Britain, the poor are frequently black.)

CRITICAL THOUGHTS

Single parent families are seen by many as disorganised or inadequate families; however they may be seen as *different* rather than as problem families. Marriage in the Caribbean and among black families here is later than for the population as a whole. The single mother and one child is a common outcome of relationships which may remain stable or change into a marital relationship. Indeed the proportion of single parent families is rising faster for white families than black families. In the Caribbean there is often support for single mothers from other females, such as grandmothers. Traditional types of behaviour might only be expected to persist if they are of value to individuals and the group.

The majority of black families have two parents in the household. Conventional families are most common among the middle class and church goers.

"WESTERN WAYS ARE BAD"

The following extract shows that it is not only the lives of minorities which are subject to stereotypes.

... South Asians perceived English family life as cold and insecure, lacking in affection and in respect for the older generation. Families were small, young adults left home to make their own way, old people lived alone or were put into homes without good reason; marital breakdowns and sexual licence were rife. By Asian standards it all seemed outrageously immoral and inhumane.

(J. E. Goldthorpe, *Family life in Western Societies* (C.U.P. 1987))

6 > ALTERNATIVES TO THE FAMILY

Is there an alternative to the family?

Most people have experience of family life. Many sociologists have suggested that the family is a universal institution. Although it is clear that not everyone spends their whole lives living in families and not all families are successful, it seems difficult to imagine an alternative arrangement.

One of the few organised alternatives is the Israeli *Kibbutz*. These are communal settlements where there is mutual support for all members. The establishing of such settlements was encouraged by Socialist and nationalist political beliefs. They were rarely religious communities.

Children are raised collectively by child carers, usually eating with the whole Kibbutz in a communal dining room and sleeping away from parents in a children's house. Although there tends to be some sexual division of labour, women, including mothers, work full-time alongside men. Work is also available for the old and for those with disabilities as the people work for the community and are not employed for wages.

There have been critical accounts written about Kibbutzim which identify positive features such as the absence of family conflicts and violence and negative features which suggest that both children and adults are deprived of intimate contacts. Nowadays the Kibbutz ideal seems to be challenged by materialistic desires to own private property and the desires of parents to have more time with their offspring.

Sociologists have written about the systematic attempts to undermine family life in Communist societies. The experiment in Russia immediately after the revolution was short lived as the government became concerned about women's reluctance to have children and the difficulty of finding adequate child-care arrangements outside the family.

EXAMINATION QUESTIONS

Q.1   Study ITEM A and ITEM B. Then answer the questions which follow.

ITEM A

FAMILY LIFE IN EAST LONDON

[An extract from a study which looked at the family in the London boroughs of Bethnal Green and Woodford, mainly working class and middle class respectively, almost 25 years after Willmott and Young's classic study of family life.]

One striking difference was how home-centred most Bethnal Green families had now become. In the 1950s, this had been a feature of the Woodford families. Mothers with a three-month-old child are, of course, likely to spend more time in the home than outside it. But it was noticeable how many husbands in Bethnal Green today were almost as much around, when they could be, as Woodford husbands. Do-it-yourself, even in rented property, and television – not to mention the baby – were clearly strong competitors of the pub and the football ground.

Source: *Family and homes in East London,* ANTHEA HOLME, New Society, 12 July, 1985

ITEM B

MARRIAGES AND REMARRIAGES IN THE UNITED KINGDOM

	1961	1971	1981	1989
Total marriages (in 000s)	397	459	398	392
Remarriages as a percentage of all marriages	14	20	34	36

(Source: adapted from *Social Trends,* 1991)

a) Study **ITEM A** and state:
   i) in what way the Bethnal Green families of 1985 were similar to the Woodford families of the 1950s;
   ii) what evidence is offered for the statement that the Bethnal Green families of 1985 were home-centred. (2)

b) Study **ITEM B** and state:
   i) the number of marriages which took place in the United Kingdom in 1981;
   ii) the trend between 1961 and 1989 in the percentage of marriages which were first time marriages. (2)

c) Identify and explain two ways in which shared (or joint) conjugal roles may affect family life. (4)

d) Identify and explain two reasons why women's roles have changed in the last 20 years. (4)

e) What explanations do sociologists give for the existence of different types of family in Britain today? (8)

(SEG, June 1992)

Q.2 Socialisation, Culture and the Individual

The family pattern has been changing in Great Britain.

Everyone has an extended family, but they may not keep in touch with the members of it, or may only meet some of its members occasionally. However, the extended family is still an important feature of life in many long-established communities, particularly in the North of England and among ethnic groups that have settled in Britain recently, especially Indian and Pakistani families. There is a growing tendency, however, for the more usual family type to consist of just a husband, wife and their own children living together with no relations near by. This family is called a nuclear family.

(Gerard O'Donnell, *Sociology Today*, C.U.P. 1993)

a) What is an extended family? Describe TWO functions performed by the extended family. (4)

b) Explain the reasons for the gradual disappearance of the extended family as the main household unit and its replacement by the nuclear family. (7)

c) The modern "model" family of television advertising is a husband, a wife and two children. How typical is this of life in Great Britain today? (9)

(MEG, June 1993)

Q.3

Petitions filed (thousands)	1961	1966	1971	1976	1981	1986
By Husband	14	18	44	43	47	50
By Wife	18	28	67	101	123	131
Total	32	46	111	144	170	181

(Adapted from *Social Trends* 1989)

a) How many petitions for divorce were filed in 1981? (1)
b) Explain the large rise in petitions filed in 1971. (2)
c) What trends can be identified over the period shown? (2)
d) Explain why age may influence the likelihood of divorce. (4)
e) In what ways has the changing role of women in society had an effect on the divorce rate? (6)

(15 marks)

(ULEAC, June 1992)

Q.4 Study ITEMS A and B. Then answer the questions which follow.

WOMEN AND THEIR FAMILIES

ITEM A

Percentage of women having a particular number of children

Year of woman's birth	None %	One child %	Two children %	Three children %	Four or more children %	Total %
1920	21	21	28	15	15	100
1925	17	22	29	16	16	100
1930	14	18	30	18	20	100
1935	11	15	33	21	20	100
1940	11	12	36	23	18	100
1945	11	13	43	21	12	100

(Source: adapted from *Social Trends,* HMSO (1990))

ITEM B

More women are marrying and marrying younger. The percentage of women who marry has risen steadily from 85% in 1900 to 95% in the 1970s. Whereas in the 1950s only 1 in 6 were married by the age of 20, this proportion increased to about one-quarter in the early 1970s. Consequently there is a far smaller pool of unmarried women available for employment at a time when there is a greater than ever demand for "women-power".

(Source: adapted from *Sociology. An Introduction for Nurses, Midwives and Health Visitors,* Caroline Cox, Butterworth)

a) Look at ITEM A. For women born between 1920 and 1945, what has happened to the percentage having only one child? *(1)*

b) Look at ITEM A. According to the table, how many children were women born in 1945 most likely to have? *(1)*

c) Look at ITEM B.

   i) From the information given, what proportion of women were married by the age of 20 in the early 1970s? *(1)*
   ii) According to the information given, what is the consequence of women getting married younger? *(1)*

d) Identify and explain **two** reasons why women are having fewer children today than they were 50 years ago. *(4)*

e) Identify and explain **two** roles that the family plays in society today. *(4)*

f) Identify and fully explain **one** reason why the number of women seeking divorce has considerably increased in the last 50 years. *(4)*

g) Identify and fully explain **one** problem likely to be faced by single-parent families with dependent children today. *(4)*

(SEG, June 1992)

ANSWERS TO EXAMINATION QUESTIONS

Q.1

a) i) They were home-centred

   ii) The husbands spent a lot of time at home

b) i) 398,000

   ii) There was a smaller proportion of 1st time marriages

c) There is greater equality between husbands and wives. Sharing the roles of breadwinner and doing housework may encourage partners to share decision making.

   There will be less gender difference in the socialisation of children. Children will see their mothers working and their fathers doing some childcare and housework. This may well influence their future expectations.

d) There is more employment available for women. Heavy manufacturing industries have contracted and service industries which offer employment considered to be more suitable for women have expanded. Earning money has made women more independent.

   Attitudes toward gender roles has changed. The women's movement has influenced the way we think about gender roles so that women expect equal treatment e.g. at work or in school and inequality is no longer seen as natural.

e) There is a wide variety of family types in Britain today. Although many people still live in nuclear families. Families vary in structure and roles. Even within the nuclear family there has been a move towards a more equal relationship between husband and wife although feminists think this move has been overstated.

   The increased number of single parent families is largely the result of a rising divorce rate. This has been encouraged by the increased independence of women who are now more prepared to end an unsatisfactory marriage as they are more able to support themselves. Rising expectations of marriage produce more marriages that are considered to be unsatisfactory. A decline in the influence of religion has made people more willing to consider divorce.

   As well as more single parent families a rising divorce rate also produces more reconstituted families when people remarry.

   Immigration during the 1960s and 1970s increased the numbers of ethnic minority families in Britain. Many of these families are now three generations. There are many types of family found amongst ethnic minorities for example three generation extended family households are common amongst Sikhs and extended families based on relationships between brothers common amongst Moslems.

   The number of childless households has increased. Women are postponing or even abandoning having children in order to pursue careers. Longer life expectancy means that there are many "empty nest" families after children have left home.

Q.2

a) Definition should mention distinction between extended and nuclear family and indicate there are different types of extended family. Describe functions such as mutual economic and social support found in traditional working class communities and amongst ethnic minorities. Housing, child care, care of dependent old could all be explained.

b) Less need for sharing housing and care of dependents because of rising living standards and the Welfare State.

   Rising divorce rate loosens ties between grandparents and grandchildren.

   Geographic and social mobility means children move away from their families.

   Media present a view of the nuclear family as normal.

   (Question c) might actually challenge the idea that the nuclear family is the dominant type.)

c) Most people do live in a nuclear family for certain periods of their life. As children and later perhaps as parents.

Their relationships with wider kin vary; families are not either nuclear or extended but often more or less extended. Telephone, cars and air travel may link separate households of the same extended family.

Only a minority of families at any one time follow the model described. Family diversity can be discussed here mentioning the whole range of possible households including: Single members, childless couples, single parents, many children, co-habiting couples with or without children, different types of extended families, communal living etc.

Q.3

a) 170,000 (remember the unit is thousands).

b) The change in the divorce law which made more separated couples eligible for divorce.

(Don't worry if you do not know all the details of the various divorce laws. You should have some idea that it has become progressively easier and cheaper.)

c) Describe the trend for the total number of petitions i.e. upwards. Describe the differences between husbands and wives i.e. the figure has risen much faster for wives.

d) (Explain at least two points)

Young marriages may be subject to more economic and housing problems. People change quickly as they leave adolescence and couples may grow apart.

People live longer and spend more of their married life without children; this may reduce their commitment to marriage.

Older women who have not worked outside the home for a long time may be reluctant to initiate divorce as they would find it difficult to support themselves.

e) (Explain at least three points)

You could discuss women working and economic independence. Changing expectations of marriage and the challenging of men's "rights" which no longer include violence and sexual relations without consent. Divorced women no longer carry a social stigma. Fewer children means that women have to consider dependent children for a shorter time.

STUDENT'S ANSWER WITH EXAMINER'S COMMENTS

Q.4

a) Look at ITEM A. For women born between 1920 and 1945, what has happened to the percentage having only one child? *(1)*

> It has decreased.

b) Look at ITEM A. According to the table, how many children were women born in 1945 most likely to have? *(1)*

> 2

c) Look at ITEM B.

i) From the information given, what proportion of women were married by the age of 20 in the early 1970s? *(1)*

> One quarter

ii) According to the information given, what is the consequence of women getting married younger? *(1)*

> A smaller pool of women available for work.

❝ Good. 4/4 so far ❞

d) Identify and explain two reasons why women are having fewer children today than 50 years ago. *(4)*

> Reasonable points, but a little more explanation would help. 3/4

■ Contraception.
Contraception is widely available and it is acceptable to use it.

■ Financial reasons.
People are aware that having fewer children may be an advantage as they are expensive to raise. Mothers can get back to work quicker.

e) Identify and explain two roles that the family plays in society today.

(4)

> Good, but a little more explanation here also. 3/4

■ Raising children.
The nuclear family feeds, clothes and takes responsibility for children.
■ Sexual role.
The family discourages promiscuity and may help limit the spread of AIDS.

f) Identify and fully explain one reason why the number of women seeking divorce has considerably increased in the last 50 years. (4)

> On the right lines. Point about financial support not clear. 3/4

Financial support is available. Women are no longer dependent on their husband's income. There is more part-time work available and social security provides some support.

g) Identify and fully explain one problem likely to be faced by single-parent families with dependent children today (4)

> Not clear which one problem is being explained. 2/4

Single mothers cannot earn enough to afford child care. Even women with qualifications who earn relatively high pay for women (but less than men) find child care very expensive.

> Overall a well-informed answer. 15/20

NB The Review Sheet at the end of Chapter 8 will also cover the material in this chapter.

CHAPTER 8

EDUCATION

CHANGING FUNCTIONS OF EDUCATION

FORMAL AND INFORMAL EDUCATION

DIFFERENTIAL ACHIEVEMENT

EDUCATION, SOCIAL ISSUES AND SOCIAL POLICY

GETTING STARTED

The sociology of education is an area where all sociology students and teachers share some common experience. It provides students with the opportunity to use sociology to analyse their own experiences and in turn to use their own experiences to "check" sociological findings and theories.

This topic illustrates the relationships between sociology, current social issues and social policy, such as encouraging the expansion of opportunity. For example, the recognition of gender and ethnic inequality and policies to correct this have changed the experience of pupils and their levels of achievement.

The main issues in the sociology of education include:

- EXAMINING THE CHANGING FUNCTIONS OF EDUCATION.
- EXAMINING THE RELATIONSHIP BETWEEN FORMAL AND INFORMAL EDUCATION.
- EVALUATING COMPETING EXPLANATIONS OF DIFFERENT EDUCATIONAL ACHIEVEMENTS.

Education in Britain is going through a period of rapid change. Any topic will be of far more interest to you if you attempt to keep up-to-date with some of the more important contemporary issues. This can be done by looking at the Times Educational Supplement and the weekly education pages found in the broadsheet newspapers. Teachers are also more aware of developments in education than in most other social issues.

DEFINITIONS

THE CURRICULUM. This is the sum of learning experiences offered by schools.

THE HIDDEN CURRICULUM. Refers to the unofficial consequences of school experience. It includes knowledge gained in classrooms but also what is experienced as a result of the organisation of the school.

THE NATIONAL CURRICULUM. This is a compulsory framework set by the government outlining what pupils must learn in school.

MERITOCRACY. This is a system where rewards depend on merit, that is, on ability and effort. The alternative is rewarding particular characteristics, such as gender or family wealth.

VOCATIONAL EDUCATION. This is learning which is directly related to the role of being a worker. It is either training for a specific job or preparation for employment in general.

THE TRIPARTITE SYSTEM. This was the system of secondary education introduced in 1944. Pupils took selection tests and were allocated to one of three types of school; secondary, technical, grammar.

COMPREHENSIVE SCHOOLS. These admit a wide range of pupils and have largely replaced the selective schools of the tripartite system.

Related topics include types of social inequality (class, race and gender) and socialisation in the family, media and religion. The influence of peer groups can also be looked at when studying youth culture and deviance.

ESSENTIAL PRINCIPLES

1 ⟩ **THE CHANGING FUNCTIONS OF EDUCATION**

Sociologists have studied the relationship between education and the wider society. Functionalist sociologists see all the different parts of society fitting together and serving the interests of the population as a whole. However both Marxist and Feminist sociologists argue that social institutions and the ideas they transmit serve the interests of particular groups and not the whole population.

Thus Marxists see the education system as serving the interests of the Ruling Class at the expense of the Working Class, and Feminists see the system as helping to maintain the dominance of men over women. They call this dominance *patriarchy* (see ch. 3).

EDUCATION AND THE ECONOMY

The education system prepares people for the world of work. This may involve:

1. Specific training for a particular job

Many FE colleges prepare students for National Vocational Qualifications (NVQs) which indicate that the students can perform particular skills required by employers, e.g. word processing, catering and beauty therapy.

2. General training for work

❝❝Preparing people for work ❞❞

Language, numeracy and the ability to solve problems may be helpful in a variety of jobs. Similarly the ability to learn new skills is important to employers who cannot predict the specific skills required for jobs in the future at a time of rapid technological change. GCSE, A-levels and General National Vocational Qualifications (GNVQs) may all provide this general preparation.

3. Selection and role allocation

The examination system is used by employers to select suitable workers. There is competition for higher paid and otherwise desirable jobs and as educational standards rise the entry qualifications to enter a profession also rise. Professions such as law and accountancy used to recruit trainees with O-levels at 16, now they only recruit graduates.

4. Preparing suitable workers

Employers have indicated that they want workers with suitable attitudes to work. Schools and colleges may help students develop social skills, including dealing with the public and dressing suitably. Punctuality, good attendance and meeting deadlines to complete work are values shared by school and work.

5. The Marxist view

The "correspondence" between school and work is described by Marxists in a more critical fashion. The school is seen as producing a low skilled, docile workforce who expect little satisfaction from work and have little ambition to succeed. They claim that schools teach pupils to rely on the authority of the teacher and learn things for rewards rather than for their own sake. They will then work for cash rather than job satisfaction. The pointlessness of education for many pupils prepares them for the pointlessness of work.

THE SOCIALISATION FUNCTION

We have defined socialisation as the transmission of culture. In modern industrial societies such as Britain the education system plays an increasingly important role in this process.

Sometimes the teaching of the knowledge, beliefs, norms and values of the society is deliberate and formal. The state system in Britain includes schools and colleges which are run by particular religious denominations. These are mostly Christian, occasionally Jewish and, at the time of writing, not yet Moslem or from any other Eastern religion. Such schools usually provide appropriate religious education. In Northern Ireland most children go to specifically Roman Catholic or Protestant schools. In the USA and France, both apparently more religious countries than Britain, prayer is excluded from state schools. In this country religious assemblies and education remain compulsory.

Pupils learn appropriate behaviour (*i.e. roles*) related to gender, age and class. They may learn a patriotic interpretation of history and to appreciate the literature of the society.

The content of text books has been criticised for being narrowly nationalistic, sexist and racist. The Sociologist David Marsland has become well known for claiming that Sociology was "biased against business" and favoured a left-wing critical view of capitalism, rather than appreciating the benefits of Western free-market economies.

SOCIALISATION AND THE HIDDEN CURRICULUM

The hidden curriculum includes:

- *Attitudes and ideas* which are taught informally or found in the way text books are written, as mentioned above.

- *Organisation of the school or college.* This may itself be a source of learning for pupils. Most organisations are based on a hierarchy, where people at the top exercise authority over those below.

- *Rules.* Teachers are seen to control both time and space. Pupils may not be allowed to pass time unless it is on an approved activity. Teachers may refer to classrooms as "my room" and many spaces are denied to pupils altogether. Toilets are often seen by pupils as a refuge from teacher authority but even this space is open to teacher inspection. There may also be rules about students' appearance and conduct out of school as well as in school.

- *The relationships between teachers and pupils,* and between pupils themselves. As described above, these may reinforce attitudes on gender and race.

- *Competition.* In both academic and sports activities, competition may be seen as part of a hidden curriculum. Of course in some cases competition may be discussed openly and become part of the official curriculum.

THE SOCIAL CONTROL FUNCTION

The school can be seen as providing a child minding service which at various times, including the present, has allowed women to work. Many mothers would argue that it is not an adequate service in this respect and restricts them to part-time work and requires them to seek additional childcare. Before the introduction of compulsory education in 1870 it was customary for children to work on the land or in the factory. The earlier restriction on child labour made it difficult for mothers to work. Schooling from 5 to 16 is compulsory and the Government is currently trying to persuade schools to be stricter about enforcing attendance. Truancy has been seen as a cause of crime.

The rapid expansion of post 16 education and training (see below) has been interpreted by some left wing critics as a way of keeping youth off the streets rather than of providing them with the skills for modern technologically advanced society. The urban riots of the 1980s are discussed in the chapter on urban life.

2 ▷ FORMAL AND INFORMAL EDUCATION

INFORMAL EDUCATION

Informal education is not acquired from teaching professionals in purpose built institutions at particular times of the day, week and year. In both simple and modern societies the FAMILY is the most important place for learning. We talk of *primary socialisation* in the family which is then followed by *secondary socialisation* in schools. Other agents of socialisation are discussed elsewhere and include peer groups and the mass media.

 Informal socialisation

Much of the learning is unplanned and not consciously organised. Children learn by imitating and later working with parents. This could involve activities as varied as learning hunting skills or serving customers in a shop.

In pre-literate societies, learning is often by observation and by knowledge passed on by word of mouth. In literate societies, much learning involves the printed word although we may see in the future the possible dominance of electronic media.

FORMAL EDUCATION AND TRAINING

We tend to think of *education* as always being provided by organisations which have been set up for this purpose. In Britain the State is by far the most important provider of education although there are private schools and colleges.

We also tend to distinguish education from *training,* although the distinction is rather blurred. Training is seen as being specifically work related whereas education has a variety of purposes. However a common criticism of education has been its failure to provide a suitably skilled and motivated workforce. Training is provided by the State, private training businesses or within the workplace by all sorts of employers. The NHS, for example, trains and educates large numbers of workers, particularly professionals such as Nurses. FE colleges are large providers of both education and training and frequently combine them in vocational courses.

Formal education has a very long history but only in providing for a small minority. Mass education began in Britain in 1870 with the Foster Education Act which introduced compulsory education from 5 to 10. The school leaving age has been gradually raised and is currently 16, though in practice the normal leaving age has crept up to 18.

The idea that formal education begins at 5 and finishes forever at 16 (or 18 or even 21) has become outdated. About half of those entering higher education for the first time are classified as mature students. It seems that both education and training will become lifelong activities with people returning to learn for a variety of reasons related to work or non-work.

The distinction between formal and informal education has become less clear.

A less clear distinction between formal and informal

1 Parents may copy the methods of the school and buy school-like materials to help their children before they begin school and during their school lives.
2 State and private organisations provide courses for home study which may or may not lead to recognised qualifications. The Open University is Britain's largest provider of Higher Education.
3 Colleges will now assess learning gained informally at work or at home and may give credits which go towards gaining formal qualifications. The media have made fun of credit given for home management skills and claimed they are "degrees in washing-up".
4 The State and private industry have begun to offer formal teaching in every-day skills and leisure activities which many people have learned informally. Teaching foreign languages for business or pleasure is a huge industry.

3 ▷ DIFFERENTIAL EDUCATIONAL ACHIEVEMENT

Sociologists have tried to explain the relationship between educational achievement and class, ethnicity and gender. Explanations can be grouped under these broad headings:

■ Innate ability.
■ Out-of-school factors.
■ In-school factors.

INNATE ABILITY

Innate ability refers to talents and skills which the individual is born with rather than acquires through socialisation. Sociologists tend to underplay the importance of innate differences in explaining different levels of achievement. It seems that genetic difference might explain the performance of *individuals* but it is unlikely to explain differences between large *populations,* such as ethnic or gender groups. This view is supported by the rapid changes in the *relative* performance of boys and girls in recent times now that girls receive more encouragement in education. Female performance has improved relative to males in a consistent way over a short-period of time, yet there has clearly been no equivalent genetic changes.

Why some succeed

Some functionalist sociologists assume, rather than demonstrate, natural inequality in order to support the meritocratic view of education, i.e. selecting the most able students for the most important jobs. The system of selection at 11 years assumes that ability and the potential for achievement is innate, or at least fixed at an early age. Postponing selection to a later date recognises the importance of experience, both in and out of school.

The influence of innate factors becomes more important as equality of opportunity increases. It seems very likely that extreme variations of ability may be influenced by genetic factors. Some children show exceptional musical or mathematical talents at very young ages, even when their parents have not encouraged them. The same applies to some learning difficulties, such as dyslexia.

OUT OF SCHOOL FACTORS

These explanations identify a variety of influences under two broad headings:

■ Material deprivation.
■ Cultural deprivation.

66 Material factors 99

Material influences are those related to family income. A number of material factors have been mentioned in research, including the effects of poverty and bad housing on educational achievement.

66 Cultural factors 99

Cultural influences include parental expectations, values and child rearing styles which vary between classes. Language development and usage has also been identified as important. Most of the research in Britain has been on class differences, whereas in the USA race has always been a major concern. These studies tend to play-down the significance of individual differences and the experience of school and locate the problem in the family and neighbourhood.

IN-SCHOOL FACTORS

Education provision can also influence success. Schools vary in the quality of staff and buildings. However most explanations which identify the school as the most significant factor in explaining educational achievement tend to focus on the teacher-pupil relationship.

66 Sub-cultures 99

There are also studies of pupil sub-cultures which tend to associate anti-school attitudes with the working class and underachievement. More recently such studies have examined the ways in which girls are disadvantaged.

TEN WARNINGS to consider when looking at evidence.

1 Findings of studies carried out at the same time are sometimes contradictory.
2 The nature and extent of differential achievement sometimes changes over time. Groups previously seen as disadvantaged have often improved their performance. Therefore the dates of studies are relevant.

66 Look carefully at the evidence 99

3 Definitions of class and ethnic groups vary.
4 Classes are divided by race and gender.
5 Ethnic groups are divided by class and gender.
6 Gender groups are divided by class and ethnicity.
7 Different ethnic groups perform differently.
8 Ethnic minorities and females may succeed in terms of examination results but still be disadvantaged if schools reinforce stereotypes and allow discrimination.
10 If the issue is the existence of a meritocratic society, then it must be noted that educational success does not eliminate inequality in the job market.

GENDER

66 Gender matters 99

Although in many respects females are disadvantaged compared to males, girls tend to do better than boys in school and most measures indicate that they are improving faster than boys. Older studies tried to explain why girls had performed worse, and in many cases the results of these studies no longer apply. In fact as long ago as 1971 girls were seen to be doing better at the equivalent of GCSE (O-level) than were boys.

Out-of-school influences

The family, peer group and media can socialise girls into early leaving, marriage and what are seen as "women's jobs". These jobs, e.g. nursing and secretarial work, may have lower entry qualifications than equivalent male professions or skilled jobs and this may encourage underachievement.

The continued importance of the housewife-mother role as an incentive for early leaving is indicated by sociological research. A famous study by SHARPE (1976) described how girls learned the priorities of love, marriage, husbands, children, jobs and careers (in that order). GRIFFIN (1985) suggested that early leaving was seen by working class girls as an escape from their responsibility for housework, as paid employment raised their status in the family.

The higher number of girls of Bangladeshi origin who are neither in full-time education nor work suggests that ethnicity also influences the chances of young women taking up full-time housework and child-care as either wives or daughters.

It should be noted that despite differential treatment at home, girls are raised in the same families as boys and therefore the influence of the family on such things as language will be less significant than it is for different class and ethnic groups.

In-school influences

Comprehensive schools, the national curriculum and the policy of individual schools has encouraged boys and girls to take the same subjects. Nevertheless there are still differences in the subjects that boys and girls take and succeed at. 1980s research, before the National Curriculum, indicated that girls were encouraged into "feminine" subjects. However girls were more likely to take sciences in single-sex schools than in mixed schools.

Relationships between teachers and pupils.

These are a significant factor in achievement, according to many sociologists. Their findings have concentrated on a variety of factors which you may have experienced yourselves. It has been suggested that:

1 Girls are taught to smile at male teachers.
2 Girls learn that hitting other children does not get attention.
3 Girls learn self control earlier than boys.
4 Teachers pay more attention to boys.
5 Maths teachers perceive boys as being more able than girls even when girls results are better.
6 The Youth Training Scheme (YTS) pushed girls into feminine jobs.

Relationships between pupil and pupil are also significant. Both boys and girls share the sexist attitudes of the society. WHYTE showed how boys denied girls access to bricks in nursery school and science equipment in secondary school. LEES (1988) wrote that sexist language such as "slags and sluts" is used by girls as well as boys to control the behaviour of girls. She also reports physical intimidation of girls in school.

Teacher–pupil relationships and gender

ETHNICITY AND RACE

American studies of the 1960s tended to replace the notion of innate intelligence as a cause of black underachievement with descriptions of a deficient culture and pathological family life. However LABOV (1975) challenged the idea that black dialects were inferior. REX and MOORE (1967) explained underachievement in class rather than cultural terms. Most recent studies have concentrated on the teacher and school as the source of inequality. COARD (1971) saw racism as the explanation of the over-representation of black children in Educationally Sub Normal (ESN) schools whilst Pakistani children were under-represented. Performance in relevant tests failed to explain these differences. TOMLINSON (1972) found evidence of low teacher expectations for ethnic minority pupils. DRIVER (1981) found evidence that, despite considerable improvements in the numbers getting 5 or more higher grade CSEs or O-levels and at A-level, children of West Indian origin still underachieve. GREEN showed that white boys got more attention from teachers than girls or ethnic minority pupils.

Ethnic influences

Separate small scale studies in London and Bradford in the late 1980s have actually shown pupils from most ethnic minorities achieving more than their white class mates. These studies need careful consideration of the class of children, as do all studies on this issue.

CLASS

Sociologists became concerned about the effects of class on achievement long before they considered gender or ethnicity. But whereas there have been dramatic improvements in the performance of girls and some ethnic minorities, the problem of class remains. The rather pessimistic view is that none of the major reforms since 1944 have had much effect on improving the relative performance of working class pupils.

The underachievement of working class pupils can be identified throughout their educational careers.

They are:

1 more likely to be poor at maths and reading.
2 more likely to leave school without any qualification.
3 less likely to get good GCSE passes.
4 more likely to leave school at 16.
5 less likely to get good A-levels.
6 less likely to go into Higher education.

 Types of underachievement for working class pupils

Sociologists do not agree whether schools or home-life are more important factors in explaining class differences in education. HALSEY suggested that neither "material circumstances" (housing, father's class etc.) nor "family climate" (parental encouragement, linguistic competence etc.) have a strong influence if children were in the *same* school. In other words, Halsey is suggesting that schools are the main influence on educational achievement. However a study of 75 schools in Nottinghamshire showed that most of the differences between schools' examination results *were* the result of the social class of the intake, rather than the quality of the school.

Studies of in-school factors have suggested that a pupil's success is influenced by:

1. Teachers' expectations.

A famous experiment by Rosenthal and Jacobson in California involved teachers being deceived into thinking that, following an aptitude test, a particular group of pupils were likely to improve their performance. There was in fact no real reason why this should happen as the pupils had been chosen at random. When the pupils were re-tested two years later, those selected as being likely to improve had in fact improved more than the other children. Because teachers had expected that group to improve, they had.

2. Sub-cultures.

The development of pupil sub-cultures which may be anti-school may influence success. Such sub-cultures seem related to streaming within schools as well as to class. Paul Willis wrote how that some boys were particularly resentful of the authority the school imposed on them and resisted it. He also showed how this anti-school culture prepared the boys for low skilled manual jobs when they left. Studies have not, as yet, identified similar anti-school sub-cultures amongst girls. There are also ethnically based sub-cultures which can influence how pupils experience school.

4 ▶ EDUCATION, SOCIAL ISSUES AND SOCIAL POLICY

The social problems associated with education have changed with the political views on Governments. The Labour Governments of the 1960s were keen on encouraging equality through promoting Comprehensive schools, and later in the 1970s tried to tackle the disadvantages associated with gender, ethnicity and disability.

The Conservative Governments since 1979 have been concerned with training people for jobs, raising standards through the National Curriculum and testing and encouraging a "market" in education with increased parental choice outside Local Authority control.

1. Selective or comprehensive schools

The 1944 Education Act introduced free Secondary Schooling for all. Children were selected by the 11-plus examination to go to one of three types of school. (This is why it is referred to as the Tripartite System.) These were:

Types of school

■ **Grammar Schools** which provided an academic education for those who gained the highest scores in the examination.
■ **Technical Schools** for those with lower scores who were seen as suitable for a technical education. This was often secretarial studies for girls and engineering for boys.

■ **Secondary Modern Schools** which offered a general education for the majority of children.

By the early 1970s most of these secondary schools had been replaced by comprehensive schools which did not select at the age of 11 but took children with a wide range of ability. After 1981, increasing numbers of children who had been previously educated in schools for those with Special Needs were increasingly integrated into the comprehensive system.

The arguments for and against selective schooling are both social and educational.

2. Vocational training

Both Labour and Conservative governments are convinced that the education system should contribute to economic growth by producing a more skilled and thus more productive work force. There have been a variety of curriculum initiatives to make education more work-related. The Conservatives are very keen to give employers a bigger say in education and training by encouraging them to be School and College Governors, join government bodies who control the curriculum and assessment and letting them spend public money on training through the Training and Enterprise Councils (TECs).

There is disagreement on whether education should be mainly about job training at all and, if so, what are the necessary skills required in the future. Colleges which have committed themselves to specific training have found that the demand for skills can rapidly change, e.g. the recession of 1988–93 led to a spectacular fall in the demand for construction workers.

3. Religion and schools

Up to 1933 the Government had refused to provide State funding for Islamic Schools. There is not a general prohibition but individual applications have been turned down. There are, of course, a large number of state funded schools for various Christian denominations and a few Jewish schools.

Religious education remains compulsory in English schools and is generally supposed to be of "a primarily Christian nature". Parents may withdraw their children from RE and assemblies and where there are substantial numbers of non-Christian children some variation is allowed.

4. The expansion of Higher Education

The number of students in Higher Education has increased dramatically during the 1990s. Many of the new students enter from non-traditional routes, i.e. they are not middle-class 18 year olds who have taken A-levels. There are large numbers of adult students. At the same time spending per student by Universities and in the form of maintenance grants has fallen.

Nearly half of HE students are women. There is still a gender bias in certain subjects but previously male-dominated professions like Law and Medicine will be recruiting almost equal numbers of women in the future.

5. The National Curriculum and testing

Since 1988 the Central Government has increased its control over what is taught in schools. The National Curriculum and the system of testing associated with it is still being modified. However the principle of the State laying down a framework for what is learned in schools and measuring standards of achievement is now generally accepted. The publishing of league tables is more controversial.

The removal of schools from Local Education Authority control through the "opting out" process remains a Government aim. By 1993, Higher Education, Further Education and Sixth-Form Colleges were all outside Local Authority Control and funded by Central Government.

6. Increased nursery provision

Since 1966, the number of under fives in Education has risen from about 15% to over 50%. Many of these are not, however, all day in Nursery Schools for the 3–5s but either attending part of the day or attending primary schools along with 5 year olds. Nursery schooling of some sort or other seems to improve the child's performance in education. There is an obvious relationship between nursery schooling and mothers being available for work.

7. Spending on education

Britain is low in any international league table of spending on education. Despite the rising participation rates of pre-school children, 16–19 year olds and those in higher education during the 1980s and 1990s, spending as a proportion of GDP (National Income) remains lower than our economic competitors.

EXAMINATION QUESTIONS

Q.1 Study extracts A, B, C and D and answer the questions below.

a) Name the method of presenting information used in Extract A. *(1)*
b) What percentage of pupils went to private schools in 1990? *(1)*
c) What trend does the information in Extract A show? *(1)*
d) What is the different between a private school and a state school? *(2)*
e) Look at Extract B
   i) What percentage of privately educated children come from lower middle class backgrounds? *(1)*
   ii) Give one example of a lower middle class occupation. *(1)*
   iii) Which social class are the majority of privately educated pupils likely to come from? *(1)*
f) Extract B suggests that an increasing number of pupils from lower middle class backgrounds are going to private schools. Using information from extracts C and D and your own knowledge, explain why this is happening. *(10)*
g) Explain some of the factors, other than those shown in Extract C and D, which might influence how well children do in school. *(12)*

Extract A

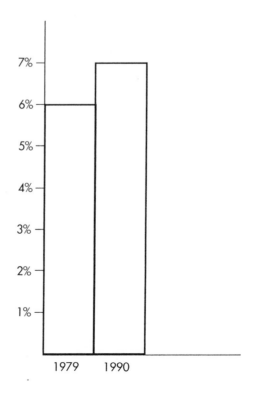

Percentage of pupils educated at private schools 1979–80

Source: M. Denscombe, *Sociology Update 1991*

Extract B

The private schools are drawing pupils away from the state system. A recent survey about the social class backgrounds of pupils who attend private schools found two main changes:

■ an increase to 40% of private school pupils whose parents were both educated in the state sector

■ an increase to 30% of pupils in private schools who come from lower middle class backgrounds.

Extract C

Percentage of students attaining GCE A-level passes on leaving school. An A-level is an advanced course which is studied after GCSE and lasts between one or two years, after which an A-level examination is taken, usually at the age of eighteen.

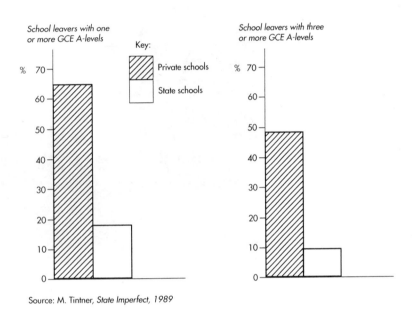

Source: M. Tintner, *State Imperfect, 1989*

Extract D
Average class sizes

State schools

Private schools

Source: M. Tintner, *State Imperfect*, 1989

(NEAB, June 1992

Q.2 "In an academic sub-culture, the teacher is able to exert great control over the peer group. The pupils behave as teachers expect and their two sets of values are shared. In a delinquent sub-culture, the teacher has little control because of the conflict which exists between teacher and pupil values."

Adapted from Education, Schools and Schooling by R. Burgess, published by Macmillan 1985.

a) According to the Source, why may the teacher have little control in a delinquent sub-culture? *(1)*
b) What is meant by a "sub-culture" in a school? *(4)*
c) How may a school sub-culture influence pupils? *(4)*
d) Why may sociologists find it difficult to study a sub-culture in a school? *(6)*

(15 marks)

(ULEAC, June 1992)

Q.3 Study ITEM A and ITEM B. Then answer the questions which follow.

ITEM A

ITEM B

GREEN EDUCATION SO VITAL, SAYS PRINCE

"MANKIND'S future on Earth depends on success in educating future generations about environmental issues," the Prince of Wales said yesterday.

"Schools should give the environment a higher profile in the classroom, while industry and commerce also have a key role in developing young people's awareness of the problems facing the planet," he said.

'The new National Curriculum is an ideal opportunity to make sure every pupil receives a planned environmental education."

(Source: adapted from the *Yorkshire Post,* 1991)

a) Study ITEM A and state why the newspaper cutting might be said not to show a typical image of girls. *(2)*
b) Study ITEM B and state:
    i) what kind of organisations other than school, are said to have a role in developing environmental awareness;
    ii) which recent educational reform the Prince suggests could ensure a planned environmental education for pupils. *(2)*
c) Boys and girls are more likely to be treated equally at school in the 1990s than they were in the 1950s. Identify and explain two reasons why this is so. *(4)*
d) The behaviour of some teenagers suggests that they feel frustrated and angry with society. Identify and explain two ways in which experiences at school may contribute to the development of these feelings. *(4)*
e) What are the main functions of schools in the United Kingdom today? *(8)*

(SEG, Nov. 1992)

ANSWERS TO EXAMINATION QUESTIONS

Q.1

a) a bar graph

b) 7%

c) An increased percentage of pupils attending private schools.

d) State schools are financed by the Government with public funds. Private schools are financed mainly by pupils' parents paying fees and also by charitable funds, bequests and government assisted places.

e) i)   30%

    ii)   Clerk (or any routine office work).

    iii)   Upper middle class (or class 1 or class A etc.).

f) Explain and if possible discuss 3 or 4 points. In addition to better A-level results (extract C) and smaller classes (extract D) you might mention:

Higher incomes, more two income families, increased expectations of higher education, discontent with state school standards (teaching methods, industrial disputes, discipline as well as academic achievement), desire for single sex education, smaller families, a larger lower middle class because of changes in the occupation structure etc.

g) Choose 4 or 5 points and explain them. Some critical discussion and reference to studies might improve your answer. e.g. what exactly might doing "well" at school mean.

You can select from out of school factors which may be either cultural (such as parents' expectations, parents' attitudes and values concerning education, language etc.) or material (such as housing, nutrition, books etc.).

Or in-school factors such as teacher expectations, labelling, standards of teaching and management, facilities and equipment in schools etc.

Points may be linked to the differential achievement of class, ethnic and gender groups.

Q.2

a) Because of the conflict between teacher and pupil values.

b) Define, explain and illustrate.

Sub-cultures are groups which differ from the mainstream culture in terms of attitudes, values, beliefs and maybe language. They can be based on class, ethnicity as well as youth itself.

c) Explain and discuss two points (or more).

They may encourage or discourage academic work and/or conformity to school rules. They may provide support for girls, ethnic minorities or those labelled failures.

d) Think about what methods might be used and assess difficulties.

Participant observation may be difficult because of age, size, gender or ethnicity.

Survey work using questionnaires or interviews may not reveal "deviant behaviour" or subjects may "show off". The presence of the researcher may influence behaviour etc. (See Methods chapter for more suggestions).

STUDENT'S ANSWER WITH EXAMINER'S COMMENTS

Question 3

a) Study ITEM A and state why the newspaper cutting might be said not to show a typical image of girls. *(2)*

A little more here. 1/2

> Girls do not usually play rugby.

b) Study ITEM B and state:
   i) what kinds of organisations, other than schools, are said to have a role in developing environmental awareness; *(1)*

1/1

> Industry and commerce have a key role in developing environmental awareness.

   ii) which recent educational reform the Prince suggests could ensure a planned environmental education for pupils. *(1)*

1/1

> The National Curriculum.

c) Boys and girls are more likely to be treated equally at school in the 1990s than they were in the 1950s. Identify and explain two reasons why this is so. *(4)*

Rather 'thin' explanation. Not enough on schools. 2/4

> In the 1950s were not treated equally because boys were given more encouragement to do well. They had to get a good education to support their family in future years. Girls were prepared to be housewives and mothers. They were taught subjects such as home economics.
>
> The national curriculum means boys and girls must do the same subjects and this means that girls do "boys" subjects like science.

d) The behaviour of some teenagers suggests that they feel frustrated and angry with society. Identify and explain two ways in which experiences at school may contribute to the development of these feelings. *(4)*

Not related to school

Some good points here, 4/4

> Teenagers feel frustrated with society because adults look down on them because of their age and lack of experience. There is a generation gap and parents and children do not understand each other.
>
> Teachers also restrict what teenagers can do and students don't always like being told what to do.
>
> Another cause of frustration is racism at school from other students and even teachers. This makes the victims angry and frustrated and want to take it out on society.

e) What are the main functions of schools in the UK today? *(8)*

Identifies 3 functions but points could have been better developed. 5/8

> Schools teach children reading, writing and arithmetic. This helps them to get jobs. They also help them to get other qualifications.
>
> Schools also continue to socialise children. Socialisation begins in the home but continues at school. Schools teach morals and rules. You also learn to get on with your friends and this helps you when you leave.
>
> Education helps us to be socially mobile. Qualifications help us to get better jobs than our parents. But labelling may stop working class children from succeeding.

Overall, quite a good piece of work, with the exception of part (c). A few points could have been taken a little further. 14/20

REVIEW SHEET

This Review Sheet covers the material in Chapter 7 (The Family) and Chapter 8 (Education).

■ List, and briefly explain, 4 important functions of the family

1 _____

2 _____

3 _____

4 _____

■ Briefly write about the modern symmetrical (Stage 3) Family:

_____

_____

_____

■ List some of the causes of family disorganisation

1 _____

2 _____

3 _____

4 _____

■ Briefly explain some of the likely causes of the rising divorce rate

1 _____

2 _____

3 _____

4 _____

■ Briefly explain some of the likely *effects* of a rising divorce rate

1 _____

2 _____

3 _____

4 _____

■ List some of the characteristics of *Asian* family life.

1 _____

2 _____

3 _____

4 _____

■ Look back at the table for Item B in Question 1 of Chapter 7.

1 What pattern can you see in the figures?

_____

2 Work out the *actual number* of *re-marriages* in each yea

_____

3 Work out the *actual number* of *first-time* marriages in each year.

_____

■ Look back at the table for Question 3 of Chapter 7. Compare the *percentage* of petitions filed for divorce by the wife in 1961 to that by the wife in 1986.

■ Look back at the table for Item A in Question 4 of Chapter 7.

1 Use the figures to show what has happened to families with 3 or more children over time.

2 Use the figures to show what has happened to families with *one or no* children over time.

■ Briefly explain what is meant by the "hidden curriculum".

■ Briefly compare the methods of learning in *pre-literate* simple societies with those of today in a modern economy.

■ Define *innate abilities.*

■ List two *out-of-school* factors which might affect educational achievement.

■ List two *in-school* factors which might affect educational achievement.

■ Look back to Fig. 8.1 in Item B of Question 1 (Chapter 8). Use the chart to:

1 Compare girls performance in science (Physics, Chemistry and Biology) to boys.

2 Compare girls performance in English, History and French to boys.

■ Look back to Fig. 8.3 in Extract C of Question 2 (Chapter 8). Use the chart to:

1 Show that a pupil educated at a private school has a *better chance* of leaving with one or more GCE A-Levels.

2 Show that a pupil educated at a state school has a *lesser chance* of leaving with three or more GCE A-Levels.

■ Look back to Fig. 8.4 in Extract D of Question 2 (Chapter 8). Use the chart to estimate the *percentage difference* in class size in a state school compared to a private school.

WORK

GETTING STARTED

This chapter deals with only half of the issues related to work. It concentrates on what happens within the workplace to individuals and to organised groups of workers in Trade Unions. We look at the factors which lead to job satisfaction on the one hand and alienation on the other. Industrial relations and conflict will be discussed and the role of unions in dealing with conflict examined.

Finally we shall look at changes in the occupational structure of the country and consider some of the effects of such changes, not just on the experience of work but also on family life.

The major themes in this chapter are:

■ EXPLANATIONS OF THE WORKERS' EXPERIENCE OF WORK

■ THE INFLUENCE OF TECHNOLOGY ON JOB SATISFACTION

■ THE EFFECTS OF NEW TECHNOLOGY

■ INDUSTRIAL RELATIONS

■ CHANGES IN THE OCCUPATIONAL STRUCTURE

DEFINITIONS

ALIENATION. This is the feeling of loss on humanity brought about by meaningless work which is performed for money and no other reason.

INDUSTRIAL CONFLICT. Describes the disputes between different groups in the workplace such as employers and employees or managers and workers. It occurs in a variety of forms, not just strikes.

TECHNOLOGY. Describes the machinery used in the production of goods and services and the ways in which it is used (processes).

NEW TECHNOLOGY. At the moment New Technology is a term used to describe the application of computers to production and management. This may soon be old technology!

ESSENTIAL PRINCIPLES

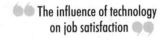
JOB SATISFACTION

For many people work is a boring and tiring experience which brings little or no reward, except for payment. Sociologists have called this lack of job satisfaction ALIENATION. Mostly they have written about factory work but similar accounts exist of office and shop work as well as housework.

MARXIST EXPLANATIONS

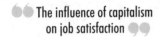
The influence of capitalism on job satisfaction

Marxists see work in capitalist societies as a very miserable experience. They use the term ALIENATION to describe the workers' experience of work. Alienation describes the difference between the creative and satisfying working lives we should have and the miserable existence we actually do have.

The absence of any job satisfaction in capitalist societies is caused by:

1 THE WAGE SYSTEM. Workers are exploited. Wages are only a small part of the value workers produce.
2 THE NATURE OF THE WORK ITSELF. Work tasks are designed and controlled to produce profit rather than socially useful products and satisfying working lives. The worker does not work out of any interest in the job but only for money.

Criticism of Marxist View

Unsatisfying work may be the unfortunate result of the factories and of technological advances associated with industrialization rather than exploitation.
Goldthorpe and Lockwood argued that workers may choose to work for money rather than satisfaction and thus not feel alienated.

BLAUNER'S EXPLANATION (1964)

The influence of technology on job satisfaction

Blauner blamed the lack of job satisfaction on the type of technology used in work. He claimed that the most complex forms of technology might even improve the level of job satisfaction. However, he described the feeling of alienation in similar terms to the Marxists. He said workers experienced **meaninglessness, powerlessness, isolation** and **self-estrangement.**

1 MEANINGLESSNESS
   Jobs were broken down into minute repetitive tasks and the worker was de-skilled.
2 POWERLESSNESS
   The workers had no control over what they produced, how it was produced or the pace of work.
3 ISOLATION
   The workers felt cut-off from their work-mates and bosses. They might stand in a fixed position on a noisy assembly line.
4 SELF-ESTRANGEMENT
   This means that the worker has to deny his true self and pretend to be someone else. Shop workers may have to adopt a false personality and pretend to like customers. Behind the customer's back they may admit their true feelings of irritation and contempt. Perhaps this experience is shared by teachers and students.

   Some businesses have tried to reduce alienation of their work forces because they wish to reduce symptoms of dissatisfaction. Volvo replaced the conventional assembly line in one factory. They set up groups of workers who were responsible for building a whole car and were allowed to allocate jobs between themselves and vary the pace of work. Many Japanese car companies also use similar work-group techniques.

Criticism of Blauner's View

Marxists do not share his optimism about advanced technology and see alienation continuing while workers are exploited.

Goldthorpe and Lockwood, as stated above, see the worker's attitude to work as more important than the type of technology in the work place.

INSTRUMENTAL ATTITUDES TO WORK: WORKING FOR MONEY

Goldthorpe and Lockwood et al described workers in three Luton factories as having an *instrumental attitue* to work. This means that they did not seek any satisfaction in the job itself but saw work as a means to earn money. This attitude applied to both factory and office workers in firms using different kinds of technology.

These new (in 1968) affluent workers were seen as being different from the traditional working class. Their instrumental attitude developed outside work and came from their desire to support a "privatised" home-centred family life. The work of Goldthorpe and Lockwood challenges both Marxist and Blauner's views on alienation.

<table>
<tr><td>**2**</td><td>**THE EFFECTS OF NEW TECHNOLOGY**</td></tr>
</table>

The debate about the relationship between technology and job satisfaction has, until recently, been focused on the work of Blauner and his critics. This means that it is not only discussing the technology of the 1950s and early 1960s but also tends to be restricted to manufacturing rather than service industries and office work (or even home working and housework). This is a problem with much of the sociology of work. As technology is changing very quickly, always note the dates of studies.

WHAT IS NEW TECHNOLOGY?

A convenient description would be to consider the use of information technology for:

■ Computer Aided Manufacture (CAM) such as robots.
■ Computer Aided Design (CAD) which can test buildings and cars before they are built.
■ Information processing in offices, such as word processors.

There are conflicting views on the effects of new technology on job satisfaction.

EFFECTS ON MANUFACTURING

Fordism

This is named after Henry Ford who pioneered the assembly line production of cars in the 1920s. It is used to describe the old use of technology for mass production of standardised products using a de-skilled work force.

Post-Fordism

Fordism and post-Fordism

This is a term used to describe the nature of work using new technology. The effect on workers depends on the way in which new technology is used. New technology is not just used to replace workers with machines and produce more goods more cheaply. It can be used to stimulate the design and manufacture of new products for specialised markets, e.g. Benetton use technology for stock control and marketing and are able to get new fashions into shops all over the world before their competitors. However traditional methods are still used to make their clothes.

Phizacklea (1990) wrote that new technology had been introduced in the fashion industry to replace expensive skilled men but low-paid, often ethnic minority, women still used simple sewing machines as they were still cheaper than machines. But she did describe the use of "intelligent sewing machines" programmed by copying the most skilled women which could be used by less-skilled women.

EFFECTS ON OFFICE WORK

The optimistic view

New Technology and office work

Daniel (1987) saw the possibility of increased skills and responsibility. Jobs could be enriched and workers paid more. Pringle (1983) wrote that secretaries have retained skills and power despite feminisation and mechanisation of their job. She saw the possibility of technology removing boring routine jobs, like copy typing. But others note that it may remove jobs altogether or lead to more demands being made on secretaries as it is assumed that corrections and extra copies are no problem.

The pessimistic view

Braverman said that office work would follow factory work and become *fragmented* and *de-skilled*. Braverman's best example of the similarity between the factory and the office is the work of key-punch operators who work as machine-minders, simply inputting "meaningless" data. But these occupations never dominated office work and have become increasingly obsolete. Gill (1985) predicted that workers would be controlled more closely, feel more isolated and lose promotion prospects.

Huws (1984) noted the alienation of female homeworkers using computers. They complained of isolation and the pressure of being constantly reminded of housework. They often worked a night shift to avoid disrupting the family.

Lockwood (1989) thought that the computerisation of large firms, like banks, was more likely to lead to job loss than de-skilling. New technology may lead to unemployment. In the past, technology only replaced low-skilled workers because machines could only perform relatively simple tasks. Computerisation allows the replacement of more complex tasks requiring intelligence and judgement, and can therefore be a threat to the jobs of more skilled workers.

In conclusion it seems that there are no inevitable results of the introduction of new technology. It depends on the ways in which managers decide to employ it. Many workers have computers on their desks but few use them all day for routine tasks, like factory workers use machines.

Industrial relations involve three major parties:

3 INDUSTRIAL RELATIONS

- EMPLOYERS and their organisations: e.g. The CBI or Institute of Directors
- WORKERS and their organisations: e.g. Trade Unions, Professional associations and the TUC.
- THE STATE, including the Government and courts.

INDUSTRIAL CONFLICT

Conflict occurs because of differences in interests between the three parties. Sometimes differences can be resolved by negotiation, sometimes differences become conflict.

Conflict takes a variety of forms:

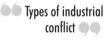

Types of industrial conflict

- Individual workers may be absent from work or leave. Theft at work may be an individual or collective activity.
- Collectively, workers may strike, work-to-rule, go-slow, sabotage machines or products.
- Employers and managers may also initiate conflict through sacking individuals or groups or temporarily locking-out workers.

It seems that these types of conflict may be alternatives. Where workers are not unionised or strikes are illegal, more covert (hidden) and individual forms of conflict occur.

Reasons for conflict

Reasons for conflict

1 PAY seems the most common reason for disputes. Employers seek to reduce wage costs and employees seek higher pay. A more efficient and productive work force could achieve both these aims. This is why *performance related pay* has become increasingly popular.
2 ALIENATION caused by the frustration of doing meaningless work may lead to workers being discontented.
3 EMPLOYERS may worsen working conditions by, for example, speeding up assembly-lines. Teachers in 1993 resisted the introduction of some tests in schools because they felt over-burdened with administrative work.
4 FEAR OF REDUNDANCY led to the biggest strike of recent years when miners went on strike for nearly a year in 1984–85. The struggle to keep pits open re-emerged in 1992, but there were marches not strikes.

The fall in strikes

Unemployment, fear of unemployment, declining union membership and new laws restricting unions have led to a decline in the number of strikes and days lost through striking. Some employers have negotiated no-strike agreements with workers.

TRADE UNIONS AND PROFESSIONAL ASSOCIATIONS

These are both workers' organisations. Some sociologists see fundamental differences between the two, arguing that professionals are a special kind of worker committed to serving the community. Critical views on the professions see Professional Associations as the Trade unions of the middle classes and serving the interests of the professional, not protecting the public. Professionals rarely strike, although lower professionals such as teachers do. They use other tactics, e.g. some dentists are withdrawing from the NHS because the Government has reduced their incomes.

Are Unions a good thing?

A first response might be "good for whom?" They serve workers' interests but challenge those of employers.

Critics of Unions have argued:

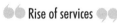 Impact of unions

1 They are (or were) too powerful.
2 They dominate the Labour Party.
3 They disrupt production.
4 They maintain inefficient practices.
5 They maintain artificially high wages and cause unemployment.
6 They are often dominated by "politically motivated" leaders.

Supporters of Unions have argued:

1 They have allowed class conflict to be peaceful.
2 They have improved working conditions and pay for large numbers of workers.
3 They help to redress the unequal relationship between powerful employers and weak individual employees.
4 Non-unionised economic interests, such as professionals, farmers and employers, are able to achieve their aims through other means.
5 Unions are democratic organisations.

4 CHANGES IN THE OCCUPATION STRUCTURE

It is conventional to distinguish three kinds of production and thus employment:

 Types of employment

- *Primary employment* is in agriculture and extractive industries, like mining and quarrying.
- *Secondary employment* is in manufacturing.
- *Tertiary employment* is in service industries, such as catering, health and financial services.

Before the industrial revolution the overwhelming majority of people worked on the land. Throughout the nineteenth century, agricultural workers left the land to work in manufacturing in the new cities. Today we are left with a tiny agricultural workforce which nevertheless produces a substantial proportion of our food needs.

The major change in the second half of the twentieth century has been the dramatic decline in the proportion of the work force employed in *manufacturing*. The two major reasons for this are:

 De-industrialisation

- firstly, increased productivity which means far fewer workers with more machinery and better work methods can produce the same amount or more.
- secondly, the increased competition from abroad from both low-wage third world manufacturers and more efficient modern industrialised rivals in Europe, Japan and the Far East.

At the same time the numbers employed in the *service* industries has increased. Some of these new jobs have been for the well-educated in highly paid full-time work in financial services, others have been insecure, low skilled, part-time and low paid jobs in catering, cleaning and caring, which are conventionally seen as women's jobs.

Rise of services

- In 1979 about 31% of workers were in manufacturing and 59% in service occupations.
- In 1991 the figures were 22% in manufacturing and 70% in service occupations.

The other major change has been the increased proportion of *women* in the work force. This has been particularly so in the service sector. In some parts of the country, e.g. Essex, more women than men were in employment in 1993. Many of these jobs are part-time.

The numbers employed in the primary sector has continued to fall. The virtual disappearance of coal mining employment is the best example. In the 1940s nearly a million men were employed in the mines, now it is about 70,000 and still falling. Even industries where production is expanding, like gas, electricity and water supply, have reduced labour forces because of privatisation and the drive for efficiency and profit.

Employment in the construction industry presents a more complex picture as it is very sensitive to overall changes in the economy. Over a long period employment has declined steadily but in the short-term, recession can lead to huge numbers of jobs being lost which are restored when the economy recovers.

There have been other changes such as:

1 More part-time jobs.
2 More homeworking.
3 More temporary jobs.
4 More self-employment.

All these changes provide a more "flexible" work force which is cheaper to employ. The Government has been accused by Unions and the Labour party of trying to make Britain more competitive by encouraging the development of a low wage economy. This explains the Government's resistance to the Social Chapter of the Maastricht treaty which gives workers protection at the expense of employers.

Rich countries have high paid workers but low wage-costs as each worker produces a lot because of the use of technology and skills.

6 6 Greater flexibility 9 9

THE EFFECTS OF CHANGES IN THE OCCUPATIONAL STRUCTURE

■ The increase in middle class jobs has allowed more opportunity for upward social mobility.
■ The decline in manufacturing employment has created pockets of regional and inner-city unemployment. This has encouraged migration within the country, e.g. from North to South.
■ More women, and sometimes fewer men, working has had a gradual effect on family life. Men may now do more housework and take greater responsibility for child care. Professional child-care is likely to be a growth industry itself.

EXAMINATION QUESTIONS

Q.1

Work and Non-Work

Union decade of decline set to continue

UNION membership fell by 3.1 million in the 10 years to 1989 and is 24 per cent below its peak, falling membership in the seven years to 1986 reflected the fall in employment.

However, while the number in employment increased by 1.4 million between 1986 and 1989, trades union membership fell by more than a third of a million in the same period.

The decline of heavy industries such as coal and shipbuilding, where unions were strong, and the growth of white-collar and leisure jobs, where they are traditionally weak, are thought to be responsible.

(Daily Telegraph, 6/6/91)

Employees in employment by industry in Thousands			
United Kingdom	1971	1983	1989
Engineering and other Manufacturing	6 783	4 707	3 455
Mining and other mineral extraction	1 282	817	67
Transport and communication	66	94	164
Banking, finance, insurance, etc.	152	217	375

Self-employed in Thousands			
United Kingdom	1971	1983	1989
All industries and services	2 026	2 221	3 240
of which			
Males	1 619	1 705	2 479
Females	407	516	761

(Adapted from *Social Trends 21*, HMSO, 1991)

a) Why did Trade Union membership fall between 1979 and 1989? (4)

b) What changes are currently taking place in the nature of employment in the United Kingdom? (7)

c) What effect is the changing nature of work in the UK likely to have on individuals? (9)

(MEG, June 1992)

Q.2 Read and study ITEM A and ITEM B. Then answer the questions which follow.

ITEM A

PROCESS	DESCRIPTION
CRAFT TECHNOLOGY	mainly hand-based, skilled production methods
MECHANISATION	use of machines, to improve production rates
AUTOMATION	machines working by themselves on tasks previously carried out or controlled by workers
MICRO-CHIP TECHNOLOGY	silicon chip and computerised control of machinery and tasks

ITEM B

a) Study ITEM A and then consider these four products:

washing machines
bottled milk
hand-made lace
cash machines.

State which one of the above products best acts as an example of each of the following:

i) CRAFT TECHNOLOGY;
ii) MICRO-CHIP TECHNOLOGY. *(2)*

b) Which processes given in ITEM A are illustrated in ITEM B? *(2)*

c) Identify and explain two ways in which automation and new technology may have affected job satisfaction. *(4)*

d) Identify and explain two functions of Trade Unions in the workplace. *(4)*

e) It is often argued that new technology is a major cause of unemployment in Britain in the 1980s. What other causes are there? *(8)*

(SEG, June 1989)

Q.3 Study ITEMS A and B. Then answer the questions which follow.

ITEM A

A sample of men and women was asked whether they felt that particular types of job were more suitable for men or for women, or were equally suitable for both sexes. The following table summarises their answers.

Great Britain   **Percentages**

	Men's answers			Women's answers		
	Suitable for men only	Suitable for women only	Equally suitable	Suitable for men only	Suitable for women only	Equally suitable
Type of job	%	%	%	%	%	%
Car mechanic	73	—	26	62	1	36
Bank manager	31	—	68	26	1	72
Secretary	1	59	39	1	50	49
Nurse	—	41	59	1	23	75
Member of Parliament	11	1	88	8	—	91
Computer programmer	5	3	91	3	1	95
Social worker	1	15	83	1	15	83

(Adapted from *British Social Attitudes Survey,*
Social and Community Planning Research)

ITEM B

Likely changes in employment in the United Kingdom show that over the period 1987 to 1995 female employment will grow by 10 per cent. Male employment will grow by only 4 per cent. More importantly, the next generation of female jobs are more likely to be in skilled categories. Women are more likely to be working in managerial, administrative, scientific, engineering, health and other professions. Less skilled categories, such as personal and sales occupations, dominated the last generation of jobs in the period 1981 to 1987. One of the key influences is the rising participation of women in higher education. Many of them will have the necessary qualifications for the skilled occupations that are earmarked for growth in the 1990s.

(From *Good Practices in the Employment of Women Returners,* Amin Rajan AND
Penny van Eupen, Institute of Manpower Studies)

a) Study **ITEM A**.
   i) What percentage of men felt that the job of car mechanic was suitable for men only? *(1)*
   ii) Which job did most women feel was equally suitable for a man or a woman? *(1)*

b) Study **ITEM B**.
   i) Which job categories dominated the 1981–87 generation of jobs? *(1)*
   ii Why is it thought that more women will participate in the growth area of skilled occupations in the 1990s? *(1)*

c) Identify and explain two reasons why changes in technology may affect people's attitudes to work. *(4)*

d) Identify two reasons why women and girls today might be more likely to enter jobs which have been traditionally thought of as men's jobs. Explain why in each case. *(4)*

e) Identify and fully explain one reason why women are less likely to be active in trade unions than men. *(4)*

f) Identify one task which trade unions perform for their members. Fully explain how this is done. *(4)*

(SEG, June 1993)

Q.4

Work and Non-work

PAY STRIKES RULED OUT BY NURSES

Ambulance crews plan fresh walk-out

[Newspaper headlines in the 1970s]

Bottom 10% of Earners Up to £7,238		Top 10% of Earners From £23,743	
Hairdresser/beautician	£6,594	Advertising & PR manager	£25,100
Dental nurse	£6,734	Bank manager	£27,560
Kitchen porter	£7,207	Underwriter	£27,628
		Solicitor	£28,319
		Medical practitioner	£32,120

(Adapted from "Scaling the Heights of Prosperity" (a comparison of earnings in Britain) in *The Independent on Sunday,* 8/3/92)

a) Why are some jobs more highly paid than others? *(4)*

b) In what ways may people who work show dissatisfaction with their jobs? *(7)*

c) Why do people work? *(9)*

(MEG, June 1993)

ANSWERS TO EXAMINATION QUESTIONS

Q.1

a) Two reasons are given. Up to 1986 a fall in employment.

After 1986 a change in the job market away from heavy industry, where unions were strong to office and leisure jobs where unions were weak.

b) (Use some of the following points and if you are interested look up the most recent available figures.)

The table shows a decline in: ■ engineering and manufacturing
■ mining

The reasons for this include recession in the early 1980s, competition from abroad and higher productivity meaning that fewer miners and factory workers were producing more goods. Government policy may have encouraged the shedding of labour in those industries.

The rise in office jobs in financial services indicates a rise in demand for their products e.g. more home buyers, more people wanting pensions, the extension of share ownership because of privatisation of nationalised industries. Growth of leisure and entertainment industries as (some) people have more time and money.

The rise in self-employment can be explained as a response to unemployment, where people cannot get other jobs and perhaps use their redundancy money to start businesses. The Conservative governments tried to encourage an "enterprise culture" where people would want to start new businesses. Women may need the flexibility of self-employment to work perhaps from home working hours that suit child care commitment.

There is some self-employment which is the result of employers refusing to employ people on a permanent basis and instead they become self-employed casual workers. e.g. Insurance companies may turn salaried employees into commission only self-employed salesmen.

c) (Develop some of these ideas.)
1 More periods of unemployment and less security may encourage savings.
2 Need for education, training and re-training throughout people's lives.
3 Changes in family life as more women are employed and fewer men are.
4 Self-employment may mean families working together.
5 Need to move home to find employment.
6 Loss of traditional community life.

Q.2

a) i) Hand made lace   ii) Cash machines
b) Micro chip technology (the desk top computer)
Automation (the robot)
c) Improved job satisfaction.

Computerisation in offices has removed the need for workers to perform many low skilled, repetitive tasks such as reading and adding cheques in banks. It also allows the production of higher quality work using desk top publishing software and printers. Much work can be done more quickly.
Reduced job satisfaction.

Managers may ask typists to redraft documents many times because they think it requires little effort using a word processor. This discourages the worker who does not feel their work is satisfactory.
d) Collective bargaining.

This means negotiating on behalf of a group of workers with the employers on issues such as pay and conditions. Acting together makes the workers more influential.
Consultation.

Trade unions may be consulted by employers where a common interest such as training or safety has been identified. The Unions can give the workers' point of view.

e) Choose TWO or THREE of the following points and develop them fully:

British industry may be less competitive than its international rivals and therefore lose sales. High wage costs, low quality and unreliable delivery may all be causes of being less competitive.

Conservative economic policy has put controlling inflation as a top priority. They have been reluctant to lower interest rates or increase public spending in order to create more jobs.

Businessmen have not invested in the development of new products to replace declining industries such as ship building and coal mining.

The education system and employers have been blamed for not producing a suitably skilled work force who would be employable when unskilled workers are not.

The number of workers available for work has increased. The numbers employed in the labour force has increased at the same time that unemployment rates have risen. The new workers are mainly married women. Frequently they are in low paid part-time work.

Q.3

a) i) 73% ii) Computer Programmer
b) i) Personal and sales occupations
   ii) Greater participation of women in higher education
c) More favourable attitudes if technology replaces hard physical labour or monotonous repetitive tasks. (Think of examples)
   Less favourable attitudes if technology de-skills workers and leads to faster pace of work and more close supervision. (Think of examples)
d) (Select TWO reasons and explain them. Emphasise that things have CHANGED.)
   Changing attitudes as women struggle for equality.
   Changing attitudes as boys and girls do similar subjects in school.
   Increased proportion of women in the labour force.
   Shortage of skilled workers.
   Employers more likely to want the best worker regardless of gender.
   Technology has replaced the need for physical strength. (Connect this to changing attitudes as women perform hard physical labour in many cultures.)
   New equal opportunities and equal pay legislation.
e) Develop one of these points or try and group more than one of them under a single reason.
   Women are employed in occupations that lack a tradition of unionisation. (Shops and offices.)
   Women are often employed part-time.
   Women have been socialised into following rather than leading.
   Men are prejudiced and resent women activists.
   Male dominated unions may have done little for women; some actively excluded women from better paid jobs.
f) Improve workers' pay and conditions.
   Explain collective bargaining, negotiation, industrial action, joint consultation with employers etc.

STUDENT'S ANSWER WITH EXAMINER'S COMMENTS

Q.4

a) Why are some jobs more highly paid than others? *(4)*

> Jobs which are paid more than others are often more skilled. They might require a long period of training like a Doctor.
>
> If you are in a business that makes a lot of money such as working in the City or being a lawyer then you will be paid more.

❝❝ Relevant points and examples. 3/4 ❞❞

b) In what ways may people who work show dissatisfaction with their jobs? *(7)*

> People who work may show dissatisfaction with their jobs by taking time off even when they are not really sick. They may "skive" when they are at work and not work hard.
>
> You could grumble at your boss but nowadays people are afraid to do this because of high unemployment and they are afraid they might lose their job.
>
> If you really dislike your job you might spend a lot of time looking for another one.

❝❝ Best to avoid slang ❞❞

❝❝ Some good points – might have been developed a little further. 5/7 ❞❞

c) Why do people work? *(9)*

> People go to work mainly to earn money. They need to support themselves and their families. If you do not work you are poor and cannot afford food and clothing. If you work you can save money.
>
> People also work to get higher social status from having a career and that is why they want to get promoted.
>
> Many women work because they get bored at home. Working means you can pay someone else to do the housework and can get out and meet other adults.

❝❝ Good ❞❞

❝❝ Good, but could illustrate with examples ❞❞

❝❝ A little more here. 6/9 ❞❞

❝❝ Many valid points made but more use could have been made of the sources: e.g. industrial action in (b), job examples in (a), etc. 14/20 overall ❞❞

NB The Review Sheet for this chapter is presented at the end of the next, related, chapter.

WORK, LEISURE AND UNEMPLOYMENT

WORK AND LEISURE

UNEMPLOYMENT

SOCIAL ASPECTS OF UNEMPLOYMENT

GETTING STARTED

Although this chapter is titled WORK, LEISURE AND UNEMPLOYMENT it is mostly about NOT working. There is an interesting discussion on what exactly is meant by work. This issue has relevance to discussions of gender and the family, as housework is not normally seen as real work. You might even consider whether crime could be "work". We talk about professional criminals for whom crime is an occupation and also refer to prostitutes as "working girls" who follow "the oldest profession".

The problem of defining work also affects our understanding of non-work obligations and leisure. The chapter examines the relationship between leisure and other aspects of our life, such as work and family responsibility.

Finally the causes and effects of unemployment are examined.

The main themes in question set on this topic area are:

■ DISCUSSING DEFINITIONS OF WORK AND LEISURE
■ EXPLAINING THE CAUSES AND CONSEQUENCES OF UNEMPLOYMENT

DEFINITIONS

WORK. Generally seen as paid employment.
NON-WORK OBLIGATIONS. Duties which have many of the characteristics of work, but are unpaid (e.g. housework).
LEISURE. Time free from obligations to others.
UNEMPLOYMENT. Officially those "unemployed and able and willing to do any suitable work".

NB. Unemployment benefit was re-named 'Job-Seekers' benefit, emphasising the government's view that actively seeking work is necessary to receive the benefit.

ESSENTIAL PRINCIPLES

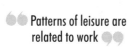
WORK AND LEISURE

Leisure is usually discussed as part of the sociology of work. Increasingly, however, leisure has developed as a topic in its own right. One reason for this is the prediction that people will have more free time because of shorter working hours, longer holidays, early retirement and the return of mass unemployment.

DEFINING WORK AND LEISURE

Sociologists do not agree on the meaning of terms such as work and leisure. S. Parker provides a useful starting point for examining the problem. He distinguishes the following:

More definitions

- **WORK.** This is paid employment. In modern industrial societies people usually go to work away from the home and work set hours. In pre-industrial societies work may be interwoven with family and religious life and not seen as a separate activity.
- **WORK OBLIGATIONS.** These are work-related activities performed outside normal working time and usually off the work premises. e.g. marking students' work.
- **EXISTENCE TIME.** This is devoted to fulfilling essential needs such as sleeping, eating and washing.
- **NON-WORK OBLIGATIONS.** These are domestic duties such as child care and housework.
- **LEISURE.** Seen by Parker as "time free from obligations either to self or to others – time in which to do as one pleases." (Parker 1983)

PARKER'S VIEW OF WORK AND LEISURE

Parker said that work was a major influence on leisure and suggested that there might be three typical ways in which people tend to relate their work to their leisure.

1. The extension pattern

Leisure activities in this pattern were often very similar to work. The function of leisure was to "develop the personality". This pattern was found where work was a central life-interest and was often associated with workers who enjoyed their work, e.g. professional Artists, musicians and athletes.

2. The neutrality pattern

Patterns of leisure are related to work

Leisure activities in this pattern were somewhat different to work. The family or leisure itself were often the central life-interest. Typically, work was not satisfying. The function of leisure was relaxation. This pattern was associated with clerical workers and factory workers.

3. The opposition pattern

Leisure activities in this pattern were definitely unlike work and the central life-interest was outside work. Work was likely to be alienating. The function of leisure was escape and recovery from work. This pattern was associated with unskilled manual workers, particularly in "extreme occupations" such as mining.

In addition to work he saw education and the amount of time available as influencing leisure. Parker (1982) argued that the rigid separation of work from leisure caused by total, rather than gradual, retirement deprived the retired of not only money and social contacts but also a sense of usefulness.

Criticism of Parker

Parker himself recognises that in some circumstances these categories may not be appropriate. He defines leisure as time free from working and this is obviously more appropriate for men in full-time work than it is for those who do not do paid work. Parker sees the unemployed and housewives as special cases, however.

A feminist view of leisure

Feminist criticism:

1 Feminist sociologists see housework as real work, usually performed by women (for men).
2 Women do not always have free time. They may enjoy leisure whilst performing an obligation, e.g. chatting at work or watching TV while ironing clothes.
3 Leisure activities are influenced by age, marriage and children. Because of child care obligations, mothers' leisure time is frequently taken up at home with the family. Single and childless women have more free time and more money as they are more likely to be in paid employment.
4 Women are limited in where they go out. Husbands, fathers and girls and women themselves have views on suitable and safe places to go. Bingo and Church are seen as more suitable than pubs. Travelling unaccompanied may be seen as a problem.
5 R. Deem suggested that leisure might be a state of mind rather than specific activities; e.g. having a relaxing meal. Activities such as cooking and eating could be work, non-work obligation or leisure, depending on why they are done.

Marxist criticism:

Marxists have criticised the view that leisure is *free*.

1 Leisure has become involved with *products* which consumers are persuaded to buy; e.g. sport have moved from the park to the Leisure centre and requires expensive kit. Consumers buy recorded music rather than play instruments.

A Marxist view of leisure

2 Leisure is a means of *social control*. The young unemployed are seen as a problem which can be solved by providing organised leisure activities to keep them off the streets and out of mischief. Many leisure activities are controlled by the State, e.g. where and when you can drink, dance or even walk.

Further problems of defining work and leisure arise when considering homeworking, housework, household production such as growing vegetables and making clothes, professional sport and artistic careers.

Conclusion

K. Roberts claimed that leisure was growing; it was no longer just a residual part of life and the use of leisure time depended on *choice* rather than class, status, work or any other single cause.

2 UNEMPLOYMENT

THE PROBLEM OF UNEMPLOYMENT

Sociology syllabuses and text books rarely mentioned unemployment until the 1980s, probably because it was seen as a problem of the 1930s which had been cured by post-war Government policy. Because of dramatic increases in the level of unemployment since the late 1970s, it is once again seen as:

■ a *social problem* (i.e. something which causes concern in society and needs to be dealt with);
■ a *sociological problem* (i.e. something which sociologists wish to study and explain).

Social problems

1 Problems experienced by the unemployed and their families. These include poverty and a sense of worthlessness.
2 Problems the unemployed are seen as causing for others. These include:
   a) the cost of paying benefits to the unemployed some of whom are seen as "scroungers";
   b) the threat of disorder from, particularly, the young unemployed.

Sociological problems

Sociologists are interested in:

1 The lives of the unemployed.
2 Defining and measuring unemployment. Criticizing unemployment statistics.
3 Examining the causes of unemployment.
4 Examining the social distribution of unemployment by class, ethnicity, gender, age and region.
5 The effects of unemployment on society.

Consider how a sociological study of unemployment and the unemployed is likely to be related to topics such as stratification, health, welfare and poverty, family relationships, work and leisure and deviance.

CAUSES OF UNEMPLOYMENT

1. New technology.

This has reduced the number of manual workers in heavy industry or factory work. In the 1990s this has begun to happen in office work. For example, Cash-point machines have replaced many bank workers. (New technology can also, however, reduce unemployment as it makes goods cheaper so more people can buy them and creates new products.)

2. International competition.

This has reduced the market share of UK firms both domestically and in international markets. (The cure is to be more efficient.)

66 Some causes of unemployment 99

3. Changes in the occupational structure.

These have led to a decline in employment in manufacturing and an increase in employment in service industries. The impact of this varies between different groups in the workforce and between different parts of the country. (The cure would include training, re-training and education so people could learn new skills.)

4. Cyclical changes in demand for goods and services.

Both nationally and internationally these lead to fluctuations in the total level of unemployment. (The cure was to use government spending as Keynes suggested, to influence demand. This was how Conservative and Labour governments controlled unemployment until the 1970s.)

5. The money supply.

This influences inflation and thereby the competitiveness of industry and thus unemployment. (The cure includes cuts in taxation and public spending and keeping wages low. This is seen as encouraging people to set up new businesses.)

THE DEFINITION AND MEASUREMENT OF UNEMPLOYMENT

You might think that it is obvious whether someone is unemployed or not. However sociologists have pointed out problems in defining unemployment.

66 Defining unemployment 99

The Department of Employment defined the total unemployed as those "unemployed and able and willing to do any suitable work" (1987). The decision of the government in 1982 to use those registering *claims for benefit* to measure the level of unemployment rather than registration as *seeking work* has not only reduced the overall level of apparent unemployment but ensured the continued underestimate of certain sections of the population (particularly married women) in the figures.

Unemployment is usually distinguished from non-employment. Unemployment suggests being available for work (i.e. both willing and able to work) and being unable to find employment.

Sociologists and politicians have debated the accuracy of the unemployment figures.

Under estimating unemployment

66 Too few unemployed? 99

1 *Married women* are unlikely to be eligible for benefit and therefore may not register as unemployed. D. Sanders and J. Reed (1976) found that less than one-third of self-defined unemployed women were actually registered as unemployed.
2 Those *under 18* are not normally eligible for benefit. They may be compelled into training schemes or be reluctant students.
3 Those *over sixty,* or *disabled* or *sick* are encouraged to claim other forms of benefit, even if still seeking work, and therefore do not count as "unemployed".
4 Those "not actively seeking work" may be refused benefit. The government itself decides what this actually means.

5 When jobs are scarce, some of those without jobs may see themselves as *unemployable* rather than unemployed.

In a depressed labour market, marginal workers such as the sick, people with disabilities, the old, the young, and those of low intelligence, may decide not to seek work, and therefore will not appear in the official statistics.

Overestimating unemployment

 **Too many unemployed**

The Government, some Newspapers and some New Right sociologists have argued that even the recent revised unemployment figures are an overestimate of the real number seeking work. They have mentioned:

1 Fraudulent claimants who work in the black economy.
2 The "workshy".
3 The high level of welfare benefit which acts as a disincentive to find work. Claimants become "Welfare dependents".

Critics of the New Right:

1 See a poverty trap caused by low wages and deductions from benefits as incomes grow, rather than high benefits.
2 Pahl estimates that the "black economy" is more likely to recruit from the ranks of the employed than from those who claim benefits. In any case increased surveillance and the threat of prosecution contains the number of "scroungers".

3 THE EXTENT AND SOCIAL DISTRIBUTION OF UNEMPLOYMENT

THE EXTENT OF UNEMPLOYMENT

1 Throughout the 1930s there was widespread unemployment until World War 2.
2 From 1945 until 1966, the rate of unemployment averaged less than 2% (representing about 350,000 unemployed) and was considered to be controllable by Government economic and fiscal policy. High unemployment was seen as both unnecessary and politically unacceptable.

Trends in unemployment

3 Subsequently, within an overall trend of increasing unemployment there have been several peaks and troughs, with the highest point occurring in 1985–86 when the unemployment figure reached about 12% (representing about 3.5 million unemployed).
4 From 1986 until 1989 the unemployment trend was downwards, but a rise began in 1990 and recession has continued to raise unemployment into 1993.

THE SOCIAL DISTRIBUTION OF UNEMPLOYMENT

"Those most likely to be unemployed are people in low-paying and insecure jobs, the very young and the oldest in the labour force, people from ethnic minorities, people from among the disabled and the handicapped, and generally those with the least skills and living in the most depressed areas."

Sinfield wrote this in 1981 and it remains true; note that his list does not consider gender. Although in the same book Sinfield does point out that women are less likely to register as unemployed.

Be prepared to discuss the relationship between unemployment and CLASS, RACE, GENDER, AGE AND DISABILITY. R. Pahl argued that it is not appropriate to stereotype the unemployed and see them as a distinct population. People go in and out of unemployment.

YOUTH UNEMPLOYMENT

During the late 1970s and early 1980s, youth unemployment increased to higher levels and at a faster rate than general unemployment. Because:

Why youth unemployment has risen

1 The increased number of married women seeking employment provided competition for school leavers.
2 The young earned adult wages during most of the post-war period of full employment, so there was little or no cost-advantage in employing school leavers.
3 New recruits may be more vulnerable to unemployment. Employers may decide not to employ new staff rather than get rid of existing workers. There is also a tradition of "last in first out". Both of these factors will disadvantage the young.
4 Training schemes replaced permanent jobs as trainees were cheap workers, lacking normal employment rights.

5 The absence of appropriate skills amongst young people has become a political and educational issue. Clarke and Willis (1984) see this as an attempt to blame unemployment on the unemployed and on schools and colleges. Youth unemployment has been reduced by the increase in 16–19 year olds in FT education.

ETHNICITY AND UNEMPLOYMENT

❝❝ Why ethnic unemployment is higher ❞❞

Unemployment tends to be higher among ethnic minorities than the population as a whole. However there are differences between different minorities. During the late 1980s the unemployment rate for those of Pakistani/Bangladeshi origin was more than twice that for those of Indian origin. This suggests that racial discrimination is not the only cause of high employment. There are also differences *within* ethnic minorities based on class, age, gender and educational qualifications.

Explanations for higher rates of ethnic unemployment include:

1 Racial discrimination by employers.
2 The extent of self-employment within a community.
3 Whether minorities live in areas of high or low unemployment. Immigrants were attracted to areas where labour was scarce and not areas where unemployment was high.
4 Levels of educational qualifications.
5 The age-distribution of the group. The high rate of joblessness amongst Afro-Caribbeans may partly be a problem of youth unemployment in a population which is relatively young.

DISABILITY AND UNEMPLOYMENT

Whereas a majority of the adult population are in paid employment a majority of people with disabilities are not seen as economically active. There are gender differences. In families where one member is disabled, wives are less likely to work than husbands, whichever is disabled. Naturally the severity of the disability has a significant effect. During recessions, some disabled people become seen as unemployable rather than unemployed.

Estimates of the unemployment rate of the disabled varies. An official rate of 23% in 1985 compared to 11% for the general population. Townsend's (1979) study showed much higher rates when overall unemployment rates were much lower.

THE SOCIAL EFFECTS OF UNEMPLOYMENT

In addition to considering the impact of unemployment on those without jobs, we can examine some of the alleged effects on the wider society.

1 **Effects on workers.**
Workers feel less secure, which permits employers to exercise more control and is likely to reduce wage demands. Mobility between jobs is reduced as workers feel safer where they are. Unemployment weakens Trade Unions and disciplines the work force.
2 **Regional unemployment.**
Specific communities may be affected, e.g. coal mining communities. The consequences of regional and local job losses tend to be cumulative as local businesses suffer from the reduced demand for goods and services. Unemployment is unevenly spread between regions. England has lower rates than the rest of the UK. The S.E. formerly had lower rates, but not during the 1990s. Within regions unemployment is concentrated in the so-called "Inner City" areas.

❝❝ Social effects of unemployment ❞❞

3 **Unemployment and social control.**
Unemployment is disproportionately experienced by particular age and ethnic groups and concentrated in specific neighbourhoods. Attempts have been made to link unemployment with crime, riots and political protest.

The disadvantaged are the most likely to experience unemployment and the most likely consequences of unemployment are the problems of poverty. *"What unemployment does before anything else is to make those who experience it poor."* (Clarke and Critcher)

EXAMINATION QUESTIONS

Q.1 Read ITEMS A and B. Then answer the questions which follow.

ITEM A

CHANGES IN EMPLOYMENT AND UNEMPLOYMENT 1979–87
Great Britain, seasonally adjusted

NOTE: The figures below are given in thousands.

		March 1979	March 1983	March 1987
1.	Manufacturing employees	7129	5485	5075
2.	Employed labour force	24699	22998	24221
3.	Unemployed	1199	2828	3116
4.	Working population	25898	25826	27337
5.	Inactive population	6672	7474	6730
6.	Working age population	32570	33300	34067

Source: adapted from Lloyds Bank Economic Bulletin, No. 105, Sept. 1987

(Source: adapted from *Discovering Sociology*, P. Langley (ed.) (Causeway))

ITEM B

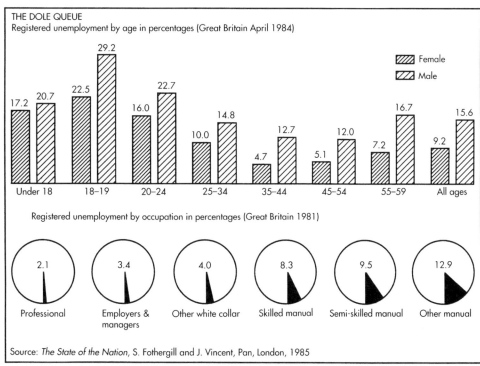

THE DOLE QUEUE
Registered unemployment by age in percentages (Great Britain April 1984)

Female
Male

| Under 18 | 18–19 | 20–24 | 25–34 | 35–44 | 45–54 | 55–59 | All ages |
| 17.2 / 20.7 | 22.5 / 29.2 | 16.0 / 22.7 | 10.0 / 14.8 | 4.7 / 12.7 | 5.1 / 12.0 | 7.2 / 16.7 | 9.2 / 15.6 |

Registered unemployment by occupation in percentages (Great Britain 1981)

| Professional | Employers & managers | Other white collar | Skilled manual | Semi-skilled manual | Other manual |
| 2.1 | 3.4 | 4.0 | 8.3 | 9.5 | 12.9 |

Source: *The State of the Nation*, S. Fothergill and J. Vincent, Pan, London, 1985

Source: *Discovering Sociology*, P. LANGLEY (ed.) (Causeway)

a) Look at ITEM A. How many people were employed in manufacturing in March 1983? *(1)*

b) Look at ITEM A. How many people were in employment in March 1987? *(1)*

c) Look at ITEM B.

   i) What percentage of women in the 25–34 age group were unemployed?

   (1)

   ii) Which kind of occupation had the lowest percentage of unemployment?

   (1)

d) Identify and explain two reasons why unemployment tends to be higher amongst some ethnic minority groups. *(4)*

e) Identify two groups of people (other than ethnic minority groups) who have a high risk of unemployment. In each case explain why this may be so. *(4)*

f) Identify and explain fully one situation where non-work cannot be seen as leisure. *(4)*

g) "The introduction of new technology will ensure an increase in employment in the years ahead."

    Identify and fully explain one way in which this view can be either supported or rejected. *(4)*

(SEG, June 1991)

Q.2 Study ITEM A and ITEM B. Then answer the questions which follow.

ITEM A

THE NUMBER OF UNEMPLOYED PEOPLE IN THE UNITED KINGDOM

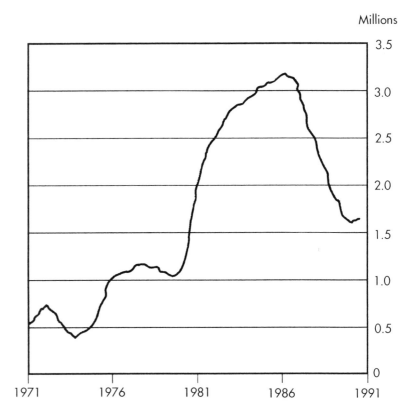

Source: *Social Trends,* 1991

ITEM B

A VIEW OF HOUSEWORK

Cleaning a house is just like working in a factory – you dust the same thing every day and it's never appreciated. I mean I could get this whole place so tidy and the kids come home from school and it's like a bomb's exploded and nothing's appreciated about it, whereas if you're decorating or teaching children there's something always gained out of it . . . as far as actual housework goes, I don't see how anyone can like it. It's boring, just like a robot.

(Shop manager's wife)

(Source: *The Sociology of Housework,* A. OAKLEY, MARTIN ROBERTSON)

(SEG, Nov. 1992)

(a) Study ITEM A and state:

    (i) the number of people who were unemployed in 1986;
    (ii) the trend in the number of people who were unemployed between 1986 and 1990. *(2 marks)*

(b) Study ITEM B and state:
    (i) in what way cleaning a house is said to be like factory work;
    (ii) in what way decorating is said to be different from cleaning. *(2 marks)*

(c) Identify and explain two ways in which housework differs from factory work. *(4 marks)*

(d) Identify two groups which are more likely than others to be unemployed. In each case explain why this is so. *(4 marks)*

(e) What are the consequences of unemployment for individuals and society in Britain today? *(8 marks)*

ANSWERS TO EXAMINATION QUESTIONS

Q.1

a) 5,485,000 (you must refer to the note and indicate thousands)

b) 24,221,000

c) i) 10% ii) Professional

d) Choose from reasons such as discrimination, concentration in the inner city, concentration in declining manufacturing industries, reduction in public sector employment, differential educational achievement, etc. Remember to explain your two points.

    e.g. Discrimination

    Although it is illegal some employers discriminate against minorities and will not give them jobs. This has been shown by research where white and black candidates with the same experience and qualifications have applied for a particular job.

e) Young people and mothers of young children are discussed above. You could also mention workers who are disabled, the old or those who live in areas of high unemployment.

f) Leisure involves choice so you could discuss a variety of non-work obligations or even what Parker called existence time. Housework is an easy one to discuss.

g) You must choose only one side of the debate.

    Agreement with the statement could involve the discussion of new markets for new and cheap electronic products.

    If you disagree you might discuss the computerisation of offices which has displaced not only routine workers but also the managers who previously supervised them.

STUDENT'S ANSWER WITH EXAMINER'S COMMENTS

Q.2

a) Study ITEM A and state:
    i) the number of people who were unemployed in 1986 *(1)*
    | 3.2 million |
    ii) the trend in the number of people who were unemployed between 1985 and 1990. *(1)*
    | Rapid decrease. |

66 1/1 99

66 3.2 million approx. 1/1 99

b)   Study ITEM B and state:

   i)   in what way cleaning a house is said to be like factory work.   *(1)*

** 1/1 **

The worker does the same thing every day and no one appreciates it.

   ii)   in what way decorating is said to be different from cleaning.   *(1)*

There is something gained out of decorating.

c)   Identify and explain two ways in which housework differs from factory work.

   (4)

** Brief, but accurate **

■ Pay.

You have to do housework but you do not get paid for it but you do for factory work.

** Good. 3/4 **

■ Working conditions.

Housework is done in your own home and you can stop when you like. Whereas factory work is done in fixed hours and possibly in bad conditions.

** Compare with others **

d)   Identify two groups which are more likely than others to be unemployed. In each case explain why this is so.   *(4)*

■ Young people.

They may aim too high, they lack work experience and they are looking for a job when there are few around.

■ Mothers of young children.

** Good explanation. 3/4 **

Low pay means they may be better off on benefits.

It is difficult to get child care and few employers provide it.

Employers may discriminate against mothers if they think they take time off with sick children or might have more children and they have to pay for maternity leave.

e)   What are the consequences of unemployment for individuals and society in Britain today?   *(8 marks)*

** List of relevant points but not always clearly explained. 5/8 **

Individuals may be trapped in poverty if they cannot get a job with adequate pay or a job at all. When someone loses their job they are entitled to benefits which are paid by the government. This means that taxes must go up and this makes others poorer. They may have to go into debt and they have no money which means that there may be less jobs as people spend less money in the shops.

   Individuals may have worse health because of poor food and housing and this costs the NHS more. Young people may turn to crime if they want things they can't get.

** Accurate and clearly argued up to part (e). Part (e) should be a mini-essay of around 200 words. 15/20 overall **

REVIEW SHEET

This Review Sheet covers the materials in Chapters 9 and 10.

■ What is meant by the term "alienation"?

_____

_____

■ How might the technology of the assembly line reduce job satisfaction?

1 _____

2 _____

3 _____

4 _____

■ List some of the main reasons (or areas) for *conflict* between employers and employees.

1 _____

2 _____

3 _____

■ List 4 reasons for *supporting* the existence of Trade Unions.

1 _____

2 _____

3 _____

4 _____

■ List 4 reasons for *opposing* the existence of powerful Trade Unions.

1 _____

2 _____

3 _____

4 _____

■ Briefly define each of the following

1 Primary employment   _____

2 Secondary employment   _____

3 Tertiary employment   _____

■ Briefly identify 3 effects of changes in the occupational structure in the UK since the Second World War.

1 _____

2 _____

3 _____

■ Look back to the Table in Question 1 of Chapter 9. Use the figures to:

1 Show the decline in the employment in engineering and manufacturing industries since 1971.

_____

_____

2 Show the rise in self-employment since 1971.

_____

_____

■ Look back to the table in Item A of Question 3, Chapter 9. Use the figures to:
1 Show men's view of the occupation of being a *secretary* compared to the women's view of that occupation.

_____

_____

2 Show how women see more jobs as equally suited to either male or female than do men.:

_____

_____

_____

■ List 4 possible causes of unemployment.

1 _____

2 _____

3 _____

4 _____

■ Give 4 reasons why official statistics might under-estimate the true extent of unemployment.

1 _____

_____

2 _____

_____

3 _____

_____

4 _____

_____

■ List some of the reasons for *youth unemployment* being higher than general unemployment.

1 _____

2 _____

3 _____

4 _____

■ Look back to the table in Item A of Question 2, Chapter 10. Use the figures in the table to:
1 Show the falling contribution of manufacturing as a *percentage* of the total working age population between 1979 and 1987.

_____

_____

2 Show the rise in the unemployed as a percentage of the total working age population between 1979 and 1987.

_____

POPULATION

BIRTH RATES

FERTILITY RATES

INFANT MORTALITY RATES

LIFE EXPECTANCY

ETHNIC DIVERSITY

GETTING STARTED

DEMOGRAPHY is the study of population. Sociologists are interested in the causes and consequences of population changes.
   The main issues examined in this chapter are:

■ EXPLAINING THE CAUSES OF CHANGES IN
   THE POPULATION.
■ EXPLAINING THE SOCIAL CONSEQUENCES OF
   SUCH CHANGES.

There are strong links between this chapter and others. If you want to study children and the effects of an ageing population, refer to the chapter on AGE (ch 2). Marriage, child bearing and care, illegitimacy and changes in the structure of households are examined in the FAMILY chapter (ch 7). The movements of populations within Britain is examined in the URBANISATION chapter (ch 12). The issues of ethnicity and immigration are discussed in the RACE AND ETHNICITY chapter (ch 4).

DEFINITIONS

BIRTH RATE. The number of live births per 1000 of the population.
FERTILITY RATE. The average number of births per women of child-bearing age.
MORTALITY OR DEATH RATE. The number of deaths per 1000 of the population.
INFANT MORTALITY RATE. The number of deaths in the 1st year of life, per 1000 live births.
RATE OF NATURAL INCREASE. The birth rate minus the death rate.
DEPENDENCY RATIO. The proportion of the population who are in dependent, rather than working, age groups. This includes the young and the old.
IMMIGRATION. People coming here from other countries.
EMIGRATION. People leaving here to go to other countries.
NET MIGRATION. The difference between immigration and emigration figures.
POPULATION CHANGE. (Births + Immigration) − (Deaths + Emigration)

ESSENTIAL PRINCIPLES

The latest complete figures for the population of Great Britain are to be found in the 1991 census. The Office of Population Censuses and Surveys (OPCS) publishes these in various forms. More recent updates based on smaller samples are published by the government as population trends statistics. In addition to the obvious statistics on total population size and household composition, the 1991 Census also included the question of ethnic origin for the first time. There is also data on the numbers of people with disabilities, the number of Welsh speakers and the condition of houses.

1 ⟩   BIRTH RATES

Crude *birth rates* are expressed as the number of births per 1000 of the population as a whole. They indicate (together with death rates) whether a population is likely to grow or fall. They do not indicate sex or age distributions of the population.

A population with a high number of women of marriageable/child bearing-age is likely to have a higher birth rate than an ageing population. Birth rates could also be expressed as births per 1000 women of *child-bearing* age. This leads us to consider fertility rates.

❝ Fertility rate is different from birth rate ❞

2 ⟩   FERTILITY RATES

Fertility refers to how many children the average woman of child-bearing age has. All *live births* are included in the calculations, but conceptions which do not result in a live birth because of miscarriage or abortion are not.

THE CAUSES OF DIFFERENT FERTILITY RATES

Explanations of changes in fertility will examine reasons why women conceive more or fewer children and also reasons why pregnancies are not completed. The fertility rate in Britain is less than two, whereas in Kenya it is nearly eight. The world average is about 4.

Explanations of the lower fertility rates found in modern industrial societies, such as Great Britain, compared to pre-industrial societies include the following:

1. An economic choice

Couples or single women CHOOSE to have fewer children because children may be an economic liability rather than an asset. In economies based on agriculture, children are seen as an asset. They can work on the land at an early age, particularly in the absence of compulsory schooling. Just as important they can care for their parents when they are too old to work, especially when there is inadequate pension provision for the old.

❝ Reasons for different fertility rates ❞

Girls may be seen as a liability and boys as an asset. According to a BBC news report it has been estimated that 3000 female foetuses are aborted daily in India following the determination of their sex by ultra-sound scanners. Female babies may even be killed. The economic reason is often related to the cost of a dowry, which may be as high as 15 years of pay.

2. Age of marriage

Young marriage is more common in pre-industrial families. Couples will marry without needing separate housing and will stay within an extended family which will share child care.

In modern industrial societies marriage may be postponed or avoided. Women increasingly find work competes with marriage and motherhood. The first child may be delayed because of the desire for a career or the need for two incomes to buy a home.

3. Status

In modern industrial societies women do not justify their existence solely by bearing children (or particularly sons), nor do men need sons to demonstrate their manliness. Success, money and consumer goods provide status in Britain.

4. Contraception

Having decided to have fewer children, modern society provides effective forms of contraception and in most countries freely available abortion to ensure that the choice becomes reality. The effects of the development of new forms of contraception, particularly the contraceptive pill, should not be exaggerated. They may make contraception simpler (for men anyway!) but the decline in fertility in this country predates the pill which was only widely available here at the end of the 1960s. Choice seems to have been the most important reason for restricting family size before the pill and cruder forms of contraception, including abstinence from sexual intercourse, were the usual means.

5. Abortion

Abortion remains a major control on fertility in some industrialised societies because of its acceptability (e.g. Japan) or the absence of efficient contraception (e.g. Eastern Europe).

6. Infant and child mortality rates

Where children are desired but their chances of survival relatively slim, mothers will bear more to ensure that a number survive.

Within Britain, fertility rates vary between social class, ethnic and religious groups. These rates are not fixed. In the past the higher the social class of the family, the fewer children they were likely to have. Now there is little difference between classes; however the greatest number of children are born to the children of the highest and the lowest classes. The lower-income middle classes have the fewest children.

THE CONSEQUENCES OF DIFFERENT FERTILITY RATES

1. Changes in the age structure of the population

Declining fertility rates decrease the numbers of dependent children in the family, but in the long term lead to an ageing population. The increased proportion of the population beyond retirement age MAY create a problem of dependency on a smaller work force. This is not, however, inevitable as the retirement age could be raised. The retirement age for women in Britain is to be raised, for those under 44 years (in 1993) to 65 years. An ageing population has implications for housing needs, as in 1991 $\frac{1}{4}$ of households were entirely made up of pensioners and $\frac{1}{3}$ contained at least one pensioner.

2. Changes in the work force

Effects of different fertility rates

The decline in the numbers of school leavers in this country during the 1990s as a result of "the birth dearth" has meant that, despite the recession, there have been increased numbers of married women entering the labour market. In the past, a shortage of labour encouraged immigration into Britain in the 1950s.

3. Government policy

The British government appears to have a neutral attitude to family size. It does, however, provide contraception, abortion and sterilisation through the NHS. The aim of such policies would be to encourage people to only have children when they wish to, and to protect people's health. Those who have difficulty conceiving children may also receive support and treatment from the NHS.

In China, the Government in some provinces has imposed penalties on those having more than one child, e.g. by withdrawing free education. Whereas in France and the old Soviet Union, a system of benefits and rewards encouraged mothers to have large families.

4. Changes in the role of women

The changing role of women is often cited as a cause of a reduced birth rate. It can also be a consequence as young women are allowed to pursue careers and middle-aged women have a long life freed of family responsibility. Both these factors could contribute to a higher divorce rate.

3 > INFANT MORTALITY RATES

Infant mortality rates refer to deaths in a baby's first year. We in fact have measures for the loss of life after 28 days following conception to 1 year after birth. Those deaths immediately following birth are called perinatal, neonatal and post-neonatal. Reduction in such deaths has been dramatic owing to improved health education for mothers and advances in intensive care for new-born babies.

Within Britain infant mortality rates correlate strongly with class. On a global basis they correlate inversely with income per head, i.e. infant mortality rates are higher in poor countries.

The reduction in infant mortality rates for all classes has been considerable throughout the 20th century. Although you do not need to know exact figures, a rough guide will indicate how dramatic the changes have been: in the 19th century the rate was 150 per 1000; before World War 2 it was 53 per 1000; in 1992 it was 7.4 per 1000, the lowest ever figure.

The major reasons for the fall in the infant mortality rate include:

Why the infant mortality rate has fallen

1 Improved diet of mothers.
2 Improved housing conditions for mothers and children.
3 Improved public hygiene has reduced epidemic disease.
4 Medical advances in pre-natal and post-natal care.
5 Vaccination to prevent child killing diseases.
6 Drugs to control disease e.g. antibiotics.

Child death rates

These have also fallen for similar reasons to infant mortality rates. They too vary between classes. Working class children are not only more susceptible to diseases, they may also receive worse medical care. This is either because they are provided with less medical care or because their parents use what is available less effectively.

Death by accident or murder is also higher for working class children. They may be allowed more freedom without supervision and thus be at risk from road and other accidents.

4 LIFE EXPECTANCY

Life expectancy has risen throughout this century. In the mid 19th century it was about 40 years, now it is nearer 80 years. Men have a shorter life expectancy than women. This sex differential has widened during the post-war period. The reasons for women living longer than men (on average 78 rather than 72) may be largely biological but *social reasons* include:

Social reasons for women living longer than men

1 Men have more hazardous jobs leading to accident or life threatening disease.
2 Men were more likely to die in war. (Although it has been claimed that war has become increasingly safe for soldiers and dangerous for civilians. The bombing of cities during World War 2 marked the shift of risk to civilian populations.) It was claimed during the Gulf War in 1990 that the risk of shooting for black American males was reduced by leaving cities in the USA to fight in the armed services.
3 More male children are conceived and born than females in Britain. However higher infant mortality rates removes any imbalance in favour of males. About 52% of the overall population is female.

5 ETHNIC DIVERSITY

The 1991 Census was the first to include a question on ethnic origins.

The results indicated that the % of the population of Great Britain from various ethnic groups was as follows:

% of G.B. population 1991		% of ethnic minority pop 1990
White	94.5	
Black Caribbean	0.9	19
Black African	0.4	4
Black other	0.3	
Indian	1.5	31
Pakistani	0.9	17
Bangladeshi	0.3	4
Chinese	0.3	5
Other Asian	0.4	
Other	0.5	

Statistics of the geographic distribution of ethnic minorities show a concentration of different ethnic groups in different places. Whereas the total percentage of ethnic minorities in Scotland is 1.3%, in Inner London it is 25.6%.

The Black Caribbean population of Britain is concentrated in London but the Pakistani population is more widely spread through the country, with concentrations in the West Midlands and Yorkshire.

Immigration and emigration

Explanations of immigration to Britain are found in the answers to question in the chapter on race (ch 4). Emigration from Britain has been encouraged by economic recession here and opportunities to improve life elsewhere. People persecuted for their religious beliefs were among the first settlers in North America. Convicts and debtors were sent to Australia. The enterprising, missionaries and civil servants travelled to the distant outposts of the British Empire.

More recently, many people who came to Britain from the Caribbean and the Indian sub-continent have returned. This appears to be less the result of racism than the desire of people to re-join families and for the old to retire in their country of origin.

EXAMINATION QUESTIONS

Q.1
Read ITEMS A and B. Then answer the questions which follow.

ITEM A

> The growth of cities in Britain really begins with industrialisation, around the end of the eighteenth century. Before 1800 only about 15 per cent of the population lived in towns and cities; 100 years later 75 per cent of the population lived in them.
>
> There has been a move away from the cities, towards the outer suburbs, New Towns and the countryside over the last ten years. Why? People prefer the better standard of housing available and the cleaner, less polluted environment of the suburbs and countryside. Cars and trains make travel into the big cities for work fairly quick and easy. However, firms are also moving out of the big cities, preferring the low costs of the New Towns to the advantage of being in the city centres.
>
> (Source: adapted from *Sociology Alive,* S. Moore (Stanley Thornes))

a)   Look at **ITEM A**. About what percentage of the population lived in towns and cities before 1800? *(1)*

b)   Look at **ITEM A**. What was the reason for the growth of cities in Britain in the eighteenth century? *(1)*

c)   Look at **ITEM B**.
    i)   Which region had the largest growth rate? *(1)*
    ii) Which non-metropolitan region had the lowest rate of population loss? *(1)*

ITEM B
Regional Population Changes in percentages (England and Wales)
1981 to 1986

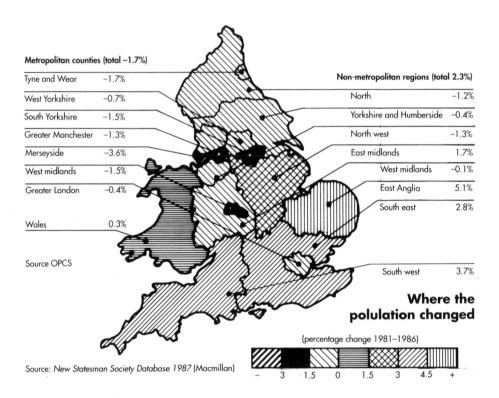

Metropolitan counties (total −1.7%)

Tyne and Wear	−1.7%
West Yorkshire	−0.7%
South Yorkshire	−1.5%
Greater Manchester	−1.3%
Merseyside	−3.6%
West midlands	−1.5%
Greater London	−0.4%
Wales	0.3%

Source OPCS

Non-metropolitan regions (total 2.3%)

North	−1.2%
Yorkshire and Humberside	−0.4%
North west	−1.3%
East midlands	1.7%
West midlands	−0.1%
East Anglia	5.1%
South east	2.8%
South west	3.7%

Where the polulation changed

(percentage change 1981–1986)

− 3 1.5 0 1.5 3 4.5 +

Source: *New Statesman Society Database 1987* (Macmillan)

d) Identify and explain two factors responsible for the decline in the population of the northern regions of the United Kingdom since 1945. *(4)*

e) Identify and explain two reasons for the increases in the population in some rural areas over the last twenty years. *(4)*

f) Identify and explain fully one factor which might be responsible for the concentration of ethnic minority groups in the inner-city areas. *(4)*

g) Identify and fully explain one social consequence of the heavy concentration of population in the southern regions of the United Kingdom. *(4)*

(SEG, June 1991)

Q.2

Read ITEMS A and B. Then answer the questions which follow.

ITEM A

Predicted Changes in the Population of the United Kingdom

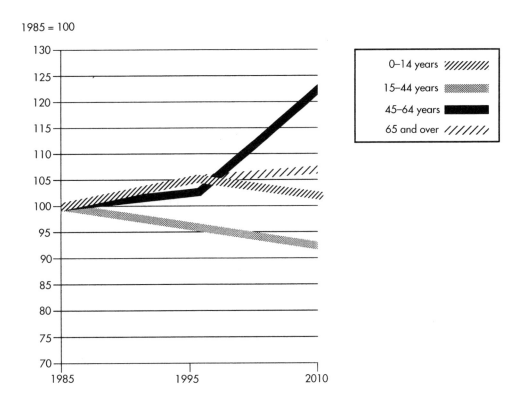

1985 = 100

Source: *The Guardian*, 22.12.1988

ITEM B

Reasons for Population Growth in the United Kingdom

Over the period 1750–1990 the main causes of death changed from the infectious epidemic diseases in the earlier period to the so-called "degenerative" or chronic diseases of today. In the 1970s and 1980s over 80% of all deaths were caused by heart and circulatory disorders, cancers and diseases of the respiratory system (bronchitis, pneumonia).

Two factors are important in explaining these changes:
1 changes in the environment, making epidemic diseases less likely,
2 changes in food production, distribution and consumption which have improved the diet for some whilst causing difficulties for other.

a)   What trend is shown, in ITEM A, for changes in the 65 and over age group?

(1)

b)   Look at ITEM A. Which age group is expected to increase the most after 1985? *(1)*

c)   Look at ITEM B.
   i)   What were the main causes of death in 1750? *(1)*
   ii) Give one major reason for the decline in epidemic diseases. *(1)*

d)   Identify and explain two problems which might arise from the actual increase in then numbers of elderly people well into the next century. *(4)*

e) Identify and explain two consequences of a low birth rate in the
   United Kingdom.   *(4)*

f) Identify and fully explain one way in which governments have acted to reduce
   the mortality (death) rate in Britain.   *(4)*

g) There is evidence to suggest that the fall in the number of 15–44 year
   olds will continue well into the next century.
   Identify and explain fully one social consequence of this trend. *(4)*

(SEG, June 1990)

Q.3
Read ITEMS A and B. Then answer the questions which follow.

ITEM A

POPULATION STATISTICS

	1871	1985
United Kingdom Total	28,055,694	56,617,800
Number of Births	913,555	723,093
Number of Marriages	214,078	382,784
Number of Deaths	589,523	654,701

(Source: *Annual Abstract of Statistics*, HMSO 1987)

ITEM B

Growth of United Kingdom Population 1801–2021

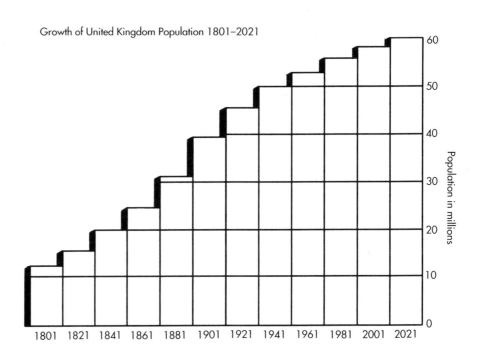

Source: *Social Studies Review*, November 1985

a) Look at ITEM A. What was the total number of births in 1871?   *(1)*

b) Look at ITEM B. Give the population size in 1941.   *(1)*

c) Look at ITEM A.
   i) Give the total number of marriages in 1871.   *(1)*
   ii) Give the total United Kingdom population for 1985.   *(1)*

d)   Identify and explain two reasons for the growth in population between
     1871 and 1985.   *(4)*

e)   Identify and explain two problems which might arise from an increase
     in the numbers of elderly people in the United Kingdom.   *(4)*

f)   Identify and explain two reasons why governments try to predict future
     population size.   *(4)*

g)   Identify and explain fully one problem which may occur with a decline
     in the birth rate.   *(4)*

(SEG, June 1989)

ANSWERS TO EXAMINATION QUESTIONS

Q.1
a)   15% lived in towns and cities
b)   Industrialisation
c)   i)   East Anglia 5.1%
     ii) West Midlands–0.1%
d)   The decline of industry.

Heavy manufacturing industries such as steel and ship building and other traditional working class occupations like coal mining have declined because of competition from abroad or reduced demand for their products. Men's jobs in particular have been lost and this has encouraged migration to the south.

New towns and job opportunities in the south.

New towns were built in the south of England to rehouse Londoners. e.g. Basildon.

These towns have attracted new industries and are often within commuting distance of London. People have moved to the south from the north to get new housing and jobs.

e)   ■ Travelling to work.

There is an increased willingness and ability to travel longer distances to work.

Car ownership has increased massively in the last twenty years. Although many railways have closed some of those that remain provide a quick service to commuters. People are more willing to commute long distances as it means they can live in nicer and cheaper places.

■ The shift of firms to greenfield sites.

Manufacturing and service industries have moved away from inner city areas. Sites are cheaper away from cities, workers may be less unionised and journey times to work are reduced.

f)   ■ Employment.

Immigrants and their descendants have different patterns of employment from the majority. Some jobs are likely to be concentrated in inner city areas.

Immigrants have higher than average rates of self-employment. Shops and restaurants may cater initially for people from the same minority. Professionals may be more likely to find clients from ethnic minorities as this avoids discrimination and overcomes potential language difficulties.

Ethnic minority employers are less likely to discriminate against minority employees. This encourages concentration in the inner city for example in the garment industry.

Public employers are more likely to employ minorities than private employers. British Rail, London Transport and the NHS all actively recruited immigrants in the 1950s and many of the jobs were in London or other Cities.

g)   The increased demand for housing as people migrated to the South of the UK from other regions or countries has caused a housing problem. Existing housing became expensive, people were forced to share houses causing the problems associated with overcrowding and some people remained homeless. In the 1980s people were observed sleeping on the streets in large numbers. Other inadequate housing was provided expensively through unsuitable bed and breakfast accommodation.

Competing for housing has increased racial tension and an extreme right wing councillor was elected on the Isle of Dogs in East London in 1993 by white residents who felt they were unfairly treated by their Local housing authority.

The fall in house prices following the recession of the early 1990s also caused housing problems as people who lost their jobs were unable to keep up mortgages or sell their homes to pay off their mortgage.

Q.2

a) Steadily increasing.

b) The 45–64 age group.

c) i) Infectious epidemic disease.
   ii) Improved sanitation.

d) Develop and explain two from this list or other suitable points.
■ Increased demand for health services OR care in the community.
■ An increase in the non-working dependent population.

e) Choose two from below and explain.
■ Smaller future work force and a greater number of dependent old.
■ Threat to teachers' jobs.
■ Increase in mothers available to work.

f) Choose from this list and write about 100 words explanation.
Health education.
Provision of health care from ante-natal to old age, including vaccination.
Safety legislation at work, on the roads, in products.
Provision of improved environment; housing, sanitation, pollution control etc.

g) Again 100 words, or more to be on the safe side, on one of the following or suitable alternative.
■ Reduced work force.
■ Increased burden of dependency.
■ Reduced crime rate.
■ Reduced demand for some goods.
■ Reduced birth rate as they become of marriageable age.

STUDENT'S ANSWER WITH EXAMINER'S COMMENTS

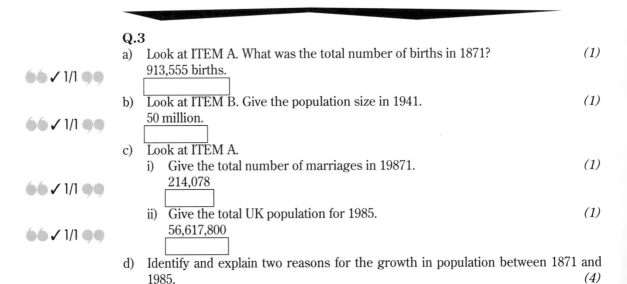

Q.3

a) Look at ITEM A. What was the total number of births in 1871? *(1)*

   66 ✓ 1/1 99   913,555 births.

b) Look at ITEM B. Give the population size in 1941. *(1)*

   66 ✓ 1/1 99   50 million.

c) Look at ITEM A.
   i) Give the total number of marriages in 19871. *(1)*

   66 ✓ 1/1 99   214,078

   ii) Give the total UK population for 1985. *(1)*

   66 ✓ 1/1 99   56,617,800

d) Identify and explain two reasons for the growth in population between 1871 and 1985. *(4)*

> *Could have been a little fuller.*

- Immigration.
  People have come to Britain from Ireland, Europe, India, Pakistan, Jamaica and other Commonwealth countries. Immigrants are often young and have lots of children.

> *Good, but refer to 1871–1985. 3/4*

- Health.
  Children are more likely to survive childhood and have children themselves because of better health. We are more healthy because of the National Health Service and new drugs. Better sewers are just as important.

e)   Identify and explain two problems which might arise from an increase in the numbers of elderly people in the UK.   *(4)*

> *Develops well.*

More Old People's Homes.
As old people live longer even if they are ill we will have to build and pay for more old people's homes. Families are not always willing or able to look after elderly parents. if they are sick the government still does not want them in hospital but cared for at home or in old people's homes.

> *Short, but accurate. 4/4*

Elderly people do not usually work so people who do work will have to pay more taxes to pay for their pensions.

f)   Identify and explain two reasons why governments try to predict future population size.   *(4)*

- Building.
  The government needs to know how many schools and hospitals to build and where in the country they are needed.

> *Relevant points made. 3/4*

- War.
  Governments may worry that their neighbours may attack them and they need soldiers for defence. If the population is falling then the government may reward people who have children. In Russia they get medals for having children.

g)   Identify and explain fully one problem which may occur with a decline in the birth rate.   *(4)*

> *Rather brief. More detail needed. 3/4*

Shortage of workers.
A declining birth rate means that when the children grow up there will be a small number of workers compared to old people. There might be a shortage of particular kinds of workers like nurses who are needed more. If people retired later it would help the problem. More workers could come from other countries.

> *Overall, good relevant points made. A few could have been explained in a little more detail. 17/20*

NB The Review Sheet for this chapter is at the end of the next chapter

URBAN AND RURAL LIFE

CAUSES OF URBANISATION

DE-URBANISATION

STAGES OF URBANISATION

URBAN/RURAL WAYS OF LIFE

POWER IN THE CITY

COMMUNITY

GETTING STARTED

Sociologists became interested in the causes and effects of the urbanisation of Western Europe during the last century. They were generally concerned with the negative effects of the city compared with the more peaceful existence of rural life.

Modern sociology has challenged this simple division between disorderly town and peaceful country. However interest remains in the negative aspects of city life, particularly when these involve conflict. We shall discuss urban riots in this chapter although any explanation must involve an understanding of other parts of the syllabus such as inequality and poverty (ch 6) and deviance (ch 4).

The main themes of questions set on this topic area are:

■ THE REASONS FOR URBANISATION AND DE-URBANISATION
■ THE EFFECTS OF URBANISATION ON:

       – HOUSING
       – SOCIAL CONFLICT
       – EMPLOYMENT
       – FAMILY LIFE

■ THE SIMILARITIES AND DIFFERENCES BETWEEN URBAN AND RURAL LIFE

■ WHETHER OR NOT THERE HAS BEEN A LOSS OF COMMUNITY

DEFINITIONS

URBANISATION. The increase in the proportion of the population who live in large towns or cities.
DE-URBANISATION. The movement of the population from old towns and cities; usually to the suburbs.
A COMMUNITY. A group of people who share a common identity or set of values and who often live in a particular geographical area.

ESSENTIAL PRINCIPLES

Urbanisation describes a situation where an *increasing proportion* of the population lives in towns and cities rather than in the countryside. It is *not* the same thing as the growth of cities. Cities can grow without an increasing proportion of the population living in them if the rural population is growing at the same rate.

1 CAUSES OF URBANISATION

The major cause of Urbanisation is people leaving the countryside to live in towns. Logically it could also be caused by:

Factors in urbanisation

1 Rural settlements growing so that they become towns. This has only a minor effect.
2 The population of the city growing more quickly than that in the country. This has NOT happened. In fact cities tend to have lower birth rates and higher death rates and so the rural population tends to grow faster. Indeed the difference during the early days of the industrial revolution was very marked, though it is hardly apparent in this country now. In Third world countries, birth rates remain higher in rural areas.
3 People migrating from the countryside to cities because of "push" as well as "pull factors".
Reasons for leaving rural areas (push):

■ The mechanisation of agriculture and the lowering of income for labourers may drive them away from the land.
■ War may make rural areas unsafe or prevent the production of food.

Reasons for going to towns (pull):

■ To find work and improve living standards.
■ to change the pattern of life.

2 DE-URBANISATION

This refers to the movement back out of cities and large towns to suburban and rural locations which has occurred since the 1950s. The reasons for these movements include:

Why move back to rural locations?

1 Families having the money to fulfil the desire to be owner occupiers and there having been many housing developments outside major towns. This has continued the trend towards a suburban life with your own house and garden which began in the 1930s.
2 Even if families did not particularly wish to leave the city, the state encouraged re-housing in New Towns or in suburban housing estates following slum clearance or war damage. This led to sociologists writing about "the loss of community".
3 Public transport, increased car ownership and a willingness to spend time commuting has allowed people to live a considerable distance from their work.
4 The decline in the physical and social environment of the inner city has encouraged those who can afford it to leave. This has left the more disadvantaged in the inner city which has discouraged the setting up of new businesses and the provision of services. The decline of the inner city is then both a cause and an effect of people leaving.
5 The decline of employment in old industries which were based in the inner city and which were often the reason why the city itself developed. New employment tends to be in service industries rather than in manufacturing, and these service sector jobs are often located on green field sites with good road links. For example, working-class communities based around the docks in London, Liverpool or elsewhere saw their employment virtually disappear during the 1960s.
6 A combination of many of the factors mentioned above has developed because of the policies of large retailers to re-locate outside cities to larger and cheaper green-field sites which provide ample car parking space. Retailing provided the major growth in economic activity during the 1980s and multiples such as Sainsbury, Tesco and Safeway have expanded the number of their out-of-town superstores dramatically. This is following the American pattern of development. Those concerned that this will lead to an irreversible decline in the shops and other businesses in towns have argued that the only way to halt these market forces is a combination of planning controls and Government investment in public transport, which might discourage the growth in car ownership necessary for the prosperity of out-of-town superstores.

Do not see de-urbanisation as the end of any process of change. Some new towns and cities are growing in population and some old cities, such as London, have begun to increase their populations, though not to the size and density of the past.

Traditional industries such as textiles, particularly fashion clothes, remain in the inner city. Often they are similar to a hundred years ago – small workshops paying very low wages to largely female and ethnic minority workers.

<table>
<tr><td>**3**</td><td>**STAGES OF URBANISATION**</td></tr>
</table>

N. Jewson (1991) has suggested that city life is best explained by looking at the development of Capitalism. He identified a series of stages in the urbanisation of Britain.

1. Before the Industrial Revolution (before 1800)

The majority of the population lived in small settlements and earned their living from the land. Fewer than 20% of the population lived in cities and these tended to be small by today's standards.

2. The industrial city (1800–1880)

This first stage was the result of the industrial revolution. Rapid urbanisation was the result of masses of workers being required for the new factories. Unplanned slum housing sprang up near the factories. There was little or no state provision of services. Life expectancy was lower than in surrounding rural areas. The urban working class did not have the right to vote, Trade Unions were weak and occasionally riots occurred. Critical views of such cities are found in studies of poverty, class and in the fiction of Dickens.

Stages in the urbanisation process

3. The metropolitan city (1880–1960s)

The move to the city has slowed or halted. The city has become very large both in terms of area and population. A few major cities dominate surrounding areas. Government now provides a wide variety of public services, such as houses, roads, gas, electricity, water, sanitation, schools, leisure activities and health care. The city was frequently divided into different zones for homes, work, entertainment etc. Slum clearance led to the break up of traditional working-class communities. The population gained political rights (see politics chapter) and political conflict tended to be restricted to industrial action and voting rather than violence.

4. "Megalopolis" the city of the present and the future? (1960s–?)

The latest development of the city is associated with de-urbanisation rather than urbanisation. It has spread over a huge area and has no clear limits. Many of the factories have gone as the old industries have disappeared and other workplaces have re-located on green-field sites. Shops have also joined the flight from the inner city and large shopping centres have grown up on the edge of towns. The population has become more sub-urban than urban and the "inner city" is seen as the home of the disadvantaged. The role of Local Government as a provider of services has diminished; e.g. council house building has virtually stopped. Riots have again become a form of disorder and perhaps protest.

<table>
<tr><td>**4**</td><td>**THE URBAN AND RURAL WAYS OF LIFE**</td></tr>
</table>

Urbanisation, as we have seen, refers to an increased proportion of a population living in town and cities. This can be caused by migration from the country or when cities have higher birth rates and/or lower death rates. In modern industrial societies, such as Britain, urbanisation has been associated with industrialisation and economic growth. Whereas in Third World countries, urbanisation has been associated with independence from colonialism and population growth, but not with industrialisation.

The problems associated with urbanisation in the Third world include:

1 The problems experienced by migrants arriving from the countryside who find it difficult to adapt to urban life.

Urbanisation problems in the Third World

2 Population explosion. Although birth rates tend to fall in cities compared with rural areas, the problems of an increasing population are more obvious.

3 The decline of the physical environment because of pressure on housing, sanitation, water supply and the social provision such as education and health care. This is exemplified in studies of "shanty towns" which grow up on the outskirts of major cities.

4 Social unrest and crime. This has often been the result of family disorganisation, as single males arrived first, and relative deprivation as their hopes for a better life were not fulfilled.

In *modern societies* a distinctive urban culture has been identified. The main features of "Urbanism as a way of life" were according to Wirth:

1 The *large size* of the population.

2 The *increased density* of population per square mile.

An urban culture

3 The *increased heterogeneity* of the population. This means greater variations in class, ethnicity, occupation, religion, etc.

These features created a segregation of groups and individuals and led to the establishing of different kinds of relationships.

Relationships in *rural* areas were based on knowing the whole person as a member of a family and church as well as a worker. Whereas in urban areas we often know people only in specialised roles, such as teacher, bus driver, neighbour, etc., these relationships tend to be more superficial and temporary. Students and lecturers are often surprised to encounter each other in different roles, such as family shopping or enjoying leisure activities.

This means that people in cities are more able to have a private life and neighbours tend to be more tolerant of private behaviour. It may also mean that we ignore problems that are seen as nothing to do with us.

The psychologist, Zimbardo, conducted an experiment which demonstrated that a car left with its bonnet up in New York City was very quickly vandalised and robbed, whereas in a suburb it was left intact. Similarly city dwellers are often unwilling to intervene when witnessing crime. This is not just through fear of being harmed, but also because we may not feel it is *our* problem.

This unfavourable description of city life has led sociologists to see the city as a lonely place where traditional informal social controls no longer operate, leading to problems of social order which need to be solved in a formal way.

Marx saw the development of cities as an inevitable part of the rise of capitalism. Although he wrote of the degradation of working class life in city slums, he did see the city as the breeding ground of class consciousness and therefore revolution. The peasant was seen as essentially conservative. There have, however, been revolutions by peasants in China, Cuba and Nicaragua.

THE SLUMS AND THE HOMELESS

The homeless are clearly at the bottom of the housing market. Unlike other countries, there is a clear preference in Britain for owner-occupation; renting from local authorities or housing associations is a second choice and renting from private landlords tends to have become less and less popular. However, just after the war, over 60% of households were in private rented accommodation.

The 1991 census showed that: (1981 in brackets)

Housing data

- Owner occupied (Owned outright or buying)   66%   (56%)
- Rented from Local Authority or New Town Association   21%   (31%)
- Privately rented (includes Housing Associations)   13%   (12%)

Although all major political parties now support the policy of increasing home ownership, it has been argued that electorally the increase helped the Conservatives in 1983 and 1987. Certainly the Tories encouraged the sale of council houses with large subsidies. The recession of the early 1990s left many new home owners unable to afford mortgage repayments because of unemployment and unable even to sell their houses to pay off their debts.

Housing as a social problem was, until recently, seen as the problem of the "slums". That is, housing which was unsuitable because of its age, condition and facilities. The proportion of households without sole use of a bath or shower and without an indoor lavatory has now fallen to 1%, compared to 3% ten years earlier.

Slum clearance by Local Authorities began in the last century and was well advanced before the Second World War. The demolition of large areas, rather than individual houses, reached its height in the 1960s and there were many complaints from inner-city dwellers about the destruction of traditional working class communities, the separation of families and their being re-housed in unsuitable places without jobs, shops or recreational facilities. Frequently good housing was destroyed with the bad, and fewer homes were made available than those demolished.

The 1990s saw an increase in those who were obviously homeless, in the sense that they were sleeping in the streets of large cities. There is also the less visible problem of those housed by Local Authorities in totally unsuitable bed-and-breakfast accommodation. This accommodation is paid for by the State and is associated with overcrowding, poor health, family disorganisation and insecurity.

GENTRIFICATION

Gentrification describes the process where previously run-down areas become occupied by well-off professionals and managers who choose to live in the inner city. They may occupy whole houses which were previously shared by more than one household and are owner-occupiers rather than tenants. The attraction of "gentrified" areas may be a combination of access to facilities and to employment, and to living in houses and districts with "character". The avoidance of the need to commute is balanced by the expense of buying in central areas. Many middle class inner-city residents also choose to have their children privately educated to avoid their going to inner-city schools with low levels of achievement.

66 Gentrification 99

The benefits of gentrification are generally shared by the new middle class residents and by property developers. Working class residents may find themselves priced out of the area. Developments in London Docklands have been one example of such gentrification.

URBAN RIOTS

Studies of urban life have become more popular since the riots of the early 1980s. There are debates as to whether they should be explained in terms of race, poverty, power or delinquency. Northern Ireland in the late 1960s gave an indication of the potential for violence in cities directed against the police and army. The army has not been deployed in similar circumstances in Britain, but tear-gas has been used and other forms of control such as water-cannon deployed.

The Scarman report, written by a Lord Chief Justice for the government after the Brixton disorders in 1981, saw the explanation for the start of the riots as lying in the relationship between the police and young black people.

66 Causes of the Brixton riots 99

"The riots were essentially an outburst of anger and resentment by young black people against the police . . . " "They were neither premeditated nor planned . . . " " . . . outsiders did participate and played a significant part in intensifying the riots by making and distributing petrol bombs. Some of them were clearly identified as whites.

Firstly . . . (the police) . . . were partly to blame for the breakdown in community relations. Secondly, there were instances of harassment and racial prejudice among junior officers on the streets of Brixton . . . Thirdly, there was the failure to adjust policies and methods to meet the needs of policing a multi-racial society."

(The Scarman Report: The Brixton Disorders 10th–12th April 1981)

Scarman was criticised from many sides. The police felt that they were being criticised for rising street crime and at the same time for their response to it which was "saturation policing", that is, lots of police on the street stopping and searching young men.

Conflict theorists did not accept Scarman's view that racism was an isolated problem found only in the lower ranks of the police rather than being embedded in the wider society.

Scarman wrote that:

"Institutional racism does not exist in Britain; but racial disadvantage and its nasty associate racial discrimination, have not yet been eliminated."

Scarman recommended recruiting more police from ethnic minorities but the proportion remains tiny. In 1985 there was further disorder on the streets of Brixton following the accidental shooting of a black woman, Cherry Groce. Almost immediately another black woman, Cynthia Jarret, died after being pushed whilst her home in Tottenham was being searched by police. This led to a riot on the Broadwater Farm Estate and to the death of PC Blakelock. The riot was explained from different political viewpoints, including "wickedness" (Norman Tebbit; Conservative) and "Oppressive policing" (Bernie Grant; then the leader of the local council, now one of the few Black MPs).

The death of an illegal immigrant from Jamaica following her arrest and being bound and gagged in 1993, did not trigger a riot as her family, Bernie Grant and the Commissioner of the Metropolitan police all attempted to channel protest into less violent forms.

It should be noted that not all street disorder occurs in cities and even when it does it is not invariably associated with race issues. The 1980s also saw violent disorder over the poll tax and the reporting of "lager lout" disturbances in country towns rather than inner cities. The largely white housing estates were the location of many disputes.

5 ▷ POWER IN THE CITY

Government is often seen as representing the interests of all the community. Planners claim to encourage building to meet the needs of the whole community. Critics have suggested, however, that it is power which influences decisions about planning and the allocation of resources in the city.

Power may be held by:

1 Business people who decide whether to invest in factories, offices, and shops and thus provide employment. Many inner-city problems are the result of unemployment caused by the loss of jobs from the city or their re-location elsewhere. Of course social problems themselves discourage investment. Governments may encourage investment in parts of cities damaged by riots, but business people may need a lot of inducements.

Holders of power in the city

2 Central government which has restricted the funds available to local government to build and provide services. However it has encouraged business by removing some restrictions on their activities in some areas of the country, such as the London Docklands.

3 Local government. This was a major influence on the development of housing and services in cities but their power has been curtailed by central government since 1979. Some Local authorities, such as the Greater London Council, were abolished. Local government managers are part of the group that Pahl called "GATE-KEEPERS". This group also includes those who lend money for housing or to business, such as Bank and Building Society managers, and those who control access to homes, such as Councils and Housing Associations.

Such people cannot, of course, be seen as a *single* group with uniform interests. There are, however, a variety of ways available to them to shape their urban environment. These range from spending money in local shops rather than in out-of-town supermarkets to discouraging disorder on the streets. Generally, as suggested in the politics chapter, those from higher social classes have more influence, e.g. in preventing unwelcome developments near their homes. The public may form organisations to protect their interests over a long period, such as tenants' associations, or to meet an immediate threat, like an unwelcome new road. In 1993, newsworthy local organisations included the development of the so-called vigilantes to protect communities against crime and anti-motorway protesters using direct action to hinder road building schemes.

ARE CITY AND COUNTRYSIDE SO DIFFERENT?

Some sociologists have rejected the view that there is a clear distinction between urban and rural life. They have argued that:

1 There is a *rural-urban continuum*, i.e. communities are more or less urban or rural, not simply one or the other. Large rural settlements may become urban.

Similarities between urban and rural life

2 The *urban-rural distinction* is not very important as there are inequalities and social problems in rural areas as well as in towns. Cities are not all the same. Townsend's study of poverty showed that in the 1970s, poor Salford had nearly twice the death rates at various ages as rich Oxford.

3 Industrialisation or capitalism influences social relationships more than urbanism. This would suggest that life in modern Britain is essentially similar, whether in town or country, and is markedly different from life in the Third World, whether in town or country.

4 Communities have been identified in urban areas. WILLMOTT and YOUNG found a thriving community in the midst of a major city. They described the "Mum-centred" family in Bethnall Green in East London as the key feature of a close-knit neighbourhood. Later, Willmott's study in Dagenham saw an East-End type of community being reborn after being broken down by re-housing policies which had brought East-Enders to a new town away from London. Other urban communities have been identified with the unifying links being ethnic or occupational.

5 The *commuter* is evidence of the disappearance of the distinction between the rural and urban ways of life. Commuters from rural dormitory towns and villages may have threatened the sense of community in those places. Think of the effects on housing prices which exclude the children of local people from competing for housing, as well as the lack of family and neighbourhood ties of many commuters.

6 Life in the suburbs has ingredients of both town and country. Communities are less varied and settlement is less dense than in the city.

ETHNIC MINORITY COMMUNITIES IN THE CITY

REX and MOORE described the lives of ethnic communities based on class. The geographic concentration of ethnic minorities in inner-city areas was seen as a result of their weakness in the housing market. Whereas PAHL argued that it was not just economic factors which confined immigrants to ghetto areas but the policies and practices of "urban managers" who allocate resources. These include Banks, Building Societies and estate agents, as well as local authority planners and housing managers. Both these explanations ignore the element of choice. Originally immigrants were helped to settle by kinship groups and later minorities may continue to choose to live together in order to support each other and enjoy specialised facilities such as religious buildings and shops.

HOUSING AND BEHAVIOUR

Does building influence behaviour? In the 1960s American writers suggested that social behaviour was influenced by architecture and planning. Tower blocks and housing with shared access and public spaces was seen as encouraging crime, fear of crime and vandalism. The solutions to such problems were identified as returning to more traditional forms of low rise housing with no shared entrances, lifts, or walkways. This was described as "Defensible space" (O. Newman). Encouraging people to walk was also seen as a way of getting back "eyes on the street" (J. Jacobs).

66 Housing can affect behaviour 99

In the 1980s similar ideas were proposed by Alice Coleman, an English professor of geography who, supported by Margaret Thatcher, encouraged local authorities to replace or modify tower block housing to reduce crime.

There is some evidence that local authorities in Britain concentrate "problem Families" in their worst housing. These areas become stigmatised by the public, press and police, perhaps encouraging further deviance and certainly dissuading those who have a choice from living there.

6 > THE CONCEPT OF COMMUNITY

66 The idea of community 99

Sociologists have used the word *community* in three rather different ways:
1 Close relationships based on a locality. Usually they present a rather romantic view of village life.
2 A pattern of close-knit relationships based on kinship or perhaps on a shared occupation such as fishing or coal mining.
3 A shared identity which might define, for example, an ethnic community.

Has there been a loss of community?

This has been suggested by those who see the feeling of shared identity and traditional sense of community undermined by such social processes as industrialisation, modernisation and urbanisation.

It has been opposed by:

1 Studies which have been able to identify thriving communities, whether in cities, suburbs or amongst the poor.

2 Marxists who see the real basis of community as CLASS. They would see ethnic and other communities as dividing the working class and as based on false consciousness (see ch 5).

3 Durkheim saw the solidarity (or integration) of rural pre-industrial society as being based on shared beliefs and values as the people were more or less the same and worked together on the land. Solidarity also existed in industrialised societies but was based on people who did *different* jobs (i.e. the division of labour) being dependent on each other. The social unrest in Paris in the Revolution of 1789 and again in the 19th century roused fears of social disorganisation and conflict (Durkheim called this ANOMIE) in cities.

EXAMINATION QUESTIONS

Q.1

Change and Stability

**How your home rates.
Are you in a break-in blackspot?**
the league table of offences

Police Regions	Total offences per 100 000	Unemployment rate population
Gt. Manchester	10 577	15.5
Northumbria	10 515	17.6
Merseyside	10 356	21.2
London	10 000	10.2
Warwicks	4581	12.8
Devon, Cornwall	4483	16.7
Suffolk	4163	10.0
Dyfed, Powys	3575	15.9

(Note: 1: The Northumbria Police region includes Newcastle.
2: There are no large towns in Dyfed/Powys.)

(Adapted from: *Sunday Mirror*, 24/3/85)

Metropolitan areas are mainly urban. The populations of all metropolitan areas fell between 1981 and 1989, but rates of decline in Greater London, Greater Manchester and West Yorkshire were small.

In the same period, the population of most non-metropolitan areas grew. The fastest growing areas were East Anglia (1.0 per cent per annum) and the South West (0.75 per cent per annum).

(*Social Trends 21*, HMSO, 1991)

---

a) Explain, using examples, the meaning of the term urbanisation.   (*4*)

b) Describe the movement of population with England and Wales during the past 20 years. Give reasons for this movement.   (*7*)

c) What major differences would you expect to find in the behaviour and lifestyles of people in urban and rural areas?   (*9*)

(MEG, June 1992)

Q.2 Study ITEMS A and B. Then answer the questions which follow.

LIVING IN TOWNS AND CITIES

World Urbanisation 1800–1970

Population living in towns of more than 20 000 people

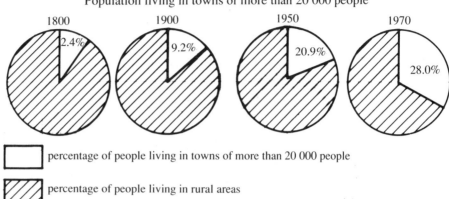

1800 1900 1950 1970

2.4% 9.2% 20.9% 28.0%

☐ percentage of people living in towns of more than 20 000 people

▨ percentage of people living in rural areas

ITEM B

Population Change by County, 1971–1981

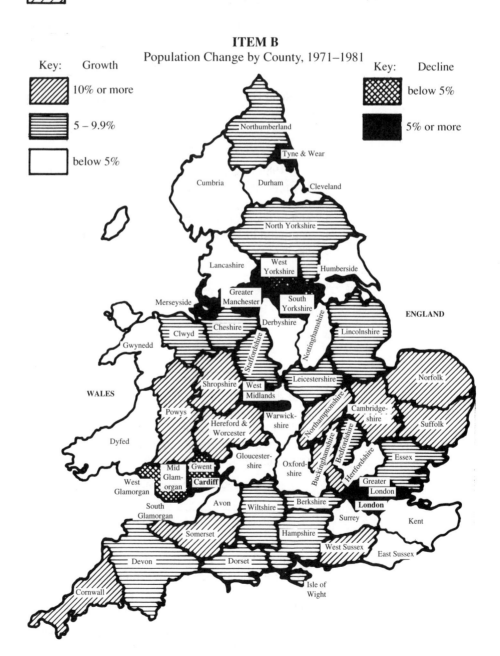

Key: Growth
▨ 10% or more
▤ 5 – 9.9%
☐ below 5%

Key: Decline
▨ below 5%
■ 5% or more

Source: adapted from *State of the Nation*, S. FOTHERGILL and J. VINCENT, Pluto Press

a)   Look at ITEM A. According to the pie charts, what percentage of the world's population was living in towns in 1900?   *(1)*

b)   Look at ITEM A. According to the pie charts, what was the increase in the percentage of the world's population living in towns between 1950 and 1970?

                                                                                  (1)

c)   Look at ITEM B.
     i)   From the diagram identify **one** county whose population declined by 5% or more
     between 1971 and 1981.   *(1)*
     ii) From the diagram identify **one** county whose population grew by 10% or more
     between 1971 and 1981.   *(1)*

d)   Identify and explain **two** reasons why people migrate from one area to another.

                                                                                  (4)

e)   Identify and explain **two** consequences of the rapid growth and development of cities.   *(4)*

f)   Identify and fully explain **one** major social problem existing in Britain's inner cities today.   *(4)*

g)   Identify and fully explain **one** factor which may affect the development of a "sense of community" in an area.   *(4)*

                                                              (SEG, June 1992)

Q.3   Read ITEMS A and B. Then answer the questions which follow.

ITEM A

The 1986 English House Condition Survey estimated that 2.9 million dwellings in England were in a poor condition. This was 15 per cent of all dwellings. Three measures of poor condition were used: unfit dwellings, lacking basic amenities, and in poor repair. Private rented dwellings were the most likely to be in a poor condition in 1986 (42 per cent) and housing association dwellings were the least likely (7 per cent)

(From *Social Trends,* 1991)

ITEM B

The death rate in Sheffield is still above the national average by about 10 per cent. Life expectancy is on average 68.4 years for men, 74.9 for women but is still unequally distributed. The central areas of the city have much higher death rates than other areas. Life is healthier generally in Sheffield today but still very unequal. Working-class people are most likely to live in the unhealthy districts.

(Adapted from *Survivors of Steel City,* Geoffrey Beattie, Chatto & Windus)

a)   Study **ITEM A.** From the information given, state
     i)   the percentage of all dwellings estimated to be in a poor condition in 1986;
                                                                                  (1)
     ii) which dwellings were most likely to be in a poor condition.   *(1)*

b)   Study **ITEM B.** From the information given, state
     i)   by how much the death rate in Sheffield is above the national average;
                                                                                  (1)

ii) in which districts working-class people are more likely to live. *(1)*

c) Identify and explain **two** reasons why people living in some districts are likely to be less healthy. *(4)*

d) Welfare services do not always reach the people they are intended to help. Identify and explain **two** reasons why people may not get the help to which they are entitled. *(4)*

e) Sociologists hold various views of why poverty exists in Britain. Identify and fully explain **one** of these views. *(4)*

f) Identify **one** voluntary organisation which attempts to fight poverty in Britain. Fully explain how it does so. *(4)*

ANSWERS TO EXAMINATION QUESTIONS

Q.1
a) Define urbanisation (see beginning of chapter).
Illustrate with an example of a town or city which developed because of industrialisation and a New Town developed because of a Government decision.
b) Choose 3 kinds of movement and explain each.
Possibilities include:

1 Flight from inner city because of lack of jobs, fear of crime etc.
2 Move to New Towns because of desire to be owner occupiers (slum clearance has been less common in the last 20 years).
3 Continued move from North to South because of job loss in the 1970s and 1980s in traditional industries.
4 Move to rural areas by commuters which has been made possible by improved transport or greater willingness to travel.
5 Movement to seaside resorts by the retired who sell houses to buy smaller homes. n.b. Some of these population movements have similar explanations so try and make distinct points and not repeat yourself.
c) Describe some major differences such as:
■ Lack of community in urban areas more personal and full relationships in rural areas.
■ Variety of population in urban areas in terms of jobs, ethnicity.
■ Greater concentration of social problems such as homelessness and crime in urban areas etc.
Suggest that differences between town and country may be exaggerated:
■ There is considerable diversity within both rural and urban areas.
■ There are social problems in the country.
■ Rural villages may house commuters who work in the city.
■ Close-knit communities have been identified in cities etc.

Q.2
a) 9.2% (The dates are above each pie chart.)
b) 7.1 percentage points.
(You express it as percentage points because the increase from 20.9% to 28% is about a third i.e. 30%. If in doubt refer to your sociology or mathematics teacher. I have heard examiners arguing over this!)
c) i) Merseyside.
(Choose one of the three with the appropriate shading i.e. Greater London, Merseyside or West Midlands. Incidentally these all contain large traditional industrial cities which helps explain their decline.)
ii) Cornwall.
(There are lots to choose from. Take the opportunity to think about the different reasons for growth in East Anglia and elsewhere.)
d) ■ The re-housing of young couples on new housing estates led to feeling of isolation until a new generation was able to be housed alongside their parents.

■ The inability of young married people in rural villages to afford houses in competition with commuters has also led to young people having to move away from their families and community.

e) If the growth is unplanned the public services such as water and sanitation may be inadequate for the increased population.

Competition for housing may lead to overcrowding and high costs, resulting perhaps in poverty and ill health.

(You may refer to recent evidence of rapid growth in the Third World as well as the UK.)

f) Racial conflict is seen as an inner city problem.

Ethnic minorities are often concentrated in particular districts of the inner city and this may mean competition for jobs and housing is seen in terms of race. Local politicians may encourage this view.

(In 1993 a BNP candidate was elected to a council seat in East London. The main issue at the election was allocation of housing to different ethnic groups.)

The police force remains overwhelmingly white and their relationships with ethnic minorities have been poor. The police may perceive minorities as more criminal than the white majority. The minorities may see the police as a force of outsiders who fail to protect them and oppress their youth.

g) The opportunity for extended families to live near each other affects the development of a sense of community. The close relationship between mothers and their married daughters was seen by Willmott and Young in their study of East London as the basis of a traditional working-class community. Immigrants have often chosen to live with family and kin.

Q.3

a) i) 15% Remember to state percentage not the total number.
   ii) Private rented dwellings were most likely to be in poor condition.

b) i) The first sentence states "about 10%".
   ii) Unhealthy districts which are often in central areas of the city.
   The remaining parts of the question are focused on the issue of poverty and welfare so, if necessary, refer back to chapter 6.

c) Just two reasons. A mark for identifying and another for explaining in each case.
   Poor housing may encourage disease.
   The lack of jobs may mean low household income and poor standards of nutrition.
   You might also discuss overcrowding, pollution, stress etc.
   There is a variation in provision of health care.

d) Explain in at least one full sentence for each reason. You might mention that the system is difficult to understand and that some individuals are too proud to want to be dependent. e.g. they might resent the feeling of lost independence if they take meals on wheels.

e) One view only from culture of poverty, class inequality, inadequacy of welfare benefits, dependency on the State etc.
   "Fully explain" means in a few lines as you only have 5 or 6 minutes.

f) One mark for choosing an organisation and three for how it works. Look at the section on pressure groups in chapter 14 as well as the discussion of voluntary organisations in the poverty chapter. n.b. Poverty is a popular topic. This question shows that you may have to discuss related areas of syllabuses and also that less popular parts of the syllabus like Voluntary organisations can be examined. Learning enough topics to have a choice in the examination may allow you to avoid an unpredictable question. If caught unprepared do not leave out part of a question but make an attempt based on your overall understanding of sociology and your general knowledge.

REVIEW SHEET

(SEG, June 1993)

This Review Sheet covers the material in Chapter 11 (Population) and Chapter 12 (Urban and Rural Life).

■ Give 4 *reasons* which might explain why the fertility rate is lower in a modern industrial society compared to pre-industrial societies.

1 _____

2 _____

3 _____

4 _____

■ Give 4 *consequences* for a society of a fall in the fertility rate.

1 _____

2 _____

3 _____

4 _____

■ Give 4 *reasons* for the observed fall in the infant mortality rate during this century for the UK.

1 _____

2 _____

3 _____

4 _____

■ Look back at Fig. 11.1 in Item B of Question 1, Chapter 11. Use the information to answer these questions.

1 Which region had the highest rate of *population decline?*

2 Which region had the most stable population over the period?

_____

Use the data to compare East Anglia with Merseyside.

_____

■ Look back at Fig. 11.2, in Item A of Question 2, Chapter 11.

1 What happens to the 15–44 years age group after 1985?

_____

2 What happens to the 0–14 years age group between 1985 and 1995 and between 1995 and 2010?

_____

3 What is happening to the elderly in this chart?

_____

4 This chart is based on 1985=100. How would you interpret an index number of 122 for the elderly in 2010?

_____

■ List 3 causes of *urbanisation.*

1 _____

2 _____

3 _____

■ List 3 causes of de-urbanisation.

1 _____

2 _____

3 _____

■ What do you understand by "gentrification"

_____

■ In what ways might urban and rural life be *similar?*

1 _____

2 _____

3 _____

■ How might housing affect behaviour?

1 _____

2 _____

■ Look back to the table in Question 1 of Chapter 12. Use the information to consider whether the number of break-ins is related to unemployment.

_____

■ Look back to the pie charts shown in Item A of Question 2, Chapter 12. Use the information to explain what has happened to people living in rural areas.

_____

■ Look carefully at the chart below.

Births and deaths

United Kingdom

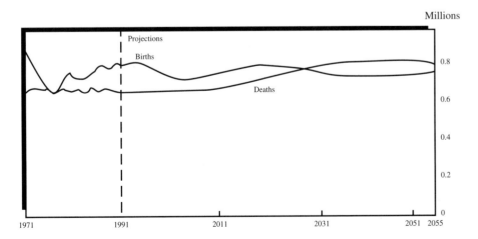

1 What would we expect to happen to UK population size in:

a 1991 ______________________________

b 2031 ______________________________

c 2058 ______________________________

■ Look carefully at the Table below

Deaths: by age and sex

United Kingdom

	Death rates per 1,000 in each age group					
	Under 1	1–14	15–39	Females 40–59 males 40–64	Females 60–79 males 65–79	80 and over
1961						
Males	24.8	0.6	1.3	11.8	66.1	190.7
Females	19.3	0.4	0.8	4.9	32.2	136.7
1971						
Males	20.2	0.5	1.1	11.4	59.9	174.0
Females	15.5	0.4	0.6	4.8	27.5	132.9
1981						
Males	12.7	0.4	1.0	10.1	56.1	167.5
Females	9.6	0.3	0.5	4.4	26.4	126.2
1991						
Males	8.3	0.3	1.0	7.4	48.7	149.4
Females	6.3	0.2	0.5	3.2	24.1	116.2

Use the figures to show:

1 What has happened to the death rate for infants under 1 since 1961.

____

____

2 What has happened to the death rate for males between 40 and 64 years since 1961.

____

____

3 Why you would expect more elderly females than males over 80 years.

____

____

POWER AND POLITICS

POWER AND AUTHORITY

VOTING BEHAVIOUR

VOTING SYSTEMS

POLITICAL PARTIES

PRESSURE GROUPS

POLITICAL ACTION

OPINION POLLS

MEDIA

POLITICAL SOCIALISATION

DEMOCRATIC/TOTALITARIAN GOVERNMENT

HUMAN RIGHTS

GETTING STARTED

Politics is about who gets what, when and how. We argue with each other about who gets scarce resources. Political relationships exist wherever and whenever people have conflicting interests. Usually politics is studied at national level but political relationships exist in families, schools, churches and workplaces. Feminists talk about sexual politics and claim that the personal issue is a political issue if marriage and the family oppress women. Children may also compete with parents for power.

Major themes for questions set on this topic include:

- IDEAS ON POWER AND AUTHORITY
- POLITICAL PARTICIPATION
- VOTING SYSTEMS AND VOTING BEHAVIOUR
- POLITICAL PARTIES
- PRESSURE GROUPS
- ROLE OF THE MEDIA
- DEMOCRACY AND HUMAN RIGHTS

DEFINITIONS

POWER. The ability to get others to do as you wish.

AUTHORITY. Legitimate power which ultimately requires consent.

COERCION. The use of force or threat. It does not need consent.

IDEOLOGY. A set of ideas, based on values, which serve particular interests.

DEMOCRACY. A system of government where the people participate in decision making.

TOTALITARIANISM. A system of Government where the people do not participate but are controlled by a strong, unrepresentative few.

THE RULING CLASS. A Marxist term describing those who have political power because they own the means of production.

ELITES. Small groups who rule and whose power or influence is based on factors other than ownership.

PARTIES. Organisations which seek to govern in order to achieve their common aims.

PRESSURE GROUPS. Organisations which seek to influence Government decisions but not actually to govern.

Related topics include stratification and the mass media, as well as the family and education.

1 **POWER AND AUTHORITY**

ESSENTIAL PRINCIPLES

■ *Power* is the ability to achieve your will against the will of others. The teacher exercises power over her class when she gets a class that wants to talk about the weekend to read a sociology book quietly. Parents exercise power over children when they are able to get them to return home earlier than they wanted to after a night out. Employers and managers have power to control the lives of workers at work and may decide not to employ them at all.

■ *Authority* is a type of power. It exists when the person being ordered accepts the right of the person in power to control them. Sociologists call this *legitimate power.* It exists when people give their consent to being controlled. For example we may consent to being ruled by a government which has been elected by a majority. Students accept the right of teachers to order them, because they accept the rules rather than admire the individual.

Max Weber identified *three types of authority* which depended on the idea that people accepted the legitimacy of the ruler:

1 Charismatic authority. This rested on affection and personal devotion to the leader, not his position. A good example would be the late Ayatollah Khomeini who led the Iranian revolution in 1979. Religious leaders have often exercised charismatic authority.

2 Traditional authority. This rested on habit and the acceptance of an established pattern of social order. Children obey parents and the young may respect the rights of older heads of the family to make decisions. Tribal chiefs in some African countries exercise traditional authority.

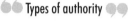
Types of authority

3 Rational-legal (or Bureaucratic) authority. This depends on the idea that laws can be enacted and changed by an accepted procedure. Obedience is not to individuals but to rules. Leaders of political parties and officials appointed by the State have this sort of authority.

Authority could depend on a combination of these sources. All our Prime Ministers have "bureaucratic authority" but some are more charismatic than others. Where leaders come from the old aristocratic families there is an element of traditional authority, like that exercised by the Queen.

2 **VOTING BEHAVIOUR**

POLITICAL PARTICIPATION

Voting is only one type of political behaviour. Individuals and groups may *participate* in the political process in a variety of ways. They may be members of political parties or pressure groups. This may involve just paying a subscription or a higher level of commitment, such as attending meetings, lobbying politicians or even demonstrating. Some people seek or hold political office as an appointed official or an elected representative. In less democratic States, opportunities for participation are much more limited and may be secretive or violent. Participants in the political system tend to come from more advantaged groups who feel that they are "insiders" in the society. More often than not this means white, middle-aged, higher class males. There are obvious exceptions to this rule, including organisations for ethnic minorities, women's groups and Trade Unions. The social characteristics of decision makers are described below.

NON-VOTERS

The right to vote in Britain has been acquired relatively recently and previously did not apply to all. It was only in 1884 that most males over 21 could vote. Women over 35 were first able to vote in 1918 and women over 21 in 1928. Eighteen year olds were given the right to vote in 1969. Some groups are still not entitled to vote, including the under 18s, the Queen and Peers, prisoners and some psychiatric patients.

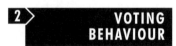
Reasons for non-voting

Some people are not registered to vote and of those who are, about 25% do not vote in general elections. This has varied between 84% and 72% in the post-war period. Voting in by-elections is usually lower and in local government elections much lower. The number of voters is generally fewer in the summer months for elections as people are often on holiday and fail to arrange postal votes.

It has been argued that the Poll tax, which was replaced in 1993 by a more traditional Council tax on property, persuaded many people not to put their names on the electoral register. This may have affected the poor and young adults more than other groups.

Non-voters may lack interest in the issues or outcomes of elections or may have made a more active decision that no party represents their interests. Those under 30, particularly males, are less likely to vote. International comparisons show high levels where voting is *compulsory,* e.g. Australia, and a low level in certain other countries e.g. in the USA with between 50% and 60% voting in presidential elections.

EXPLANATIONS OF VOTING BEHAVIOUR

The main explanations can be considered under the following headings:

1 CLASS AND VOTING.
2 OTHER SOCIAL CHARACTERISTICS.
3 CONSUMER CHOICE.

Remember that votes do not translate directly into seats in Parliament.

Class and voting

The key issue in the study of voting behaviour has remained the relationship between *class* and party allegiance. The traditional assumption about British voting was that the middle classes voted Conservative and the working classes voted Labour. The working class were defined as manual workers and the middle class as non-manual workers.

Sociological concern has often been directed towards the so-called "deviant", i.e. cross-class voters who were seen as explaining Conservative electoral successes despite there being a working class majority.

The explanations for deviant voting included:

❝❞ Reasons for deviant voting ❞❞

1 The *embourgeoisement* of the working class (See chapter 5).
2 *Deferential working class* voters who saw Conservative leaders as their social superiors.
3 *Instrumental voters* who calculated their individual interests and were not loyal to parties.
4 The existence of *"middle class radicals"* who voted Labour. These tended to be better educated, in the caring professions and often employed in the public sector.
5 *Social mobility* may have meant that voters stayed loyal to the party of their youth rather than that associated with their new social position.

Class dealignment

However, since 1974 the link between class and voting has become so weak that the concept of deviant voting is no longer useful and the debate has now broadened to consider a variety of explanations of voting behaviour. The failure of the Labour party in the last four elections has led to the revival of old theories such as embourgeoisement (see ch 5) and new explanations of voting behaviour which still see class as significant. These include:

a) Changes in the occupational structure which have led to the shrinking of the traditional working class who remain loyal to Labour. Crewe distinguished:

❝❞ Breaking of the voting link with class ❞❞

   ■ The Old Working Class of public sector workers, council house dwellers living in the North and Scotland (perhaps he should have added Wales).
   ■ The New Working Class who work in the private sector are owner occupiers and live in the South.

b) The middle classes have also become divided. Routine clerical workers, particularly those in unions and working in the public sector, are less loyal to the Conservatives. Many of these are women.

c) All classes have become increasingly affluent. Ownership of homes and shares and optimism about the economic future are often associated with voting Conservative.

Other social characteristics of voting patterns

1 Cultural differences, such as nationality, religion, language and ethnicity. Nationalism is a major political issue in Wales and Scotland. The politics of Northern Ireland appears quite distinct from the rest of the UK with the major parties dividing on religious lines.

2 Geographical divisions based on regions or housing in urban, suburban or rural areas. The recent elections up to 1992 show that: Labour is strong in Scotland, Wales and the North of England. The Conservatives are strong throughout the South East, South West and East Midlands. The West Midlands is divided between these parties. The Liberal Democrats and previous third parties have suffered by having their supporters spread relatively evenly throughout the country and thus are not able to win seats because of the first past the post system. Labour is strong in inner London, but outer London is overwhelmingly Conservative. Owner occupiers are more likely to vote Conservative than Council tenants.

3 Generation rather than age itself may influence voting. The old appear to be more likely to vote Conservative but this may be because the middle classes and women both live longer. Many voters, though fewer than in the past, stay loyal to the same party throughout their lives.

4 Gender has correlated with voting in the past. Women were more likely to vote Conservative than Labour. This was probably because they were less likely to be in paid employment, less likely to be manual workers and less likely to be in Trade Unions. Since 1983, women have been less likely to vote Conservative than men.

5 Ethnicity is an increasingly important influence as the number of minority group voters increases. Asian and particularly Afro-Caribbean communities are more likely to vote Labour. This applies even when allowance is made for class. The Labour party may appear more sympathetic to minority interests but all parties endorse strict immigration control.

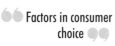
Social aspects of voting patterns

Consumer Choice

These explanations suggest that voters behave like consumers in the market place. They "choose their product" i.e. vote for a party based on their views about:

- Party leaders.
- Party image.
- Party policies.
- Party competence.

Factors in consumer choice

In 1951 the psychologist H. Eysenck suggested that political attitudes could be measured on two separate scales. *Economic issues* separated left and right wing views whereas *humanitarian social issues* (e.g. punishment and immigration) separated "tough" from "tender" views. Working classes tended to have left wing and tough views. The extent to which this still applies would help to explain working class Conservatives who favour tough policies and middle class Labour voters who favour tender ones. The consumer choice model does not mean that class has no influence on voting, as the social characteristics described above may help to explain how people choose.

Dunleavy and Husbands (1985) suggested that voters' attitudes could be influenced by the media and whether they worked in the public or private sector.

Views on recent election from Crewe (1987) and King (1992) suggest that although the public favour Labour policies for the country as a whole, they may vote Conservative out of economic self-interest. The major success of the Conservative campaign in 1992 was to associate the Labour party with high taxes.

3 > VOTING SYSTEMS

Britain has a first-past-the-post electoral system with MPs being elected for specific constituencies. This system has been criticised for being undemocratic and in particular as being unfair to third parties. Most alternative electoral systems would produce numbers of seats in parliament which more closely represented the numbers of votes cast for the parties. These systems are described as *proportional representation* and come in a variety of forms.

The problems of the first-past-the-post system can be illustrated by looking at some specific election results.

- In 1951 the Conservatives won most seats in parliament with fewer votes than Labour.

■ In February 1974 the reverse happened and the Labour victors got fewer votes than the outgoing Conservative government.

■ In no election since 1945 has the winning party gained 50% of the vote. This means that even when governments have had huge parliamentary majorities and claimed a mandate for major reforms, they have had fewer votes than the combined opposition.

■ In most constituencies the winner attracts a minority of votes.

Problems with first-past-the-post

The Conservative and Labour parties have been beneficiaries of this system and therefore have not been inclined to amend it, although 4 consecutive defeats have encouraged Labour to consider alternatives. It is the parties of the centre (Liberal, Social Democrat, Liberal Democrat) which have suffered most from the system. This is most clearly demonstrated by the 1983 election.

1983 Election	% Share of vote	number of seats
Conservative	43.5	397
Labour	28.3	209
Lib/SDP	25.4	23

In 1987 the Liberal/SDP Alliance gained 23% of the vote and 3.4% of the seats. Many people may have been dissuaded from voting for them because their votes may then appear to be wasted.

The advantage of the system to the country as a whole, rather than the victorious parties, is the claim that it produces a clear majority in parliament and thus a decisive Government. In the USA, where usually only two parties stand, the results seem fairer. However there does not seem to be a clear link between electoral systems and political stability. Proportional representation has produced stable coalition Governments in Germany and Scandinavia, but not in Italy. (A coalition government contains more than one party who act in alliance.) The British system has sometimes failed to produce decisive majorities or on some occasions, most recently in February 1974, any majority at all.

Perhaps proportional representation and the possibility of coalition government that follows is more likely to produce decisions based on consensus rather than reinforcing divisions in society. In the USA "weak" government, limited by all sorts of checks and balances is seen as preferable to strong government which may tend to act undemocratically.

4 ▷ POLITICAL PARTIES

Political parties are a relatively new development in the politics of Britain. They now dominate the political system at local as well as national level. Government is drawn from the leadership of the most successful political party and therefore the way that the party chooses MPs and its leaders is important. Only the last three Conservative leaders (all Prime Ministers) were elected. Before that they were chosen secretly. Only MPs vote in the election of Conservative leaders.

There are still arguments in the Labour party about who should be able to vote for leaders and policies. There has been a shift in power away from Trade Unions, who still however support the labour party financially.

Political parties can be distinguished by the *ideologies* (their beliefs) and they *policies* (their aims). Parties are the main link between the public and the government.

They represent the people in two main ways:

1 They select candidates for office whom the voters can choose.
2 They adopt policies for voters to choose from.

PARTY IDEOLOGIES

Conservative and Labour

There may be a difference between the public's image of what a political party stands for and the views of its members and leadership. In 1955 a study showed that Labour and Conservative voters had quite different views on what their party and the other party stood for. This is important, as it is thought that *party image* may influence voters more than actual issues.

Party images

■ Labour voters thought that the Labour party was for the working class and the Welfare State, whereas Conservative voters thought it was for nationalisation and was impractical and extravagant.

■ Conservative voters thought that the Conservative party was for all classes and for free enterprise and business. Labour voters saw them as a party for the rich and big business.

The discussion about the voter as a *consumer* in this chapter indicates that voters do not just see parties in terms of right or left economic policies but also as being tough or liberal. In the past the Labour party was seen as having a fairly clear socialist ideology. It was committed to public ownership, the Welfare state and greater equality of income and wealth. Having lost the last four elections, policies are much less rigid now and the emphasis is on getting re-elected. Unpopular policies, such as uni-lateral nuclear disarmament, have been ditched.

Conversely the Conservative party was seen as a party that wanted to govern and adopted the policies which would get it elected. However since Mrs Thatcher a much clearer ideology has emerged. The party is seen to be committed to the free market, which has led to privatisation of nationalised industries, selling council houses, lower direct taxes (but higher indirect ones) and the reduction of Trade Union power.

OTHER PARTIES

The Liberal Democrat party

This is the successor to the centre parties which have been growing since the 1970s. It is the only party consistently in favour of British membership of the European Community. It criticises the main parties for being dominated by their pay-masters in business or the Trade Unions. Not having a major interest group supporting them, they are usually short of money.

Nationalist parties

These support a degree of independence, e.g. for Scotland and Wales. The preservation of a national language and culture is very important to Welsh nationalists (Plaid Cymru) whereas economic and political independence are favoured by the Scottish National Party. Both have seats in parliament.

In Northern Ireland the parties represent sectarian interests. The Unionist parties are supported by Protestants who wish to stay part of the UK or possibly independent. The SDLP is supported by Catholics who oppose their disadvantaged economic and political position and in many cases favour unification with the Irish Republic. Sinn Fein is associated with the IRA and wishes to see Irish unity.

Fringe parties

These are parties of the right and left which are seen as extremist and are not usually represented in parliament or on local councils. There are parties of the far right which are more or less racist though some would prefer to be called nationalist. These parties are not usually committed to democracy and offer authoritarian policies. They have been successful to the degree that the main parties all now support rigid immigration policies.

There are also a variety of Marxist-influenced parties with small memberships but some have in the past gained influence within the trade union movement.

Since the 1970s Green Parties have been committed to protecting the environment and have enjoyed popularity but have not got candidates elected. Many of their policies have been adopted by the major parties.

5 ▷ PRESSURE GROUPS

In modern industrial societies with populations of millions it is clearly difficult for an isolated individual to make governments hear their views. Knowing that individuals vote every few years may constrain the behaviour of governments but it does not allow the citizen to participate in the everyday business of politics.

Along with political parties *pressure groups* allow individuals to make their views known. The role of pressure groups is to influence government in line with their views. They may want the government to do something, such as provide adequate housing for the homeless or *not* to do something, such as not build a motorway through a wood.

Political sociologists have distinguished different kinds of pressure groups:

Promotional pressure groups.

These have a specific cause and their membership is open to those who share their views. For example, Amnesty International campaigns to promote human rights; its members write to governments about individual cases of abuse. Promotional groups often have rivals promoting opposite causes, such as over the abortion issue.

Protective pressure groups.

These try to influence government whenever they feel the interests of their members are affected. They are sometimes called *interest groups*. The members tend to have something in common, like a particular occupation. The major examples in Britain include Trade Unions, Professional Associations and Employers Organisations, such as the CBI and the Institute of Directors.

Pressure groups can influence governments in a number of ways:

1 Influencing public opinion through media campaigns. Politicians worry about public support.
2 Bargaining behind the scenes with politicians and civil servants in parliamentary committees.
3 Recruiting MPs to their cause who will then speak on their behalf. This may cause some concern when ex-ministers become employees of organisations they have dealt with. During the 1980s and 1990s some Conservative ex-ministers have joined the Boards of businesses they helped to privatise or banks who were involved with privatisation. Similar criticism has been levelled at Labour MPs who are sponsored by Trade Unions.
4 Extra-parliamentary activities such as marches.
5 Members may be mobilised to write to MPs and Ministers, for example complaining about sex and violence on TV or smoking in public places.

Activities of pressure groups

Because the main activity of the pressure group is to *influence* government rather than *be* a government, they are sometimes called *Lobbies*. This reflects their attempts to persuade MPs in the lobbies of parliament (or Representatives and Senators in the US Congress). Rich and well-organised pressure groups are the most successful, if not always the most worthy.

6 > POLITICAL ACTION OUTSIDE THE SYSTEM

As we have seen, modern industrial societies have complex institutions and rules for fighting political battles. These include parties and pressure groups. Many of the arguments take place in the parliamentary system, either in the Houses of Commons and Lords or in the Cabinet where the most important ministers meet.

However some individuals and groups in society do not have access to these more accepted channels of political dispute and fight their battles outside "the system". The behaviour of such groups is sometimes called *extra-parliamentary* activity. (This means outside parliament.) Governments generally disapprove of such activities, and do not see it as legitimate and may condemn those who take part. The range of activities includes demonstrations, direct action such as blocking roads or chaining yourself to railings, even terrorism and revolution. Peaceful campaigns of direct action were led by Gandhi in India and carried out by the Civil Rights movement in the USA who fought for the end of segregation in the Southern States. In both cases the groups involved were excluded from the normal political process and did not enjoy full legal rights. Women in Britain fought similar battles to get the vote in the first half of the 20th century and women at Greenham Common tried to obstruct the movement of cruise missiles during the 1980s.

Extra-parliamentary action

Violent political movements are often judged according to their success. Many national leaders began as "terrorists" or "freedom fighters", according to one's point of view, and fought to free their countries from colonial rule. Both France and the USA are proud of their revolutionary history but tried to suppress freedom movements abroad and, on occasions, citizens' rights at home.

7 > OPINION POLLS

WHAT ARE OPINION POLLS?

Opinion polls are a type of survey research. Usually only a sample of the relevant population are questioned. The techniques for asking subjects include structured interviews, which may be face to face, telephone enquiries, and questionnaires completed by the subjects themselves.

The most discussed form of opinion polls are those that ask about *voting intentions.* Other information can be gathered from exit-polls where actual voting behaviour is questioned as the voter leaves the polling station and may be correlated with the voter's class, gender etc. Politicians and newspapers may also poll the population for opinions on particular issues and policies and on the popularity of politicians.

THE USE AND LIMITATIONS OF OPINION POLLS

The media often commission and publish surveys, as they may produce newsworthy results. Politicians may commission surveys but keep the results secret. They use them to help choose a suitable election date and to identify key groups of voters, e.g. by class or constituency who can be targeted in the campaign. The polls may also identify key issues and voters' attitudes to them and this information can be used in election campaigns. In between elections, parties can test the popularity of policies and decisions although there is little evidence that Governments feel the need to be popular unless a general election is imminent; e.g. privatisation, grant maintained schools and NHS trusts were never popular but were enacted with determination by recent Conservative governments.

Critics of opinion polls claim that they may influence voting behaviour not just measure it. There may be a *bandwagon effect* where voters turn to the party likely to win or perhaps there may be a desire to support the underdog. Where a cause seems hopeless, people may not bother to vote. Alternatively, opinion polls may encourage tactical voting where voters choose the candidate likely to defeat the person they dislike the most. Whether any of these things are undesirable is a matter of opinion. You may feel that polls just help voters to make more informed decisions. In France, polls are banned in the period just before the election.

WHY DO POLLS MAKE MISTAKES?

The research organisations only make limited claims for the accuracy of a sample survey. When conducting most research into attitudes or behaviour a small margin of error may be unimportant. However General Elections are often decided by small margins so that the poll predictions of who will be the victors are sometimes wrong. This happened in 1970, February 1974 and most dramatically in 1992.

The possible sources of error include:

1 Sampling errors.
2 Secretive subjects who do not respond.
3 Subjects who lie.
4 Subjects who change their mind. Polls are more accurate very near elections.
5 "Don't knows" who may not divide evenly between parties.
6 Subjects may express a preference but not turn out to vote.
7 Questions may be unclear or leading.
8 There is the possibility of interviewer bias.

> Why polls may be wrong

You can use this list to criticise surveys in questions about methods and in thinking about your own research.

8 ▶ THE INFLUENCE OF THE MEDIA

It has been argued that examination and even criticism of government policy and actions should be part of the function of a free press and healthy for democracy. MEDIA BIAS means that the media do not report events in a fair and balanced way but give a selective or distorted view which favours particular interests. Party politicians tend to see the media as biased against them. Legislation requires that both the BBC and Independent TV should report political events in an impartial manner. However both major parties have criticised TV news and current affairs, particularly when they are in government. Newspapers are legitimately partisan and most support the Conservative Party. This may help to shape public opinion but does not seem to determine voting behaviour. Like all research on the effects of the media, the relationship between the political views expressed in newspapers and those of their readers is inconclusive.

People's political views may lead them to choose a newspaper which shares those views. The Daily Express consistently supports the Conservative party and has a high proportion of Conservative voters amongst its readers. The Daily Mirror supports the

Labour party (though this loyalty has been questioned since the new ownership and management in 1993) and has a high proportion of Labour voting readers.

Readers' views may be independent of the views expressed in their Newspaper. They may not even be aware of the paper's political stance. Tabloid newspapers devote little space to party politics. The Sun, with a largely working class readership, has consistently supported the Conservatives and perhaps more significantly fiercely criticised Labour policies and politicians. Despite this, Sun readers are still more likely to vote Labour than Conservative; however the readership is much less pro-Labour than Mirror readers.

Before the 1992 election, readers of both The Independent and The Guardian intended voting Labour rather than Conservative, whereas the reverse was true for The Times and The Telegraph.

Impact of the media

9 > POLITICAL SOCIALISATION

In addition to the mass media there are other influences on people's political views.

- THE FAMILY. This appears to influence voting behaviour, particularly if both parents support the same party. The young were once thought to be rebellious because of their youth but a study of CND supporters showed that radical youth often had radical parents.

- THE SCHOOL. In some countries the school has the responsibility for direct political education (or, if you disapprove, you might say indoctrination). Before 1989, schools in the Soviet Union taught different aspects of communist doctrine and Russian patriotism at different ages as part of a national curriculum. Even in nursery schools cooperation was encouraged and individualism discouraged.

  In Britain, party political values are not taught but critics often accuse teachers and text books of political bias. Sociology, for example, has been criticised for being left-wing and biased against business in Britain, but right-wing and uncritical of capitalism in America.

- THE WORK PLACE. Workers in the public sector and in large organisations where many workers perform the same task together are more likely to be in trade unions and share a sense of solidarity. Such workers are more likely to support the Labour Party than workers in the private sector and in small firms.

Other influences on voting

10 > DEMOCRACY

Democracy means "people power". It is a form of Government where citizens have a considerable influence over political decisions. The idea originated in ancient Greece and described a system where all qualified citizens were allowed or even required to participate in Government. Slaves, women and children were not qualified to participate. This idea of citizenship being restricted was also found in the revolutionary constitution of the USA which excluded slaves. The Declaration of Independence claimed that "all men are created equal" but slavery was not abolished until after the Civil war and civil rights for the Black population were fought for in the 1960s.

Direct democracy would involve all citizens actually playing an active political role. This is seen as impractical in a country like Britain with a very large population and therefore we claim to have a *Representative democracy,* where the citizens choose people to represent their interests (usually members of major political parties) and to influence decisions.

The characteristics of a modern Liberal Democratic State are usually seen to include these factors:

1 Government power depends on the consent of the people.
2 The job of government is to maintain the rights of the people and to help achieve their chosen goals, such as security, welfare and economic well-being.
3 The people have the right to vote and there are regular elections.
4 Various freedoms and rights exist (see below).
5 Power is not concentrated in the hands of a small minority such as a *Ruling Class* or an *Elite.*
6 Power is dispersed between competing groups such as political parties and pressure groups.
7 Power is dispersed between different branches of government, e.g. the Judiciary is free of political control.

The Liberal Democratic State

Britain and the USA

Power is more concentrated in Great Britain than it is in the USA. The USA is a *Federal State* where the 50 States have considerable independence from the central federal government, e.g. they make and enforce their own criminal law. At both Federal and State levels the law making (legislative) function is separated from the administrative (executive) function. So that the power of the President, who heads the executive, is limited by Congress who make the law and approve the Budget. Often the President is in the other party from the majorities in Congress. In Britain, the Government is formed from the largest party in Parliament so that the Prime Minister heads *both* legislature and executive.

Citizen rights are guaranteed by a *written constitution* and Supreme court in the USA. In Britain there is no written constitution or Bill of Rights and our freedom depends on a collection of Statutes, common law and customs.

11 TOTALITARIAN GOVERNMENT

❝❝ The Totalitarian State ❞❞

This exists where the essential characteristics of democracy are absent. A single elite rules, controlling the life of the citizen. The citizen is powerless and there are no competing parties or pressure groups. There tends to be an absence of freedom in such countries and the citizens are oppressed rather than protected by the law.

Liberal democracies in the Western mould such as Britain and the USA are fairly rare. We tend to see other systems as totalitarian whereas they may themselves claim to be democratic.

Communist totalitarianism or Proletarian democracy?

During the 20th century, Communism appeared to be a serious rival for liberal democracies. Since 1989, most communist states have fallen and those that remain are unstable. These countries claimed to be democracies where the communist party ruled *on behalf of* the proletariat. The new regimes in such countries are often far from democratic and the oppression of minorities continues in some of them.

Democracy in the third world

Few third world countries have parliamentary democracies with competing political parties. Many have one-party states and some military governments. Where States had their boundaries drawn by colonial powers such as the British and French, they often have internal divisions based on tribe, ethnicity and religion. Strong central governments based on a single nationalist party of the military have claimed to offer stability.

12 HUMAN RIGHTS

"All human beings are born free and equal in dignity and rights" (Universal Declaration of Human Rights 1948).

A common test of democracy is to look at the human rights enjoyed by citizens of a particular state. It is common to make some distinction between FREEDOMS and RIGHTS. *Freedom* is the absence of restrictions by others, usually the State. For example freedom of speech means that the State does not censor the media and freedom of movement means that citizens could travel as they wished inside or outside the State. Sometimes one person's freedom interferes with the freedom of others, for example we may accept rules which limit how we drive or listen to loud music because these activities may harm others. There is certainly a tension between those who argue for a free press and politicians who support laws against libel or protecting privacy. The controversy over the publishing of Salman Rushdie's "Satanic Verses" shows the conflict between freedom of speech and offending citizens.

Rights are what the individual is entitled to as a citizen of a State or even as a member of humanity. Some people think humans have natural *rights* which become legal or political rights, such as the right to a fair trial or the right to vote. There is an argument that other animals have natural rights, which is part of the debate about using animals for scientific research, eating meat or hunting.

The Universal Declaration of Human Rights was adopted by the general assembly of the UN in 1948 and all member states are committed to observing it. It includes prohibitions on racial, religious and sex discrimination and outlaws slavery. it claims that all people have positive rights such as adequate food, clothing, housing, medical care and education. There are also articles dealing with freedom of speech, religion and association.

Citizens may have three sorts of rights or freedoms:

- *Civil rights.* These include the right to fair legal treatment and freedom of speech and religion.
- *Political rights.* These include the right to vote and stand for public office.
- *Social rights.* These include the right to economic security and this is provided in part by the Welfare State. The issue of the Welfare State is discussed in the poverty chapter (ch 6).

> Types of human right

Many States have laws which allow their citizens rights and freedoms but do not in practice keep to them. Amnesty International is a pressure group with branches in many countries which monitors human rights and publishes reports on offending countries which deny their citizens rights by, for example, persecuting minorities, imprisoning people without trial and torturing detainees.

EXAMINATION QUESTIONS

Q.1 Write an essay about power and authority in society.
You may choose to include reference to any of the following.

> The difference between power and authority.
>
> Different types of power and authority (e.g. coercive, bureaucratic, charismatic).
>
> Ways in which power and authority are maintained in various social settings,
> such as: the family,
>   the peer group,
>   the school,
>   the workplace.

Credit will be given for appropriate evidence.

(NEA, June 1992)

Q.2

Power and Authority

Pressure groups can appeal to the emotions of those in power; presenting feelings as well as facts.

(From: Gerard O'Donnell, Mastering Sociology (Macmillan) 1985)

a) Explain, with two examples, what a Pressure Group is. *(4)*

b) Explain the various methods used by Pressure Groups in order to influence people. Give examples to support your answer. *(7)*

c) What are the advantages and disadvantages of Pressure Groups? *(9)*

(MEG, June 1992)

ANSWERS TO EXAMINATION QUESTIONS

Q.1

There are some very useful suggestions in the question indicating what the examiner would like to see.

You will probably want to discuss power and authority exercised by Government as well as in the less obvious settings suggested.

You have 30 minutes and with good planning should be able to produce up to two sides of average size writing.

Define and explain power and authority. Give clear examples of each. If you have learned the different types of authority you can describe and illustrate those but they are not essential.

You could explain how voting produces legitimate government.

If you want to adopt a critical tone you can remind the examiner of the exercise of power at home, school and work even when its legitimacy is not accepted e.g. domestic violence.

STUDENT'S ANSWER WITH EXAMINER'S COMMENTS

Q.2

a)   Explain with two examples, what a Pressure group is.   (4)

> A Pressure Group is a group of people who can appeal to those in power to get their own way. The NSPCC appeals to the public's emotions to help children.

Definition O.K. but only one example given. 3/4

b)   Explain the various methods used by Pressure groups in order to influence people. Give examples to support your answer.   (7)

> Pressure groups use lots of methods to influence people. Members go on marches or rallies to get their message across to the public. If people wanted to stop testing products on animals they could walk the streets shouting for people to stop buying products tested on animals. They could also collect signatures and take a petition to parliament.

Methods identified but little explanation of how they influence people; few examples given. 4/7

c)   What are the advantages and disadvantages of pressure groups?   (9)

> The advantages of pressure groups are that they allow people to stand up for what they believe in and get their point across to others. They can show their feelings as well as show the facts.
>
> The disadvantages of pressure groups are that they can go too far. For example the poll tax rally. They could start a riot and get arrested.
>
> People might not want to hear about causes they do not care about and people who make a lot of fuss might get their own way because ordinary people don't say anything.

More needed here – e.g. technical ideas of 'participation', 'democracy' etc. and role of pressure groups. Not fully developed. 4/9

Some reasonable points made, but often not fully explained or clearly illustrated with examples. 11/20

NB The Review Sheet for this chapter is at the end of Chapter 14.

DEVIANCE AND SOCIAL CONTROL

SOCIAL ORDER

SOCIAL CONTROL

CRIME AND DEVIANCE

CRIME STATISTICS

CONFORMITY, DEVIANCE AND CRIME

GETTING STARTED

It seems that, in common with the Sunday newspapers, sociology examiners and often sociology students are more concerned with deviance than social order. Many sociologists find the study of crime and criminals exciting. The sociological study of crime has a long history. Sharing the experiences of criminals as a sociological method because popular in pre-war Chicago and has continued since then. There have been numerous studies of street gangs in both the USA and Britain and, more recently, studies using covert (undercover) participant observation of football hooligans and informal interviews with professional criminals.

A comparative approach will demonstrate that what is seen as deviant varies historically and between different cultures.

The main themes of questions set on this topic area are:

- THE NATURE OF SOCIAL ORDER.
- FORMAL AND INFORMAL SOCIAL CONTROL.
- THE DISTINCTION BETWEEN CRIME AND DEVIANCE.
- HOW USEFUL ARE CRIME STATISTICS TO SOCIOLOGISTS AND OTHERS?
- THE SOCIAL DEFINITION OF DEVIANCE; VARIES FROM TIME TO TIME AND PLACE TO PLACE.
- EVALUATION OF SOCIOLOGICAL EXPLANATIONS OF DEVIANCE.

Related topics include other institutions which provide social control such as: Religion, the media, the family, education, and work.

Deviance studies also offer a rich source of examples to evaluate *methods* such as participant observation and to illustrate research problems, for example the use of official statistics. Sub-cultural theories of deviance also contribute to discussions of education and youth cultures.

As expected class, race and gender inequalities can be discussed in the sociology of deviance. Consideration of power and politics may also help us to understand who makes the rules which define deviance.

DEFINITIONS:

The absence of a generally agreed definition of deviance is a major problem in studying this topic.

SOCIAL ORDER. This exists when social life continues without major disruptions. Most people are conforming to most rules most of the time.

DEVIANCE. The real or imagined breaking of rules.

CRIME. The breaking of rules which have been made part of a formal legal criminal code.

SOCIAL CONTROL. The imposition of social order on individuals or groups. It can be formal or informal.

ESSENTIAL PRINCIPLES

1 > SOCIAL ORDER

Social Order may be based on *agreed values* because most of the population share the same goals and accept that there needs to be rules about how we achieve those goals. For example we may agree that we wish to enjoy a high standard of living and that we should work to achieve this but not steal from others. If we wish to live peacefully and safely, we may agree to pay taxes to maintain a policy force which then limits our freedom of movement by enforcing laws against drunk driving.

Social Order may also be *imposed* by the more powerful on the less powerful. Thus although some degree of social order is necessary for the survival and stability of a society we may not always agree that the form it takes is desirable. Marxists argue that the Ruling Class imposes order on the Working Class and Feminists argue that men impose order on women. Until recently, order in Eastern Europe was imposed by the national Communist parties often with the support of the Soviet Union. Although the collapse of this Communist control may have been welcomed by many, the disintegration of social order in the old USSR and Yugoslavia has led to war between national, ethnic and religious groups.

⁶⁶ Imposed social order ⁹⁹

2 > SOCIAL CONTROL

Where there is the possibility of rule breaking there is often *social control*. In simple pre-industrial societies this tended to be informal, whereas in modern societies it becomes increasingly formal.

In a close-knit society simple disapproval can be a major sanction. Offenders disgrace themselves and their families. These *informal* controls may be supported by religious institutions and beliefs (see Chapter 15).

⁶⁶ Types of social control: formal and informal ⁹⁹

FORMAL SOCIAL CONTROL

Modern industrial societies such as Britain have seen a growth in *formal* agencies set up specifically to impose social control. These include the police, courts, prisons, traffic wardens and a number of specialist organisations who deal with particular activities or occupations. Professions may have special bodies which can punish those who break their own rules, perhaps by excluding them from the profession. This applies to Doctors, lawyers and priests but not to teachers or lecturers.

Social control is imposed by systems of rewards and punishments. Many rules become "internalised" and individuals keep to them without thinking. This is because many agencies of social control try to convince people to behave properly, rather than threaten them with force.

Marxists and Feminists have argued that convincing people to accept capitalist or patriarchal society is a form of *ideological control* imposed by the family, school, Church or media. This control serves the interests of the powerful (men or the Ruling Class) and the weak need to be made aware of their position in society before they can change it.

3 > CRIME AND DEVIANCE

The distinction between crime and other forms of deviance is more important to lawyers than sociologists. Often serious acts of deviance are also illegal but this is not always the case.

	DEVIANT	NOT (very) DEVIANT
CRIMINAL	Armed robbery	Stealing pens from work
NOT CRIMINAL	Prostitution Being a New Age Traveller	Studying Sociology

If you are not happy with my examples choose your own. The test of whether an act is *deviant* is to consider the moral outrage it provokes. To discover if an act is *illegal,* ask a lawyer.

Blasphemy is only illegal in Britain if it offends against Christianity. This law has hardly ever been used during the 20th Century. The newspaper "Gay News" was prosecuted for blasphemy in the 1970s. The British author Salman Rushdie has been in hiding for several years following his condemnation by the late Iranian religious leader of writing the *Satanic Verses*. This book is seen by most Moslems as blasphemous.

●● **Blasphemy** ●●

UNEMPLOYMENT AND CRIME

It is unlikely that there is a single cause of rising crime. But there does seem to be a relationship between crime rates and the level of unemployment. Low levels of unemployment during the 1940s and 1950s saw a reduction in crime compared to the depression of the 1930s. Crime has increased since the 1960s. Higher rates of increase have coincided with the peaks in unemployment.

●● **Links between crime and unemployment** ●●

Conservative governments have resisted accepting this link. They prefer explanations based on individual morality and responsibility. John Major said that crime should be condemned more and explained less. He felt that links with levels of unemployment were insulting to the unemployed. The Home Office has, however, published research showing a statistical relationship between crime rates, the location of crime and unemployment.

4 > CRIME STATISTICS

Sociologists have criticised crime statistics on the basis of whether they are:

■ RELIABLE: Have they been collected accurately?
■ VALID: What do they mean? Do they tell us about crime and criminals or about the practices of the police and courts?
■ REPRESENTATIVE: As only some crimes are recorded are they typical of all crime committed?

Conventionally, crime figures have been the *official* collections of crimes known to the police (CKP) and data about convicted criminals. Following criticism from the interactionist school, both sociologists and Governments have become interested in alternative types of figures.

Self-report studies

These have permitted a check on the reliability of CKP figures by asking representative samples of groups whether they have committed a variety of offences. A study in the USA found that 93% of a sample of your people had offended and hardly any of tens of thousands of offences had been detected and even fewer acted upon.

D. J. WEST in a study of delinquent boys in London used self-reporting to overcome the criticism made of conventional studies linking delinquency to deprivation. Critics had said that social disadvantage explained arrest and conviction rather than the committing of offences. West identified differences between offenders and non-offenders *before* the offenders had become known to the police.

Victim studies

These ask representative groups of the public whether they have been victims of crime over a particular period. They include the British Crime Survey and YOUNG and LEA's work in Islington and on Merseyside. These have shown a greater extent of crime that the CKP figures suggested and have also produced data on the *fear* of crime rather than crime itself.

Non-officiaïl sources

These include Rape Crisis Centres, Women's Refuges, and telephone help lines for abused children. All indicate that most crime goes unreported. Only about 1 in 8 rapes appear to be reported, although this proportion is increasing as police treatment of victims is seen as being more sympathetic.

The reasons for *not reporting crime* include:

●● **Reasons for non-reporting** ●●

1   Victims being afraid or ashamed, e.g. rape, domestic violence and incest. Illegal immigrants in California began to report crime when their residents' status was no longer threatened. The Islington Crime Survey found that only about 1 in 5 sexual offences were reported to the police and only 1 in 10 officially recorded.

2 Victims see reporting as a waste of time where the offence is trivial, there is no chance of detection or property is uninsured, e.g. indecent exposure and petty theft. As insurance becomes more widespread the amount of reported, though not actual, crime will rise. An increase in telephones has encouraged crime reporting.

3 Victims are unaware or unconcerned, e.g. theft from work.

4 "Victimless" crimes are seldom reported and require detection by the police, e.g. prostitution, under-age sex, importuning in public lavatories, drug abuse and bribery.

The reasons for the authoritiesnot recording crime include:

Reasons for non-recording

1 The police not responding to reports.

2 The police judging no crime has been committed.

3 The police deciding the offence is not important or the offender is underage or should be "let off[+2]" for some other reason.

4 Prosecuting agencies may decide there is insufficient evidence for trial.

5 Trials do not always lead to convictions. This may indicate no crime has been committed or that there is insufficient evidence to convict.

The size of the police force, their administrative support, the numbers of telephones, radios, computers and the use of video surveillance have all led to an increase in recorded crime. The reduction in the number of police employed in London owing to spending cuts in the 1970s produced the only reduction in recorded crime of recent years.

Another complication is, of course, the fact that the innocent may be convicted and included in the statistics. The conviction of a significant proportion of those convicted for IRA bombing offences has proved wrongful or unsafe.

The Discussion of crime figures above indicates that crime rates vary between different societies, between different times, and between different groups in the same society. Some of the explanations for deviance are considered below and applied to the different rates of recorded crime for age, class, gender and ethnic groups. In general the explanations either concentrate on why some people break the rules or on why they get caught.

5 > EXPLANATIONS OF CONFORMITY, DEVIANCE AND CRIME

■ Non-sociological explanations
■ Traditional sociological explanations
■ Interactionist theories
■ Marxist theories
■ Feminist theories

NON SOCIOLOGICAL EXPLANATIONS

Sometimes these explanations have been called "Biographical Approaches" because of the methods they use. The characteristics of known offenders are compared with those of "normal" non-offenders and differences identified. These differences include physical characteristics, psychological factors and the social background of the offender. It is only the last which many would see as a sociological explanation and it is considered below.

A biological approach

Modern versions of the biological approach have identified Pre-Menstrual Syndrome as explaining the timing of some crimes by women and an extra Y Chromosome as explaining aggressive crime by "super male" men. Biologists are more able to identify the functions of specific genes and many are confident that this knowledge can be used to explain behaviour.

Psychological explanations have tried to link family upbringing with a tendency to be delinquent. There are also perceived links between some mental illness and some violent crime. In some cases it may be that being criminal leads to the diagnosis of mental illness. Defining mental illness has caused sociologists as much of a problem as defining deviance.

TRADITIONAL SOCIOLOGICAL EXPLANATIONS

These theories assume that the rules are based on shared beliefs about right or wrong. They try to explain why some individuals, groups or even whole societies are more likely to break the rules than others. Many of these studies depend upon the reliability and validity of published crime statistics.

Anomic theory

Sociology theories of crime.

The high rate of crime in the USA was explained in the 1930s by arguing that most of the population was committed to achieving a high standard of living but some individuals lacked the opportunities to achieve this goal by lawful means and therefore adopted illegal means or even stopped trying to achieve the goals at all. Crime was therefore lower in societies where people had lower ambitions.

A more modern version of this has talked about *relative* deprivation where individuals or groups are unable to achieve standards of living which are accepted as normal in the society as a whole.

Sub-cultural theories

These are similar in approach to the explanations above but they explain the behaviour of *groups* rather than individuals. Deviant sub-cultures have norms and values which are different from the wider society. Members of the group conform to sub-cultural rather than majority rules.

The sub-culture may be a *counter culture* which rebels against the rules of the wider society, or perhaps an exaggerated version of the social norms of the wider society. Counter culture have been identified in schools where the values of hard work and conformity to school rules are rejected. In many films there is the portrayal of a division between "good youth" who are studious and athletic and "dangerous youth" who wear leather jackets or their contemporary equivalent. Sometimes the media also present this as fact as well as fiction.

The idea that sub-cultures may not reject the wider society but be an exaggerated version of working class culture has also been argued, originally by the American W. Miller in 1962. He talks about the lower class concern with toughness, masculinity, smartness, and excitement and a dislike for authority. This list has been used to explain the behaviour of football hooligans in this country. They have also adopted a crude nationalism and dislike for outsiders which is mirrored in some sections of the tabloid press. Most males will have been exposed to some of these values in their youth and the ability to fight as a nation, if not as individuals, remains much valued in British culture.

Interactionist theory

Interactionist or labelling theories are more concerned with the social reaction to real or imagined deviance than they are with deviant acts themselves. Instead of asking why individuals or groups break rules these theories ask why the "offenders" are treated as deviant by the authorities. Put more simply, they ask why the offender got caught rather than why they committed the crime.

Critics find this aspect of interactionist theory unsatisfactory as there is a failure to explain why some people commit crimes. However the supporters of interactionist theory argue that there is no such thing as deviance until there has been a social reaction.

There is a lot of interest amongst interactionists in the behaviour of the police, the courts and other institutions such as the media who define what is crime and who are criminals.

	rulebreakers	not rule breakers
labelled deviant	1. convicted bank robber	2. innocent but falsely convicted
not labelled deviant	3. bank robber who is not caught	4. conformists

The above table shows the difference between traditional explanations of deviance which define deviants as rulebreakers (1. and 3.) and interactionist theories which define deviants as offenders who have been caught and labelled (1. and 2.).

Numerous studies have indicated that the police can choose where to patrol and how to treat different kinds of offenders. These questions can be applied to the study of class, age, ethnicity or gender and crime.

Marxist theories

These contain elements of both traditional and interactionist theories. They may explain some working class crime as the result of economic exploitation. Marxists do not see deviance as the breaking of consensual rules as they do not accept that the rules are based on agreement but instead see them as imposed by the ruling class.

Like the interactionists they do not see the behaviour of the police and courts as neutral but see them as enforcing the law on behalf of the ruling class. Marxists are interested in *who* makes the rules as well as how they are enforced.

The decision to allocate large numbers of police to the control of industrial disputes or to prevent the gathering of travellers on private or even public land has sometimes been interpreted from this Marxist viewpoint. It could be contrasted with the failure of the law to deal with large scale white collar crime like fraud or corporate crime committed by business organisations to maintain profits.

Feminist theories

Like Marxists, feminists see the law as being made and enforced to serve the interests, not of the whole society, but a section of it. The most important issue for them is rather different from the other theories. They are not trying to explain rulebreaking but instead why many more women than men conform to rules. Some feminists think that the crime statistics underestimate the extent of female crime but nevertheless accept that the male rate is much higher. Another interest of feminist writers is to examine the role of women as victims rather than offenders. Sexual offences and domestic violence have a particular interest for feminists.

EXAMINATION QUESTIONS

Q.1

Extract A

Notifiable offences recorded by the police per 100,000 population in England and Wales, 1982-88

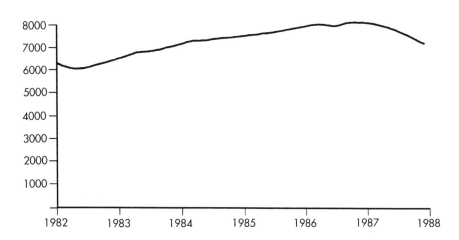

Source: Home Office, *Tackling Crime*, 1989

Extract B

Notifiable offences recorded by the police, England and Wales, 1988

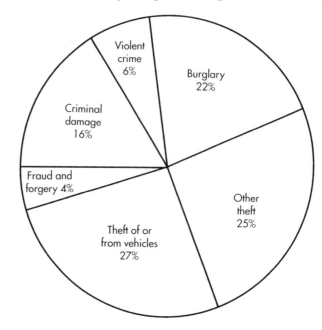

Source: Home Office, *Tackling Crime*, 1989

Extract C

Some findings from the second Islington Crime Survey

The Islington Crime Survey is based on detailed interviews with a representative sample of 1,600 people. It covers the London Borough of Islington, a socially and culturally mixed area of North London. This is what the survey found:

■ More than 90% of women between 16 and 24 years of age often take safety measures against crime. These range from avoiding certain streets to not going out alone at night.
■ 74% of women in all age groups stay at home fairly often or very often.
■ 40% of men in all age groups stay at home fairly often or very often.
■ Fear of crime is the main reason why people do not go out after dark.
■ In the three years since the first Islington Crime Survey, crime has moved from third place to the top of people's list of problems affecting the neighbourhood.
■ 80% of the sample see crime as the main problem affecting the neighbourhood.
■ 31% of the sample felt that the police are not doing very well in the fight against crime.

Source: The Guardian, Crime puts women in state of siege, 13 February 1990

a) What trends does the information in Extract A show?   *(2)*

b) Look at Extract B.
    What percentage of notifiable offences are violent crimes?   *(1)*

c) Explain two ways in which official crime statistics might underestimate the
    amount of illegal activity.   *(4)*

d) Look at Extract C.
    State three ways in which crime may affect the behaviour of people living in
    Islington.   *(3)*

e) Why might it be difficult to make generalisations from the findings in Extract C?
                                                                                            (4)

f) What do we mean by the term crime?   *(3)*

g) Give an example of criminal behaviour and explain why it might not always be regarded as deviant. *(6)*

(NEAB, June 1991)

Q.2

■ Explain why an act may be deviant in one situation but not in another. *(15)*

(ULEAC, June 1992)

Q.3 Conformity, Deviance and Social Control

> The shabby streets south of the Thames remain the home of an old and vicious form of criminal family.
>
> HERE, unlike most neighbourhoods in Britain, where police would have had strong support for their actions, the dead robbers had been seen by many as following a perfectly ordinary career.
>
> South of the river the streets, communities and most importantly families, remained more or less intact and with them the social climate that allowed crime to flourish.*
>
> The docks developed family ties, with jobs and to some extent criminal expertise being passed from father to son, uncle to nephew. Strong extended families were also to become the centre of organised crime. Intermarriage between established criminal families led to underworld dynasties that still exist.
>
> The thriving criminal sub-culture also produced increasingly violent gangs.
>
> *[Daily Telegraph, 6/8/91]*

> From the official rate we cannot tell whether the high proportion of sexual offences in Lincolnshire is because that county is a hotbed of sexual deviation or because such offences are much more likely to be reported in tight-knit rural and small town communities.
>
> [R. Davidson, Crime and Environment (Croom Helm, 1981)]

a) Explain what is meant by a criminal sub-culture. *[4]*

b) Why does crime flourish* in some areas rather than others? *[7]*

c) Why are statistics on crime likely to be unreliable? *[9]*

[* flourish means to grow and "do well"]

(MEG, June 1992)

ANSWERS TO EXAMINATION QUESTIONS

Q.1

a) Trends are broad movements not minor changes. The graph shows a steady rise in recorded offences until 1987 then a fall.

b) Simply read the 6% from the pie graph.

c) Explain and perhaps illustrate two reasons why crime is not reported and recorded. You could mention victimless crime, white collar crime, crime not reported because it is seen as trivial, the shame of victims, lack of confidence in the police, police reluctance to record reported crime etc.

d) The extract clearly identifies how people may adapt their behaviour to fear of crime. Remember the examiner is interested in behaviour not feelings or opinions although these influence behaviour. Therefore "avoiding certain streets" is correct but seeing crime as a problem is not. Three points would get the marks.

e) You can only make generalisations if your sample is representative of the population.

Islington may not be typical of London and London may be untypical of other cities and cities differ from rural areas. The class, ethnic mix and types of household may make Islington unrepresentative. Attitudes to the police may be unusual.

Two to four points should be made depending on the level of explanation given.

f) Simple definition required. The distinction from deviance is considered in the next question.

g) You need a relevant example which must be clearly criminal. If it is not deviant despite being a crime it does not provoke moral outrage and is acceptable at least to some sections of the population.

You might consider tax evasion, theft from work, receiving stolen goods, underage sex, motoring offences, drug abuse etc.

Q.2 You have 30 minutes to plan and write an essay for this answer.

i) A simple definition of deviance as rulebreaking

ii) Explain how a particular act can have different social meanings depending on:

Time: Think of acts which were deviant but are no longer.

Place: Think of acts which are deviant in some cultures but not others or even rules that apply to particular places e.g. when is nudity permissible?

Who the offender is: Age, class, profession, religion, ethnicity and gender all influence whether an act is seen as deviant.

iii) Explain how some sociologists see the social reaction to a real or imagined act as more important than the act itself in explaining deviance.

Discuss why some people in some circumstances are more likely to be caught and labelled deviant.

STUDENT'S ANSWER WITH EXAMINER'S COMMENTS

Q.3

a) Explain what is meant by a criminal sub-culture.   *(4)*

> A criminal sub-culture means a group of people who have their own way of doing things, their own values and beliefs towards society. In this case a criminal sub-culture is gangs of violent people who do criminal things because they think it is O.K. and they like it.

❝ Shows understands sub-culture idea. 3/4 ❞

b) Why does crime flourish in some areas rather than others?   *(7)*

> Crime flourishes in some areas rather than others take the example of robbery. Robbery is not going to take place in working class areas because the families are not going to be rich and have a lot of valuable things in the house. So robbery would mostly happen in rich areas e.g. where middle and upper class people live because they are more likely to have more money or valuables in the house.
>
> Taking vandalism as another example. It is most likely to take place in working class areas where there are gangs of youths who have nothing else to do. It is not as likely to take place in middle class areas because they would have other things to do.
>
> Another example is violence e.g. fights would most likely happen in working class areas because the gangs of kids might be bored and they might just start on each other, also in working class pubs where people might have drunk one too many fights might break out causing damage to the pub.

❝ Inaccurate ❞

❝ More on social control in different areas and its influence on crime. Unemployment, inner-city, policing all relevant here. 3/7 ❞

c) Why are statistics on crime likely to be unreliable?   *(9)*

> Statistics on crime are likely to be unreliable because take for example sexual offences, not every child or woman is going to admit that they have been sexually assaulted so when they say 50,000 children have been assaulted it would be wrong because not everyone has reported it. Also if you take as another example burglary not everyone will tell the police that they have been burgled so again the statistics are wrong.
>
> Statistics are also unlikely to be reliable because of people messing around saying a crime was committed when it was not. e.g. People say they were burgled to claim insurance on something.
>
> Also if the statistics were estimated they could be wrong because they could estimate too much or too little.

❝ This answer is too much about reporting crime. More on other causes of unreliability – e.g. detecting and recording crime ❞

❝ 5/9 ❞

❝ Overall a reasonable effort. More sociological ideas and evidence needed in places. 11/20 ❞

REVIEW SHEET

This Review Sheet covers the material in Chapter 13 (Power and Politics) and Chapter 14 (Deviance and Social Control).

■ List, and briefly explain 4 reasons why there might be cross-class (deviant) voting behaviour.

1 _____

_____

_____

2 _____

_____

_____

3 _____

_____

_____

4 _____

_____

_____

■ List 2 advantages of first-past-the-post voting systems.

1 _____

2 _____

■ List 2 disadvantages of first-past-the-post voting systems.

1 _____

2 _____

■ Give an example of a *promotional* pressure group.

_____

_____

_____

■ Give an example of a *protective* pressure group.

_____

_____

_____

■ List 6 reasons why opinion polls might be wrong.

1 _____

2 _____

3 _____

4 _____

5 _____

6 _____

■ List 4 characteristics of a modern *democratic* state.

1 _____

2 _____

3 _____

4 _____

■ List 2 characteristics of a *totalitarian* state.

1 _____

2 _____

■ List 3 types of criticism which could be made about crime statistics.

1 _____

2 _____

3 _____

■ List 4 reasons for *not reporting* crime.

1 _____

2 _____

3 _____

4 _____

■ List 4 reasons for the authorities *not recording* crime.

1 _____

2 _____

3 _____

4 _____

■ Give 3 reasons or theories why some groups are more likely to break the rules than others.

1 _____

_____

2 _____

_____

3 _____

_____

■ Look back to Extract B of Question 1, Chapter 14. Use the figures to compare violent crime with theft involving vehicles.

_____

_____

_____

_____

_____

_____

_____

■ Look at the table below.

Offenders cautioned: by type of offence

England & Wales			Percentages	
	1971	1981	1990	1991
Percentage of all **offenders cautioned**				
Violence against the person	3.0	5.4	10.1	10.8
Sexual offences	5.0	2.7	2.0	1.8
Burglary	16.0	10.8	8.6	7.4
Robbery	0.3	0.1	0.4	0.3
Theft and handling stolen goods	69.2	76.2	60.0	60.3
Fraud and forgery	1.3	1.3	2.8	3.1
Criminal damage	4.7	2.0	2.5	2.1
Drug offences	–	0.3	11.2	11.8
Other (excluding motoring offences)	0.4	1.3	2.3	2.3

(*Social Trends* 1993)

Use the figures in the table to:

1 Identify the most common offence in 1991.

_____

2 Identify the offence showing the largest percentage increase between 1971 and 1991.

_____

3 Identify the offence showing the largest percentage decrease between 1971 and 1991.

_____

4 Comment on the change in drug offences between 1971 and 1991.

_____

■ Look carefully at the table below.

Population under sentence on 30 June 1991: by ethnic origin, age and offence group

England & Wales		Percentages	
	White	West Indian/ Guyanese/ African	Indian/ Pakistani/ Bangladeshi
Males			
Prisoners aged under 21			
Violence against the person	86.2	7.7	3.6
Rape	76.9	14.0	8.3
Other sexual offences	87.3	3.6	7.3
Burglary	94.3	2.5	0.7
Robbery	78.1	14.8	3.2
Theft and handling stolen goods	89.6	5.5	1.2
Fraud and forgery	77.8	7.4	14.8
Drug offences	76.4	13.2	6.6
Other offences	92.3	2.9	1.8
Offences not recorded	86.6	7.7	3.0
In default of payment of a fine	93.4	2.2	2.2
All prisoners aged under 21	87.9	6.8	2.5
Total population aged 14–20	91.5	1.4	4.3

(*Social Trends*, 1993)

1 Use the data to show how the West Indian/Guyanese/African group is disadvantaged.

_____

_____

_____

2 What offence is most commonly committed by:
a) the White ethnic group

_____

b) the Indian (etc.) ethnic group

_____

c) the West Indian (etc.) ethnic group

_____

RELIGION AND THE MASS MEDIA

RELIGION IN SOCIETY

RELIGION AND SOCIAL CHANGE

SECULARISATION

OWNERSHIP/CONTROL OF MEDIA

EFFECTS OF MEDIA

GETTING STARTED

It may seem rather unusual to consider religion and the mass media in the same chapter. The reason I have chosen to do so lies in the kinds of questions that refer to these two topics. They both are rarely the subjects of an entire question. The examiner is more likely to ask you questions on SOCIALISATION or SOCIAL CONTROL where reference to religion or media is possible or necessary.

Both churches and the mass media are agents of socialisation for an adult as well as a child. They are sources of norms and values and as such are often sources of social control. This is more obviously the case with religion which claims the authority to indicate what is right or wrong. The socialisation and social control effects of the media are usually pointed out by people who are critical of their effects.

The main themes of questions set in this area are:

- SOCIALISATION
- SOCIAL CONTROL
- THE INFLUENCE OF THE MEDIA ON POLITICAL ATTITUDES
- FREEDOM OF THE PRESS AND CENSORSHIP
- OWNERSHIP AND CONTROL OF THE MEDIA
- THE MEDIA AND STEREOTYPES OF RACE AND GENDER
- THE FUNCTIONS OF RELIGION
- SECULARISATION AND SOCIAL CHANGE

DEFINITIONS

THE MASS MEDIA. The system of communication which transmits messages to large audiences. It includes TV, radio, newspapers and magazines. Some writers would also include discs, tapes, computer games as well as popular design in the definition.

MEDIA BIAS. Describes the lack of objectivity in the media. The News is often seen to be neutral facts and because of this has been studied more than other media output.

RELIGION. There is no agreed definition of religion. Not all major religions acknowledge the existence of a God or Gods. When sociologists write about religion they are usually interested in:

- Religious behaviour
- Religious institutions
- Religious beliefs
- Religious symbols.

SECULARISATION. Refers to the decline in the influence of religion on the wider society.

THE ROLE OF RELIGION IN SOCIETY

ESSENTIAL PRINCIPLES

SOCIALISATION

In many societies religion is an important agency of socialisation. Children and adults learn the norms, values and beliefs of their society either within the family or from specialised religious institutions such as schools and Churches.

In both simple tribal societies and some more modern states there is little or no separation between religious and secular life. Pakistan, for example, has moved towards a more religious society where Islamic morality and law are the basis of the rules of all social life.

In Britain children do attend religious classes and services. They have some religious education in State schools and are often taught religious beliefs and rules by parents. Despite this, the influence of religion as a source of socialisation has diminished and the influence of the school and the media has increased.

SOCIAL CONTROL

Social control describes the means by which society, or at least the powerful within society, deal with members who do not conform to the rules. Some forms of social control involve the use or threat of force. More often control is exerted over people's thoughts. We may conform because we think it is right to do so.

Religion provides mostly control over our thoughts but in other times and places Churches have used force to imprison, torture or even kill dissidents. The persecution of so-called witches in 17th century Britain and in the USA was probably more about the control of women than the control of any threat to religion. (You may have read Arthur Miller's play "The Crucible" which uses the persecution of witches in the past to condemn modern "Witch Hunts" of alleged communists in America in the 1950s.)

Some sociologists see religion as supporting the norms of the whole society. For example, they would argue that the 10 Commandments of the Old Testament provide divine backing for rules that are generally supported. The rules are then seen as being enforced by God as well as being made by him. The idea of a God who sees everything ensures that the good will be rewarded and the wicked punished in the next world, if not in this one. This is important as a form of social control as observation tells us that the evil often prosper in this life and the good suffer.

''Religion is the opiate of the masses''

Marxist sociologists believe that religion is like a drug which eases the pain of living in a Capitalist society. It also deludes people into accepting the control of the Ruling Class. Up to the 17th Century, English Kings claimed to rule by divine right. Christianity has suggested that poverty and suffering are associated with virtue. Some religious sects preach that the world will soon end and that God will intervene to end their suffering. This makes it less likely that people will get involved with political or violent struggles against their rulers.

❝❝ Views on religion as a form of social control ❞❞

Religion unites societies

Functionalist studies of religion emphasise the uniting (or INTEGRATING) function of religion. It has been suggested that religion unites society by providing shares beliefs and by encouraging people to worship together. Sacred objects and places may also have a unifying effect on the members of society.

Harmony or conflict

The view that religion unites society has been challenged. It may very well be the basis of conflict or of making existing conflicts worse.

1   There may be conflict between the religious and the non-religious: e.g. in Communist States all or just some religious groups were persecuted. In Ireland the Church has, until recently, imposed its views on abortion and contraception on the whole population and continues to prevent the legalisation of divorce.

2   There may be conflict between different groups *within* the same religion. The struggle between Catholic and Protestant goes back for hundreds of years and

continues to fuel the struggles in N. Ireland. Shia and Sunni sects of Islam continue to fight in the Middle East.

3   There may be conflict *between* different religions. Israel's disputes with its neighbours has become a conflict between Judaism and Islam as well as between nations.

<table>
<tr><td>**2** **RELIGION AND SOCIAL CHANGE**</td></tr>
</table>

When Marxists talk about religion as opium or "spiritual gin" they are suggesting that it helps to keep the working class quiet. If the workers became aware of their oppression and realised that they could do something about it. (Marx described this as becoming CLASS CONSCIOUS and no longer FALSELY CONSCIOUS)

Thus Marxists are suggesting that religion helps to prevent a communist revolution and inhibits social change. The idea that religion prevents change and helps to maintain the STATUS QUO (i.e. keeps things as they are) has been a source of debate in sociology for a long time. Weber directly criticised Marx when he wrote that Protestant religious beliefs helped to encourage the rise of Capitalism in Western Europe. He was arguing that religion *may* promote social change rather than prevent it.

There are lots of contemporary examples to support both sides of the argument.

■ In Iran, the Islamic revolution in 1979 brought about dramatic social change. Although critics may see it as turning the clock back. The left wing opposition to the Shah who ruled Iran before 1979 took part in the revolution but were later suppressed so Marxists may still argue that religion is inhibiting progress.

■ In Poland, the Roman Catholic Church which remains conservative on many religious and moral issues nonetheless helped to unify resistance to the old Communist regime and supported Solidarity in its opposition to the State.

■ In South Africa, the Dutch Reform Church helped to justify Apartheid by preaching white superiority and the need for separation. However other Churches were in the forefront of the opposition to the racist State. The Anglican Archbishop Tutu who leads a congregation of different races became the most well known black leader in South Africa whilst Mandela remained in gaol.

Religion can increase or slow down social change

WOMEN AND RELIGION

It has been argued that religious organisations and religious beliefs help to support patriarchal societies. (Those where men dominate women.)

■ Religious beliefs may justify the different gender roles suggesting that they are ordained by God or "natural".

■ Religious organisations may restrict the roles that women may play. The Church of England has recently decided after a long struggle that women may be priests but there remains strong opposition to this change and the Roman Catholic retains an all male (and unmarried) priesthood. Similarly women Rabbis exist in Reform but not Orthodox Jewish Communities. In fact men and women remain separated when they attend Orthodox synagogues.

■ Women may be excluded from some religious activities because they are seen as "unclean" in a religious sense. This may result from attitudes to menstruation.

Religion and gender

Religion, women and family life

Religion often supports gender differences (or inequalities depending on your point of view) found in family life. Rules about sexuality are frequently supported by religious attitudes and husbands and fathers may see a need to protect "their women" from the sexual desires of outsiders by restricting what they do outside the home.

A feminist pressure group, Women against Fundamentalism, has criticised religious leaders for opposing the setting up of women's refuges for the victims of domestic violence. It was argued by the religious leaders that such problems, if they existed at all, should be resolved within the family or within the community.

Feminists see religious fundamentalism as a threat to women's freedoms which are more likely to be protected in more liberal societies. They see fundamentalism as a problem whether among Christians, Moslems, Sikhs, Jews or Hindus. Religious fundamentalism either supports traditional family values and thus women's traditional roles or it condemns the outside world as immoral and corrupt and claims that women need protecting.

However there are women who see religious belief as a protection against sexism and racism. Single sex education not only appears to improve girls' academic performance but in religious schools also allows them freedom from male or racist controls.

Abortion

England, despite having a state religion, has liberal laws on abortion and contraception. These are challenged by the Roman Catholic Church and by Protestant fundamentalists. The conflict between those advocating women's "right to choose" and those who argue for the unborn child's "right to life" has been exemplified in 1992 by the legal dispute in Ireland as to whether a 14 year old rape victim had the right to leave Ireland and come to England for an abortion.

3 ▷ SECULARISATION

Although sociologists have argued about the precise meaning of the term secularisation there is a general agreement that it describes the decline in the influence of religion in society.

It could be measured by looking at:

■ RELIGIOUS PRACTICE
■ RELIGIOUS INSTITUTIONS
■ RELIGIOUS BELIEF

RELIGIOUS PRACTICE

The most obvious indication of the decline of religion in Britain is the fall in Church attendance. Although some groups can report rising membership and attendance at services the overall picture this century is quite clear and it indicates decline.

Other forms of religious behaviour which could be measured include: Religious weddings and funerals, religious practice at home such as prayer and keeping to dietary rules, identification with or active membership of a particular group and active membership of a group.

It is worth remembering when examining the decline in regular attendance at Church and other religious services that for some religions it is seen as essential, e.g. the Roman Catholic Church whereas for others such as Moslems and Jews it is not necessary even for the most observant.

Those who do attend Church are disproportionately middle class, middle aged or old and female. About 10% of the adult population attend on an average Sunday compared to 14% of children.

RELIGIOUS SCHOOLS

Whereas about 99% of children in N. Ireland attend religious schools in the rest of Great Britain the proportion is much smaller. About a quarter of state funded schools are voluntary-aided religious schools. These comprise nearly 5000 Church of England, over 2200 Roman Catholic, 30 Methodist and 22 Jewish schools. There are no state aided Muslim schools despite requests from the Muslim community.

Religious education and worship remain compulsory in English schools. In the 1990s there has been a strong movement within the Conservative party to emphasise the teaching of Christianity rather than the more non-committal multi-cultural approaches which had become common in those schools that taught religion at all.

THE INFLUENCE OF RELIGIOUS INSTITUTIONS

It is generally accepted that the influence of the Church of England over the social life of the nation has declined. In the past the Church influenced political decisions and in the middle ages Church leaders held high political office.

Nowadays the Church may criticise government but has little direct influence. The Church of England has criticised the government over poverty, inner city deprivation, unemployment etc. Although religious leaders were prominent in the Peace and nuclear disarmament campaigns of the 1950s and later, the Gulf War was supported by major churches as a "just war".

The Church of England has lost battles or ceased to fight over moral issues such as divorce, abortion and contraception. The Roman Catholic Church maintains a more traditional stance but not all members conform to its rulings on these matters.

THE PROBLEM OF STUDYING RELIGIOUS BELIEF

Unlike religious behaviour, religious beliefs cannot be directly observed. Some sociologists have suggested that the fall in Church attendance indicates a decline in religious belief. Others have suggested that belief remains but people practice at home i.e. religious activity has become more individual.

Surveys can provide the answer to questions like how many people believe in God or more specific items of religious doctrine such as asking Christians if they believe in Hell or the resurrection. What is more problematic is to discover what influence these beliefs have on people's lives.

In general it appears that scientific beliefs have been increasingly successful in challenging religious beliefs over the last 100 years. The major challenge coming from Darwin's theory of evolution.

A RELIGIOUS REVIVAL

The picture of religion in terminal decline is not quite accurate. Some religious groups are thriving. The religions of the East, which are largely followed by ethnic minorities, have increasing numbers of followers in this country.

A variety of New Religious Movements which are sometimes sects and cults but sometimes more Church-like have also been successful in recruiting and retaining members. Both the Mormon and Jehovah's Witnesses have been successful in recruiting new members. Within the more traditional churches some sub-groups flourish. The House Church movement attracts those who have found that traditional churches lack inspiration and Churches catering for Britons of African and Afro-Caribbean origin are often full.

World wide religious fundamentalism and the influence of religion on political affairs seem far from in decline. The influence of Islam in previously secular States in the Middle East, Central Asia and S.E. Asia appears to have increased with Iran and Pakistan as good examples.

The USA remains the most religious of Western societies with Britain, particularly England, the least religious. 90% of Americans identify with a Christian church and 50% attend Church on an average Sunday. Christian fundamentalism has been associated with right wing politics in the USA and issues such as abortion divide the voters.

4 ▷ OWNERSHIP AND CONTROL OF THE MEDIA

Television

Television in Britain has tended to be controlled by monopolies. The BBC was until 1955 the sole broadcaster of television in this country offering a single channel. The ITV companies which were permitted to broadcast in different areas of the country from 1955 enjoyed a near monopoly with only the BBC in competition. The BBC did not of course compete for advertising.

Until 1991 the original companies were largely successful in keeping their franchises. In press magnate Lord Thomson's words an ITV franchise was "a licence to print money." The commitment of the Thatcher government to free enterprise has opened up TV to satellite and cable channels and also required the ITV companies to bid for franchises. Twelve of the existing franchises were renewed. Soon after a second satellite TV station went on the air it was taken over by Rupert Murdoch's SKY TV.

Newspapers

Unlike the USA Britain has a number of national newspapers. In addition there are local daily and weekly papers and numerous free papers which rely on revenue from advertisements. The defeat of the Fleet Street print unions by Eddie Shah and Murdoch with the support of the Government did allow the launching of two new national daily newspapers. Today by Shah which was later taken over by Murdoch and the Independent which is a rival to the Times and other quality papers. The Independent later launched a new Sunday paper. Two Sunday papers launched since 1987 have folded.

The Murdoch media empire

Rupert Murdoch attracts criticism from many directions. Some people object to the lowering of quality standards since he began to operate in Britain. Some object specifically to the vulgarity of The Sun and its effect on competing papers and some object to the political views of his papers and the way in which they attack left wing politicians. Critics of the content of Murdoch papers should however accept that the papers only thrive because the audience reads them.

Readership of tabloid newspapers has fallen since 1981 and The Sun has lost about a $\frac{1}{4}$ million buyers. It should be noted that newspaper readership is sensitive to big events like wars and royal weddings as well as price promotions and bingo and other competitions.

A more general concern arises from the increased concentration of media ownership and control which is best exemplified by Murdoch's News International. News International owns:

■ The Sun, Today, The Times and Sunday Times, The News of the World.
■ Newspapers in the USA and Australia.
■ BSKYB the satellite station.
■ Twentieth Century Fox.
■ TV stations in the USA, Australia and Hong King.
■ Various book and magazine publishing businesses.

▟▟ Concentration of the media ▟▟

English law has tried to limit the ownership of more than 20% of a TV station by newspaper businesses. In addition it tries to prevent non-EC citizens from controlling a British TV station. Murdoch was Australian but took US citizenship to be able to operate more easily in the USA. SKY operates out of Luxembourg and is not subject to British law.

There are other international media businesses that also manufacture hardware like TV and video recorder as well as selling discs, tapes and producing programmes for broadcasting.

In the past most knowledge was local and passed on slowly through small communities. National newspapers produced a more national culture which TV has reinforced. There is a strong argument now that a global culture is emerging with brands like COCA COLA and performers like Michael Jackson and Madonna being known (and bought) world wide.

5 ▶ EFFECTS OF THE MEDIA ON THE AUDIENCE

The main public concern with the media tends to focus on its alleged effects. This is why the previous questions of ownership, control and output have become social problems. Most people who are concerned with effects tend to concentrate on harmful rather than favourable effects and assume that the harm is done not to themselves but to others who are seen as more vulnerable.

There is a general acceptance that children may need to have media output censored in some way. TV operates a time threshold system where unsuitable material is scheduled after a 10 p.m. "watershed", films and videos are given certificates indicating suitability and there may be restrictions on sales or cinema admission.

There are also laws which may involve censorship either before or after transmission or publication. These include laws of obscenity, indecency, libel and the Official Secrets Act. The campaign against pornography embraces very different political groupings from radical feminists who see pornography as oppressing women to the Christian right who see it corrupting family values.

Sociological and psychological research has examined the effects of the mass media on behaviour and attitudes. Psychologists have tried to establish a link between watching VIOLENCE on TV and subsequent violent behaviour in young men. Some studies have asked boys to remember both watching TV and later acts of violence. Some have been more scientific and tried to establish a cause and effect relationship in laboratory experiments.

Sociologists have been more interested in examining longer term cultural effects on the audience. For example the extent to which the media create, reinforce or contradict gender and ethnic stereotypes. In addition to the points made about gender and the media in the gender chapter, it might also be worth examining the fact that there were relatively few women in managerial roles in the media in the past compared with now. There are women editors of national newspapers and women producers of TV programmes and films. Of course we need to work out the *proportions* of female involvement rather than draw conclusions from a few well-known individuals.

THE REPORTING OF RAPE

A study of the reporting of rape in national newspapers suggests that the stories are presented as entertainment. They may not even bother reporting the verdict but concentrate on the defendant's account which he uses to discredit the victim. These are often presented in the language of a salacious novel rather than as a crime of violence.

Stories tend to focus on rape as a sudden violent attack by a stranger. The fear of such attacks may lead women and their husbands or fathers to restrict their movements. The Home Office figures indicate that attacks by strangers make up only a minority of reported rapes.

Juries may regard attacks by acquaintances as not really rape and judges may be more lenient in their sentences.

RACE AND THE MEDIA

Various studies have suggested that the media have "set an agenda" for discussing race issues which concentrates on conflict and social problems. There is little attention paid to the positive contributions made by members of minorities.

The more liberal newspapers and TV programmes may portray minorities as victims of violence or discrimination. The tabloid papers are more likely to write about the problems that minorities allegedly cause for the majority in the fields of housing, employment and crime. The presenting of black youth as a threat to law and order has been discussed by S. Hall in "Policing the crisis". He argued that moral panics about race and crime distract people from economic problems and the failure of the government to maintain public support.

The election of black councillors and MPs in the 1980s was followed by press attacks on so-called "loony left" policies which it was claimed favoured minorities or involved ridiculous bans on language. A false story that the nursery rhyme Baa, Baa Black Sheep had been banned by various London Councils was published all over the world.

Bernie Grant, now an MP, found himself subject to continual press attack when he became the country's first black leader of a local authority.

Headline	Newspaper	Date	Story
It's Barmy Bernie on the attack	Sun	8.10.85	Demand for resignation of officers involved in Cynthia Jarrett raid
Barmy Bernie moves in with blonde	S Mirror	13.10.85	Domestic arrangements
The darker side of Barmy Bernie	D Express	25.10.85	A feature article which compared Coun. Grant to Adolf Hitler
Barmy Bernie set to ban police*	Sun	20.11.85	Council calls for reduced policing on Broadwater Farm Estate
Barmy Bernie goes coffee potty*	Mirror	5.12.85	Haringey Council decides to order Nicaraguan coffee
Bernie takes the merry out of Christmas*	Standard	11.12.85	Haringey Council tells dust workers not to solicit tips
Racist bin liner is blacked*	Mail on Sunday	2.3.86	Unfounded story that Haringey Council stopped purchasing black dustbin liners because they are "racist"
Bernie's banter is baffling*	Mail on Sunday	25.5.86	Untrue story that Bernie Grant wants Creole to be taught in Haringey's schools

*A council decision is personified in the name of Councillor Grant

WAR AND THE MEDIA

The press has been criticised by sociologists for bias in the reporting of War and Peace. During the Falklands War the press in general was uncritically supportive of the Government. The Mirror, which was critical of the conduct of the war, was accused of treason by The Sun. Politicians got upset with the BBC for presenting what was aimed to be an objective view. For example the BBC used the terms "Government policy" rather than "British policy" and "British Forces" rather than "our forces". The Sun produced notable headlines:

"GOTCHA" when an Argentinian battle ship was sunk.

It also captioned page 3 photos "naughty nautical knickers" and "all ship shape and Bristol fashion".

The Gulf War produced a similar patriotic and uncritical account from most sources. The Guardian produced a list of phrases used by the British press in one week of the Gulf War.

The Peace movement also receives biased reporting. The women who demonstrated

Mad Dogs and Englishmen

We have	**They have**	**Our boys are motivated by**	**Their boys are motivated by**
Army, Navy and	A War machine	An old fashioned sense of duty	Fear of Saddam
Air Force		**Our boys**	**Their boys**
Reporting guidelines	Censorship	Fly into the jaws of hell	Cower in concrete bunkers
Press briefings	Propaganda	**Our ships are . . .**	**Iraq ships are . . .**
We	**They**	An armada	A navy
Take out	Destroy	**Iraeli non-retaliation is**	**Iraqi non-retaliation is**
Suppress	Destroy	An act of great statesmanship	Blundering/Cowardly
Eliminate	Kill	**The Belgians are . . .**	**The Belgians are also . . .**
Neutralise or	Kill	Yellow	Two-faced
decapitate		**Our missiles are . . .**	**Their missiles are . . .**
Decapitate	Kill	Like Luke Skywalker	Ageing duds (rhymes
Dig in	Cower in their foxholes	zapping Darth Vader	with Scuds)
We launch	**They launch**	**Our missiles cause . . .**	**Their missiles cause . . .**
First strikes	Sneak missile attacks	Collateral damage	Civilian casualties
Pre-emptively	Without provocation	**We . . .**	**They . . .**
Our men are . . .	**Their men are . . .**	Precision bomb	Fire wildly at anything in
Boys	Troops		the skies
Lads	Hordes	**Our PoWs are . . .**	**Their PoWs are . . .**
Our boys are . . .	**Theirs are . . .**	Gallant boys	Overgrown schoolchildren
Professional	Brainwashed	**George Bush is . . .**	**Saddam Hussein is . . .**
Lion-hearts	Paper tigers	At peace with himself	Demented
Cautious	Cowardly	Resolute	Defiant
Confident	Desperate	Statesmanlike	An evil tyrant
Heroes	Cornered	Assured	A crackpot monster
Dare-devils	Cannon fodder	**Our planes . . .**	**Their planes . . .**
Young knights of	Bastards of Baghdad	Suffer a high rate of attrition	Are shot out of the sky
the skies		Fail to return from missions	Are Zapped
Loyal	Blindly obedient	• All the expressions above have been used by the British press in	
Desert rats	Mad dogs	the past week.	
Resolute	Ruthless	Reprinted with thanks from: The Guardian,	
Brave	Fanatical	23 January 1991, p. 21	

outside the American Cruise missile base at Greenham Common in Berkshire found the press were more interested in condemning their personal hygiene, sexuality and neglect of mother and wife roles than they were discussing issues of war and peace.

A critical thought

The mass media may challenge as well as reinforce stereotypes. American TV has run fictional series that provide very positive images of women and ethnic minorities often challenging conventional stereotypes. You could explore this issue with your own research.

EXAMINATION QUESTIONS

Q.1

a) What is meant by the term "mass media"? *(4)*

b) Describe some of the changes in the ownership and control of the mass media which have taken place during the last five years. *(9)*

c) What is meant by the term "stereotype"? *(2)*

d) Show how the mass media present a stereotyped view of one particular group or type of people. *(10)*

(Total 25)

(NEAB, June 1992)

Q.2

From Social Science for GCSE by Jack Nobbs, published by Macmillan Education 1987

a) Which candidate won the 1978 Pontefract by-election? *(1)*

b) Explain why two papers can present the same news in totally different ways. *(4)*

c) What determines the "newsworthiness" of an item? *(4)*

d) Why is freedom of the press seen as important in a society? *(6)*

(15 marks)

(ULEAC, June 1992)

Q.3
Study **ITEMS A** and **B.** Then answer the questions which follow.

ITEM A

On an average Sunday, 10 per cent of England's adult population choose to be in church, rather than in bed, in the garden or at the DIY shop. One in seven of those go to church twice on Sunday. The English Church Census reveals that 3.7 million adults in England are churchgoers. Also, 1.2 million children under fifteen years of age attend church services or Sunday School, around 14 per cent of the child population. This means that over eight times as many people go to church each week as go to Football League matches.

(From *Parish Magazine*, Romsey Abbey)

ITEM B

Membership in thousands of selected Christian groups and non-Christian religious groups in the United Kingdom

	1970	1975	1980	1985
Non-Christian Religious Groups				
Muslims	250	400	600	853
Sikhs	75	115	150	80
Hindus	50	100	120	130
Jews	113	111	111	109
Christian Groups				
Mormons	88	80	91	81
Jehovah's Witnesses	62	80	84	101
Spiritualists	45	57	52	49

(Adapted from *Contemporary British Society,* N. Abercrombie and A.Warde, Polity Press)

a) Read **ITEM A.**
   i)   According to the information given, how many adults in England are churchgoers? *(1)*
   ii) What is the source of the information used by the magazine? *(1)*
b) Study **ITEM B.**
   i)   What is the largest non-Christian religious group in the United Kingdom? *(1)*
   ii) Which Christian group has declined in number in the period covered by the table? *(1)*
c) Identify and explain **two** reasons why statistics concerning church membership may be misleading. *(4)*
d) Identify and fully explain **two** ways in which the Established Church affects people's lives in England and Wales today. *(4)*
e) Identify and fully explain **one** function which religion performs in a society. *(4)*
f) Identify and fully explain **one** way in which people's religious beliefs affect their behaviour. *(4)*

(SEG, June 1993)

Q.4
a) Why do many people obey rules laid down by religions? *(4)*
b) In what ways can religion limit change and encourage change? Give examples. *(7)*
c) Describe THREE other *causes of social change* identified by sociologists. Give examples. *(9)*

(SEG, June 1991)

ANSWERS TO EXAMINATION QUESTIONS

Q.1

a) (Definition, explanation and examples to gain all 4 marks.)

The mass media are the means of communicating messages to large audiences. At present the communication is one way but new digital technologies that integrate TV, computers and telephones may soon allow the audience to answer back. Audiences tend to be separated from one another often in their own homes.

The most important mass media are TV, radio, newspapers, magazines, books, CDs, tapes etc.

b) Describe and try to explain the causes and consequences of three or more changes.

You might include:

1 The continued tendency for major international conglomerates to buy into a variety of media. e.g. News International, Time-life-Warner, Sony-CBS.
2 The collapse of Maxwell communications following Robert Maxwell's death.
3 The introduction of cable communications networks again owned by international consortia.
4 The launching of new independent radio stations e.g. Classic FM and Virgin radio.
5 The replacement of ITV companies such as Thames and Southern by new companies Carlton and Meridian.
6 Launching of new satellite channels or the takeover of Maxwell's BSB by Murdoch's Sky.

The causes of changes include:

1 technological developments,
2 government policy.

The consequences of changes include:
1 the increased political influence of owners
2 the lowering of quality standards.

c) (2 marks so a short answer)

An over-simplified or exaggerated image of a group of people such as a race, gender or age group. e.g. the portrayal of women as housewives.

d) You could choose women, the young, the old, an ethnic minority, an occupation such as the police, politicians, or workers during industrial action.

Describe the characteristics of the stereotype and explain why it is an oversimplification or distortion.

Refer to the material above on race and the media or gender and the media to give you an idea.

Write about one page to ensure sufficient depth to gain high marks.

Q.2

a) G. Lofthouse (Lab.)
b) Your answer should discuss media bias.

You could refer to ownership, and control.

Editors and journalists may have their own views.

The influence of advertisers.

The existing views of the papers' readers.

Examples would help and they should relate to political bias – this could cover issues like race relations.

c) You should explain at least two points.

The selection and presentation of news is influenced by:

i) Cultural factors

These influence what the editor thinks the audience is interested in. What is seen as unusual, a social problem, a human interest story etc. A story often confirms the audience's beliefs and prejudices e.g. social security scroungers, young hooligans, sexual indiscretions of the famous etc.

   ii)   Technical factors

   Was the event known about before hand so that journalists and cameras were there in advance? e.g. a royal visit or political speech. Was the event times to catch a news deadline. This is more important for newspapers than broadcast media which can include last minute and even current items.

d) You should try to develop two or three points. You could explain what freedom of the press involves, how it might be limited by law or government intervention, the importance of competition.

   The contribution of a free press to democracy can be discussed by identifying the functions of a free press such as scrutinising government, alerting the public to the misuse of power etc.

   You could discuss the consequences of not having a free press and a government allowed to manipulate public opinion.

   You could adopt a critical stance and argue whether we have a free press in Britain or whether there is a case for curbing press freedom.

Q.3

a) i)   3.7 million   (ii) The English Church Census
b) i)   Muslims   (ii) Mormons
c) The definition of membership varies between different groups. Some only count one family member usually the head of the house. Others count all adult members. Some religious groups would have a membership list of those who pay subscriptions.

   There are problems if church attendance is used to measure membership. Some people attend more than once in a day, others only for High Holydays. It has been suggested that local churches may understate their membership to avoid paying contributions to the national organisation or overstate membership to indicate the success of the clergyman. Attendance for ??

d) The Established Church is the Church of England.

   It provides, in cooperation with the State, thousands of schools. These make some contribution to the religious education of pupils although pupils of other denominations and religions may attend.

   Leaders of the Church of England make pronouncements on moral and political issues. They may do this in Church, in the House of Lords or through the mass media. Church leaders have influenced public views on strikes, pit closures, abortion, medical ethics and family life. The Church has been relatively successful in resisting Sunday trading.

e) Religion may act as a form of SOCIAL CONTROL.

   Islam and Judaism have detailed rules about virtually every aspect of life which are supported by religious belief.

   Norms may be seen as having divine origin i.e. God made the rules; and thus people are more likely to obey them.

   Religious beliefs and doctrines may provide the basis of or support for norms and morals e.g. concerning sexuality, marriage and crime. Some religions also believe in rewards and punishments in the next world. So that even if the wicked appear to prosper and the virtuous appear to suffer everyone will get their just desserts eventually.

   (You could also look at the INTEGRATION function described above)

f) Family life may be strictly governed by religious beliefs. Religion may define rules of sexuality e.g. no sexual relations outside marriage or no homosexual behaviour.

   Marriage partners may be either prescribed or forbidden by religious taboos. Sikhs are forbidden by rules against incest to marry even distant relatives whereas cousin marriage is common for Muslims.

   Relationships between husbands and wives may be influenced by religious rules. Feminist critics have argued that fundamentalist religion upholds patriarchy (i.e. male domination). The rules about divorce and re-marriage are also defined by religious beliefs.

   (You might also discuss religion and political conflict, religion and deviance, the behaviour of the clergy, monks and nuns etc.)

STUDENT'S ANSWER WITH EXAMINER'S COMMENTS

Q.4

a) Why do many people obey rules laid down by religions? *(4)*

> Many people obey rules laid down by religion because they are brought up to accept them and believe they are right.
>
> They also obey rules because it gives them a code to live by. Religion helps to fulfil missing needs in a person's life.
>
> Because religion is a common belief in a community it helps people to get along and share something.

66 Good answer to the question. 4/4 99

b) In what ways can religion limit change and encourage change? Give examples. *(7)*

> Religion can limit change and encourage change by restricting what people can do like drinking and gambling. Also in Islam restricting the showing of "permissive" films and the wearing of indecent clothes e.g. bikinis.
>
> But religion can also encourage change acting as a go-between between religion and politics. It can help the followers in the community grow together and achieve what they believe is right.
>
> If the Ayatollah is Iran's next ruler he will try to restore the old traditional Islamic beliefs but that will only work if all the people agree and then the country can work to get what it needs.

66 Good, use of source 99

66 Not enough use of examples – drifts away from the question a little. 4/7 99

c) Describe THREE other causes of social change identified by sociologists. Give examples. *(9)*

> Three other sources of social change which are identified by sociologists are peer pressure, family pressure and the law.
>
> You can be influenced by friends who want you to do things. Sometimes these may be criminal things. Social change is not always for the good.
>
> Families can pressure you into things that you don't want to do. For example some religions support arranged marriages. You may not agree with your family but feel obliged to obey.
>
> The law is the main organisation which leads to people leading better lives. Everyone conforms to that because of the consequences which may follow. Everyone agrees with the making of laws and this helps the community to get along in which ever country you come from or are in.

66 Social change is not really given enough attention – this is more about Social control. 3/9 99

66 Overall some good points but not quite enough explanation. 11/20 99

NB The Review Sheet for this chapter can be found at the end of Chapter 16

METHODS AND THEMES IN SOCIOLOGY

USING PRIMARY SOURCES

USING SECONDARY SOURCES

CASE STUDIES

DIFFERENT SOCIOLOGICAL METHODS

KEY THEMES

GETTING STARTED

From 1996 onwards there will be an increased emphasis on students *understanding* and using sociological *methodology*. This means that you should develop the skills required to DO sociology as well as learn what sociologists have done.

The following skills will be tested in examinations and in coursework:

- YOUR KNOWLEDGE AND UNDERSTANDING OF DIFFERENT METHODS.
- YOUR ABILITY TO ACQUIRE INFORMATION DIRECTLY, E.G. THROUGH OBSERVATION OR FROM SECONDARY SOURCES, E.G. PUBLISHED STATISTICS.
- YOUR ABILITY TO INTERPRET INFORMATION PRESENTED IN A VARIETY OF FORMS, E.G. GRAPHS, TABLES, EXTRACTS FROM SOCIOLOGICAL RESEARCH, OR NON SOCIOLOGICAL SOURCES LIKE NEWSPAPERS.
- YOUR ABILITY TO USE INFORMATION GATHERED BY YOURSELF OR OTHERS TO EXAMINE ISSUES AND EVALUATE ARGUMENTS.
- YOUR ABILITY TO IDENTIFY SOCIOLOGICAL RESEARCH PROBLEMS AND CHOOSE APPROPRIATE RESEARCH STRATEGIES TO INVESTIGATE THEM.

Examiners have commented that doing coursework has encouraged thorough coverage of this part of syllabuses and the quality of answers is high. Doing coursework is the subject of chapter 1. The first part of this chapter will help you to answer *examination questions* on methods. It may also help you in studying other topics to consider how sociologists have acquired their information and whether they are justified in drawing conclusions from it.

The second part of this chapter seeks to show that there are consistent themes running through the previous chapters that cut across the usual topic boundaries. I have divided this book into areas of social life which sociologists have chosen to study and examiners have decided to include in syllabuses and use as the basis for examination questions. However questions can focus on two or more topic areas and sometimes are based on an important sociological concept or theme which is useful in studying a range of topics.

The themes I shall look at in the second part of this chapter are:

CULTURE. The total way of life of a society; it includes knowledge, norms, values and material items.

SOCIALISATION. The process of learning culture. We emphasise the socialisation of children but the process carries on throughout people's lives.

SOCIAL CONTROL. The constraint exerted on our behaviour by groups or society.

SOCIAL CHANGE. Alternations in the basic structures of society, such as the economy, family, and religion.

ESSENTIAL PRINCIPLES

Primary sources are where *you* develop the information and data.

PARTICIPANT OBSERVATION

66 Observation is important 99

All sociological research depends on observation. Sociologists use their minds to interpret what they see and hear, and can study people by getting more or less involved in their lives. When the involvement is minimal we call it *observation,* and when involvement is deliberate we call it *participant observation.*

Participant observation is a popular kind of research both to do and to read about. It involves the researchers *joining in* with their subjects in order to understand, as well as simply describe, their activities. A major advantage of observation is that it allows the study of people in their natural environment rather than their merely responding to questions set by the sociologist. It can indicate what is important to the subject rather than to the sociologist. Observation may be time consuming and the findings difficult to analyse but it does produce detailed accounts of everyday life.

Interactionist sociologists have stressed the importance of discovering the motives and meanings which underlie our actions in order to explain social behaviour. Participant observation allows the researcher to "get in the shoes" of their subjects and share their feelings and experiences.

Sometimes the observer is almost a real participant and can write an autobiographical account of their experiences. Jason Ditton wrote about learning to steal whilst working as a bread salesman. You could do research into your real roles in the family, school, work place or religious organisation. The main advantage of such research is your ability to share and understand the experiences of subjects. However for some critics who prefer a more scientific approach to sociology this is also the main disadvantage. They would prefer the researcher to remain detached and report on objective behaviour rather than subjective experience.

66 Some prefer to be detached 99

Participant observation can be conducted with or without the knowledge and consent of the subjects. We refer to secret studies as *covert* research in contrast to *overt* research when the subjects are aware of being observed.

The major advantages of covert research are:

1   It allows access to groups who might exclude outsiders because their behaviour is illegal, shameful or secret. There have been studies of gangs, Freemasons and religious sects.

66 Advantages and disadvantages of covert research 99

2   It minimises the possibility of the subjects changing their behaviour because they know they are being observed. Studies revealing racial discrimination by employers would be unlikely to be successful if the employers *knew* they were being observed.

The major disadvantages of covert research are:

1   Access may be limited to groups where the researcher can pass as one of the subjects. Thus class, race, gender and age may limit opportunities. Although it must be pointed out that there are numerous famous studies where researchers disguised themselves to change their age or even skin colour. King found that being over six foot, remaining standing and avoiding contact, allowed him to move among infant school children with minimum involvement.

2   There may be a degree of danger of being discovered during research or of reprisals after publication. Researchers may find themselves witnessing criminal behaviour and have to decide whether to intervene, inform the police or do nothing. The undercover policeman may have similar problems but is clearer about the aims of the operation. Rosenhan found it difficult to get out of a secure psychiatric hospital after faking symptoms to get admitted – not many sociologists are trained to prove themselves sane!

3   There may be practical difficulties, such as not wishing to act suspiciously by asking too many questions or having to take notes secretly. As yet sociologists do

not appear to have taken much advantage of modern technology and use miniaturised electronic recording devices! There has, however, been the overt use of video cameras in a study of market traders and the use of a concealed camera in a study of racial discrimination in Bristol.

4   In any case, some sociologists think that deception itself is unethical. The determination of the sociologist as an observer can be illustrated by this extract from a pre-war study done for the Mass Observation project.

SEX IN BLACKPOOL AUGUST – OCTOBER 1937

"When we began work in Blackpool we expected to see copulation everywhere. What we found was petting . . . Observer unit combed the sands at all hours, crawled around under the piers . . . pretended to be drunk and fell in heaps on located sand couples to feel what they were doing exactly, while others hung over the sea wall and railings for hours watching couples in their hollowed out sandpits below."

THE SURVEY

The *survey* is perhaps the most common method in sociology. The survey method involves both the collection and analysis of data, with the information gathered presented in a numerical form. Surveys are often used to test hypotheses by seeking correlations between variables; e.g. the relationship between unemployment rates and ill health or crime and gender.

Comparative surveys can be:

■ *Longitudinal surveys.* Here the SAME group of subjects are compared over a period of time. The advantage here is that you can see how people CHANGE over a period of time; e.g. The NCB has conducted a survey of all the children born on a particular week in 1964 and their results have been televised by Granada at 7-year intervals.

■ *Historical surveys.* Here the behaviour of different groups at different times can be compared; e.g. The Census shows how household sizes have changed at 10-year intervals.

■ *Cross-sectional surveys.* These compare the characteristics of different groups in one society at a single moment in time; e.g. the relationship between class and educational achievement in Britain in 1987. It is worth looking carefully at the date of such studies as things may have changed since.

■ *Cross-cultural surveys.* These are a type of cross-sectional study but they compare different societies. They can demonstrate the importance of socialisation rather than nature in explaining social behaviour; e.g. differences in gender roles in different societies.

METHODS OF DATA COLLECTION USED IN SURVEYS

a)   The use of *secondary data* collected by someone else. These provide a cheap source of large quantities of information. But there may be doubts over their validity; e.g. using Home Office crime figures to examine the changes in crime rates.

b)   *Postal self-completed questionnaires.* These allow the sociologist to cover a wide area of the country at a low cost. Unfortunately the response rate tends to be low; e.g. Wallis' study of Scientologists.

 Populations and samples

c)   *Self-completed questionnaires distributed by the researcher.* These produce a better response rate, but are less convenient to distribute over a wide area. They allow more privacy for the subject than interviews; e.g. The National survey of Sexual behaviour and Attitudes (see below).

d)   *Interviews.* These can be more or less structured. The interviewer can explain any problems and ask further questions where appropriate. However interviewers may influence the subjects' responses. This is called "interviewer bias"; e.g. Willmott and Young in Bethnal Green and Oakley's study of Housework.

THE SAMPLE SURVEY

In order to save time and money you can select and study a small proportion of the population. If the sample is REPRESENTATIVE (typical) the results can be GENERALISED to the whole population. Opinion Polls are a kind of sample survey. The use of opinion polls to predict voting is discussed in the politics chapter.

- THE POPULATION is all those who could be included in the study and all those whom the study claims to describe, such as all housewives with young children.
- THE SAMPLING FRAME is a list of the population from which the sample is chosen. The register is a sampling frame of your class. Telephone directories are used as sampling frames for research into voting intentions and interviews are conducted by telephone. In the past this caused problems as higher class subjects were more likely to have telephones.
- THE SAMPLE is those selected for study.

Sampling methods are ways of choosing representative samples. They include the following

Populations and samples

a) QUOTA or STRATIFIED samples. These are chosen by dividing the population into strata with particular characteristics and selecting individuals from each strata in proportion to their numbers in the population. Thus if 53% of candidates for GCSE sociology are female, then a study of a sample would choose 53 females for every 47 males. This method is cheap and quick but the relevant strata must be known in advance; e.g. the population of a school could be broken down into age, gender or ethnic groups.

b) RANDOM samples. These are chosen mathematically from the whole population so that each unit has an equal chance of selection. (Like playing "Bingo".)

c) STRATIFIED RANDOM samples. These are chosen randomly from pre-determined strata, not the whole population. This ensures that relatively rare strata are represented even in a small sample.

d) PURPOSIVE samples. These are chosen so that specific subjects are included and may sacrifice representativeness to achieve this. This may be the only solution if no suitable sampling frame exists; e.g. Mack and Lansley found their subjects for their poverty study by choosing 3 types of neighbourhood which had already been classified as containing poor households. You might study criminals by surveying those in prison.
Why might those in prison be an unrepresentative sample of all criminals?

e) "SNOWBALL" samples. These are chosen by allowing subjects to introduce the researcher to other suitable subjects. This is unlikely to be representative but permits access to secretive subjects such as drug abusers and criminals; e.g. L. Taylor used ex-criminal John McVicar (who began to learn his sociology in prison) as a key informant to get introductions to criminals.

- List the reasons why your class might not be typical of any other GCSE class in Britain.
- Was A. Oakley justified in generalising about housework from her interviews with 40 women?

INTERVIEWS

Interviews are used by sociologists for different purposes and take a variety of forms. They may be more or less structured and more or less formal.

If the sociologist is doing a survey then the interview is likely to be *structured* and conducted in a *formal* manner. Structured interviews are really a questionnaire administered by the researcher rather than completed by the subject. Questions are asked in the same order and as far as possible in a standardised way. The advantage of structured interviews are that they allow the data to be quantified and systematically analysed. However surveys have used informal and less structured interviews in order to get subjects to trust the interviewer and discuss sensitive issues, e.g. "Violence against Wives" by Dobash and Dobash.

Interactionist sociologists are often more interested in letting the subjects speak for themselves than in the gathering of quantitative data for a survey. They prefer to use *informal and less structured* interviews which are more conversational in tone. They tend to be longer (A. Oakley's interviews in "From Here to Maternity" lasted an average of more than 2 hours) and may be conducted over a long period of time not just in a single meeting. The Oakley study began 6 months before birth and continued to six months after. Clearly the interviewer had the opportunity to build up a relationship of trust with her subjects.

Unstructured interviews are seen as less reliable but produce more natural and detailed responses.

Interviewer bias occurs when the subject responds not to the question but to the characteristics of the interviewer. Research indicates that the interviewer's class, race and gender can all affect responses and thus undermine the reliability of the study.

QUESTIONNAIRES

Questionnaires are lists of questions used to gather information about a subject's background, attitudes, opinions and behaviour. They are generally used to gather data for surveys. They are a relatively cheap and quick way of obtaining large amounts of quantifiable data. Questions may be closed or open. *Closed questions* can be answered by ticking boxes and the responses analysed by optical mark readers and computer. *Open questions* allow the subject to answer more fully.

The problems with questionnaires include:

1   Subjects not understanding the questions at all.
2   Subjects understanding questions differently.
3   Quite similar questions can produce very different results; e.g. opinion research on abortion commissioned by interested pressure groups has produced results supporting the interested groups' views, on both sides of the argument.

 **Problems with questionnaires**

You might collect some questionnaires from various sources, such as government forms, magazines, market research questionnaires and consider any problems you or others might have in completing them.

THE EXPERIMENT

The experiment is the dominant method used in the natural sciences. It is not commonly used in Sociology but is popular with psychologists. The experiment involves the researcher changing an independent variable (the cause) and observing what happens to the dependent variable (the effect) whilst controlling outside variables which might spoil the experiment.

W. Daniel conducted an experiment to test the extent of racial discrimination in the fields of employment, housing and the provision of services. He sent applications for jobs from imaginary subjects who were white natives of Britain, white immigrants and non-white immigrants. His CAUSE was the skin colour of the subject. The applications were identical in every other respect such as qualifications and experience. This CONTROLLED the OUTSIDE VARIABLES. He then recorded whether applicants were called for interview. This was the EFFECT.

2 > USING SECONDARY SOURCES

Secondary data is information which has not been collected by the sociologists themselves but by others. It exists in either a quantitative or qualitative form.

Secondary sources used by sociologists include:

1   OFFICIAL STATISTICS
2   ORGANISATIONAL RECORDS
3   MEDIA OUTPUT
4   DIARIES, AUTOBIOGRAPHIES AND OTHER PERSONAL DOCUMENTS
5   PUBLISHED SOCIOLOGICAL RESEARCH

1. Official statistics

Social statistics are produced by a variety of bodies. Those produced by the Government are called Official Statistics. They cover a wide variety of areas including births, marriages, divorces and deaths, crime, employment and unemployment, health and educational achievement. Non-government bodies produce statistics on similar activities and also on Church attendance, racial disadvantage and job opportunities for women. Social Trends, published annually, is extremely useful in this respect.

The major advantage of using official statistics is the availability of large quantities of data covering large populations at low cost. Census information on household types can be used to investigate changes in family life connected to divorce and the changing age structure of the population.

The disadvantages include concerns about the reliability and validity of the statistics. Some sociologists have argued that crime statistics tell us more about police and judicial practices than they do about criminals. Critics of the government have suggested that the many changing definitions of unemployment have been used to artificially lower the published figures.

 **Useful secondary sources**

2. Organisational records

Employers, schools and colleges, Churches and other organisations keep records which may be of use to the sociologist. R. Revans compared 5 Manchester hospitals by looking at their records of absenteeism, wastage of student nurses during training, labour turn over, and patients' recovery rates. He argued that these were measures of the morale in the hospital.

3. Media output

The mass media produce newspaper reports, TV and radio broadcasts, recorded music and also the output of books and magazines. Sociologists have analysed these in both quantitative and qualitative studies. Sometimes the sociologist is interested in using press reports as a source of information about subjects, e.g. what politicians say in speeches; on other occasions the interest is as much in the media themselves as the subjects they describe, e.g. the way in which TV portrays women and ethnic minorities.

Analysing media output is a popular research project for candidates. The major problems include the difficulty of giving anything more than a personal selection and interpretation of output.

4. Personal documents

We can use diaries and other personal accounts to find out how people in the past felt about issues. The complex relationship between class, race and gender can be examined by reading accounts of domestic labour written by employers, owners, servants and slaves.

5. Published sociological evidence

Murdock is famous for his argument that the family is a universal institution. He based his argument on the published research of about 20 societies. His critics also used the same published research to attack his views.

3 SOME CASE STUDIES

1. UNPACKING THE FASHION INDUSTRY

Some sociologists like to use a variety of methods. The study was part of a larger comparative survey of the fashion industry in W. Germany and France as well as Britain.

Phizacklea explains her choices of methods largely in practical terms; "A wide range of primary and secondary source material was used in compiling the information and at all stages I have used one source to check against another".

In Phizacklea's study the following methods and techniques of data collection were used:

■ Secondary source material was derived from Government statistics, statistics produced within the garment industry and the annual reports of large manufacturers.
■ Primary data collection involved a variety of techniques and sources:

1   Key informants were interviewed using a checklist.
2   These provided lists of firms as a sampling frame for further investigation using postal questionnaires, and where agreed interviews with bosses. The small sample, absence of a complete sampling frame and desire to cover a range of firms in terms of size, activity and type of technology employed, all meant that the sample was not necessarily representative.

3   Interviews were conducted with union officials and central and local government officers.
4   The interviewing of workers met through their employers seemed unsuccessful. Most employers did not provide access to workers and where they did responses seemed guarded. As an alternative interviews were arranged separate from work using Bangladeshi community workers and a Cypriot in the workers' own homes.
5   Observation was carried out by the author in many of the workplaces. Where firms selected seemed unwilling to participate she simply turned up and in some cases was able to observe and get an interview.

(A. Phizacklea 1990)

Suggest two reasons why Phizacklea decided to use Bangladeshi and Cypriot community workers to conduct interviews with the workers. Why did Phizacklea use more than one research method?

2. THE NATIONAL SURVEY OF SEXUAL ATTITUDES AND LIFESTYLES (1992)

(Wellings, Field, Wadsworth and Johnson)

The aim of this study was to identify patterns of sexual behaviour and to identify patterns of sexual attitudes with particular reference to AIDS.

METHOD: SAMPLE SURVEY
TECHNIQUES FOR GATHERING DATA: STRUCTURED INTERVIEW
                                    SELF COMPLETED QUESTIONNAIRE
(A related research project conducted in France used telephone interviews.)

POPULATION: ADULTS 15–59 GREAT BRITAIN
SAMPLE: 19,000 FROM 50,000 ADDRESSES
(This was the largest survey of sexual behaviour using interviews. It was hoped that a large sample would reveal unusual behaviour.)

SAMPLING METHOD: RANDOM
(Kinsey used volunteers for 17,000 interviews in USA in 1940s.)

RESPONSE RATE: Typical of survey research.
(The topic was not a problem. The researchers said people were more secretive about their incomes!)

PILOT STUDY: Was conducted to refine questions and
                                    see if subjects would answer.
(It was intended that the subjects, rather than the researchers, should be able to define and describe behaviour. Questions on masturbation turned out to be embarrassing for subjects and were dropped rather than risk refusals to participate.)

FUNDING: Originally the Government who dropped
                                    it for political reasons.
                                    The Wellcome Trust (a medical research
                                    charity) took over.

(They said it was "Worth doing and going to be well done." The cost according to the Press was £$\frac{1}{2}$m. It was funded because AIDS is seen as a SOCIAL PROBLEM.)

PROBLEMS OF RESEARCH INTO SEX:

■ People do not use explicit language.
■ They may not understand questions.
■ They may be embarrassed or shocked.
■ Behaviour is private.
■ People may deny or exaggerate activities.

SOLUTIONS:

The researchers:

- Used a Pilot study to ensure subjects would respond.
- Used a self-completed questionnaire, rather than interviews, for the most intimate questions.
- Allowed subject to respond using a number code instead of words.
- Subjects were guaranteed anonymity.
- Checked data against external sources; e.g. abortion records, and within the questionnaire. They noted that people are inconsistent.
- People respond to the interviewer, not the topic. Subjects were "More willing to discuss sex than earnings".

(Source: *BBC Horizon programme* 3.12.92)

4 >	A SUMMARY OF DIFFERENT SOCIOLOGICAL METHODS

(Some examples of studies using the method are given.)

PRIMARY	SECONDARY
QUANTITATIVE	
SURVEY: 1. QUESTIONNAIRE (TOWNSEND: POVERTY)	SURVEY: 1. OFFICIAL STATISTICS (Durkheim: Suicide)
2. STRUCTURED INTERVIEW school (Rowntree: Poverty) (National Sex Survey)	2. RECORDS e.g. absence from work or PRESS REPORTS (K. Pryce: Reports about Black community in St. Pauls)
3. UNSTRUCTURED INTERVIEW (Dobash and Dobash: domestic violence)	PUBLISHED SOCIOLOGICAL STUDIES (G. Murdock: comparative study of families)
4. OBSERVATION EXPERIMENTS (W. Daniel: Racial discrimination)	CONTENT ANALYSIS OF MASS MEDIA (GUMG: War and Peace news) (G. Loban: Sexism in reading schemes)
QUALITATIVE	
OBSERVATION (S. Ball: Beachside School)	CONTENT ANALYSIS OF MASS MEDIA (A. McRobbie: "Jackie")
PARTICIPANT OBSERVATION 1. COVERT (Humphreys: Homosexuals)	DIARIES, NOVELS
2. OVERT (Polsky: Criminals)	PERSONAL DOCUMENTS (Leicester University study of young people's images of attendance at football matches is both qualitative and quantitative)
UNSTRUCTURED INTERVIEW (A. Oakley: pregnant women)	
PERSONAL DOCUMENTS	
CASE STUDY (P. Willis: a school)	
EXPERIMENT (Atkinson: Coroners decisions)	

- Many studies use a *variety* of methods to get different sorts of data. (E. Barker: Moonies)
- Different methods allow checking of findings and improve reliability. (Humphreys: PO followed up by interviews)

- They may adopt different sociological perspectives which encourage particular methods.
- (A. Phizacklea: Fashion industry. Primary and secondary. Interviews and observation.)
- (W. Daniel: Racial discrimination. Experiments (objective data) and interviews (subjective data).

KEY THEMES

SOCIALISATION

The main AGENCIES OF SOCIALISATION are:

The family

It is likely that for most people the family is the first and remains the most important source of socialisation. Gender roles, language and morality are significant results of family socialisation.

The peer group

Various agencies of socialisation

The word peer means *equal*. A person's peers include the other children at nursery, school and on the street. In simple societies and on Israeli Kibbutzim children are raised in age groups and these are a strong source of identity and thus socialisation. Studies of delinquent gangs and deviant youth activities such as drug abuse tend to "blame" peer groups. It could of course be argued that drug abuse is part of the mainstream adult culture rather than just found in deviant youth sub-cultures. Adults learn from their peers at work and in other social groups such as churches and clubs.

Schools and colleges

Socialisation at school is the result of both the formal and the "hidden curriculum". Schools have become increasingly important as agents of socialisation as the customary period of education lengthens and the educational demands from employers increase. Peers as well as teachers and pupils are part of the socialisation process in school.

The mass media

The mass media have become increasingly important in the socialisation of both children and adults. Electronic media have encouraged socialisation at a national and even global level. TV ownership in Britain is more or less universal. Children watch TV for about half the time they are in school. In neither case does this indicate how much attention the child pays to TV or teacher!

Religious institutions

The extent of the influence of religion on socialisation is a subject for debate. For some people religious beliefs, norms and values dominate socialisation both in the family and in religious schools and places of worship.

The secularisation of society and the development of more rational scientific beliefs suggests that the influence of religion has declined.

Socialisation is not just a passive process. Children are not blank sheets of paper upon which culture can be imprinted. We all take an active part in our socialisation. Within your family the socialisation of members depends on the relationships between all of you. Children help to socialise mothers and fathers by helping them to learn parental roles.

CULTURE

Most human behaviour is learned. It is not genetically programmed. It is cultural rather than biological. Even basic biological behaviours such as eating, sleeping, sexuality and reproduction are influenced by cultural expectations.

Although we have to eat to live there are social rules concerning what we eat. Muslims and Jews do not eat pork for religious reasons; the English try to avoid eating horsemeat for sentimental reasons and Russians will make enormous financial sacrifices to eat caviar because they have learned to like it. Other rules of eating influence the timing of meals and perhaps the need for accompanying prayer.

Culture influences what kind of sexual behaviour is permissible, with whom and under what circumstances. Homosexuality as a form of behaviour exists in all societies. But the recognition of the homosexual as a distinct kind of person is quite unusual. The criminalisation of homosexuality varies from time to time and place to place.

Biologically there are lower and upper age limits for human reproduction. These do not coincide with cultural expectations. Women tend to avoid conception for much of their potentially child bearing life. Unmarried women are not expected to have children; married women are expected to have them (eventually). The age for first time motherhood has risen although biologically girls appear capable of child birth earlier.

There are some aspects of culture which are common to all human societies such as language, marriage, religion and property rights. These universal aspects have developed in very different ways indicating the importance of culture rather than nature. All humans may have the biological potential to learn language but whether you speak French or Japanese depends on socialisation.

Why is there a universal incest taboo?

It has been argued that "the incest taboo" i.e. the prohibition of sexual and marital relationships between close relatives is universal for biological reasons. However neither biology nor sociology lends much support to this view.

The relatives who are forbidden as partners vary enormously between cultures. Sikhs prohibit quite distant relatives whereas Muslims encourage marriage between cousins.

Some animals practice "incest" with little or no effect. Others use biological signals such as smell to prevent parent child incest. The association of incest with low intelligence or mental illness is possibly confusing cause and effect. That is the mentally ill may be more likely to break the rules or less likely to conceal rulebreaking.

The reasons for an incest taboo and the inclusion of some relatives and not others is probably based on the cultural need to preserve stable family life. Incest would create jealousy within families and also confuses role relationships such as parental roles of protection and authority.

Try and find out who is excluded as a marriage partner in different cultures. You could discuss it with students from different ethnic backgrounds or approach the clergy of different religions.

Sometimes we use the word culture to describe the values, knowledge and products of those at the top of society. "Cultured" people are those familiar with the arts and literature which we see as superior to popular tastes. Thus the Opera is seen as culture but rock music is not. Sociologists do not use the term in this way but may be interested in why different aspects of culture are seen as superior and also in the development and effects of popular culture.

Sub-culture

Is a term used by sociologists to describe the existence of a separate culture which exists within the main culture of a society. This assumes that a society like Britain has a single dominant culture.

You can use the term sub-culture to describe the different cultures of ethnic minorities in Britain and also to describe the norms and values of delinquent youth groups. Youth sub-cultures are often influenced by class (Skinhead culture is seen as an exaggeration of traditional working class concerns and styles), ethnicity (Rap and Ragga cultures have developed from communities in the USA and Jamaica) and gender (football hooliganism is seen as an extreme expression of masculine values).

CAUSES OF SOCIAL CHANGE

Social change has occurred at a rapidly accelerating pace.

Urbanisation

The flight from countryside to city (and back again?) and its effects are discussed in the urbanisation chapter.

Industrialisation

Most human society has been based on agricultural production. The changes brought about by industrialisation have been a central theme in sociology since the last century. Industrialisation was a major influence on early important writers of sociology such as Marx, Durkheim and Weber.

Secularisation

The decline of the influence of religion has increased the importance of other agencies of socialisation and social control. It has been argued that secularisation has led to a threat to social order and stable family life.

The influence of science

Scientific developments and the widespread acceptance of scientific knowledge has undermined the influence of religion. The improvements in health resulting from scientific knowledge of hygiene and diseases has had a dramatic effect on world population.

The influence of political ideas and movements

Belief in ideas such as Communism, Nationalism and Capitalism have led to political movements which have produced sudden and far reaching social change.

THE EFFECTS OF SOCIAL CHANGE

The influence of the processes described above can be found on:

Family life

Developments in family structure, functions and roles have been linked with industrialisation, urbanisation and secularisation.

Crime and deviance

Rapid social change may undermine people's commitment to social norms. Secularisation leads people to question traditional values.

Health

Science has changed the way we think about health as well as improved the life expectancy in much of the world.

Population

The size, age distribution and movements of population have been influenced by the changes described above. Population growth and movement have, themselves, been causes of change.

SOCIAL CONTROL

Social control is the discipline some members of society impose on others to maintain social order. Some sociologists think that social control is exercised in the interests of all or at least most of society. Others see it being exercised only in the interests of powerful groups.

The agencies of socialisation discussed above all help to impose social control. The controls may be:

- FORMAL such as those exercised by the police, courts and army.
- INFORMAL as experienced by members of families and other small groups.

Simple societies tended to rely more on informal controls such as expressing disapproval whereas modern industrial societies rely more and more on specialist agencies and the law.

Control over the way people think and thus to a large extent how they act is exercised by families, schools, Churches and the mass media.

EXAMINATION QUESTIONS

Q.1 Study **ITEM A** and **ITEM B.** Then answer the questions which follow.

ITEM A

Some major surveys used in "Social Trends"

Name of survey	How often survey is conducted	Who is questioned	Area covered	Response rate (percentages)
Census of Population	Every 10 years	Household Head	United Kingdom	100
British Social Attitudes Survey	Every year	Adult in Household	Great Britain	67
British Crime Survey	Occasionally	Adult in Household	England & Wales	77
General Household Survey	All the time	All adults in Household	Great Britain	84

(Adapted from *Social Trends*)

ITEM B

COUNTING UNEMPLOYED PEOPLE

The International Labour Organisation calculates that the true level of female unemployment is 1.1 million, which is 53,000 higher than the British government's figure. The International Labour Organisation's figure includes people who are not receiving benefit. These people are excluded from the British government's figure.

(Adapted from *The Independent,* 1991)

a) Study **ITEM A** and state
   i) which survey has the lowest response rate;
   ii) which survey does not cover Scotland. *(2)*
b) Study **ITEM B** and state
   i) which women classified by the International Labour Organisation as unemployed are excluded from the British government's figure;
   ii) how many women were unemployed according to the International Labour Organisation. *(2)*
c) Identify two secondary sources which may be useful to researchers studying poverty and explain why they may be useful. *(4)*
d) Identify and explain two advantages a researcher may gain by undertaking a pilot study. *(4)*
e) Why should sociologists be careful when using official statistics in their own studies? *(8)*

(SEG, June 1993)

Q.2 Sociologists sometimes use longitudinal studies (such as that described in Extract A) in their research. What are the advantages and disadvantages of longitudinal studies to sociologists investigating teenage motherhood.   (6 marks)

EXTRACT A

Ann Phoenix, with a team from the Thomas Coram Research Institute, has made a detailed longitudinal study of 79 young women who gave birth while still in their teens. The sample included young women who were married, cohabiting and single.

The two most common stereotypes of teenage mothers are: firstly, that they are likely to produce delinquent children and secondly, that they have babies because they want council housing and welfare benefits. Phoenix found no evidence of these two stereotypes in her study. Even among those who had planned their pregnancies, no-one reported that she wished to get pregnant in order to receive housing or benefits. There was no evidence that children born to teenage mothers (married or not) developed less well than those born to older women. Nor was there any evidence that early motherhood caused poverty. If anything, motherhood acted as a spur to seek education and training, so that they could earn a living in the future. However, almost all women had low expectations of paid employment. They felt, as a result, that motherhood would be the most significant and fulfilling development in their lives.

(Source: A. Coote's review of A. Phoenix's study "Young Mothers?" in *New Society* 11 December 1990)

(NEAB, June 1992)

Q.3 Study ITEMS A and B. Then answer the questions which follow.

CULTURE AND SOCIAL ORDER

ITEM A

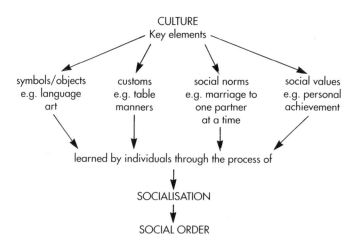

ITEM B

Social control is said to be beneficial for society because it enables its members to work together and cooperate in relative peace and harmony. However there is another side to the picture. Many aspects of social control can be seen as harmful to society and to its members.

(Source: adapted from *Sociology: A New Approach,* M. Haralambos, Causeway Books)

a)   Look at ITEM A. According to the diagram, by what process is culture learned by individuals?   *(1)*

b)   Look at ITEM A. From the diagram, give one key element of culture.   *(1)*

c) i) Look at ITEM B. According to the information given, why is social control said to be beneficial to society? *(1)*

ii) Look at ITEM A. State an example of social values. *(1)*

d) Identify and explain two ways in which social groups encourage their members to conform to their rules. *(4)*

e) Identify two agents of socialisation and explain briefly how each one passes on the norms and values of British society. *(4)*

f) Identify and fully explain one reason why young people form sub-groups or sub-cultures. *(4)*

g) Identify an example of a situation where labelling may occur and fully explain the way in which it can lead to increased non-conformity or deviance. *(4)*

(SEG, June 1992)

Q.4 Write an essay about socialisation and culture.

You may choose to include reference to any of the following.

> The influence of the family,
>> the peer group,
>> education,
>> the mass media,
>> religion.
> Socialisation in different cultures.
> The effects of being brought up without other humans.

Credit will be given for appropriate evidence.

(NEAB, June 1991)

STUDENT'S ANSWER WITH EXAMINER'S COMMENTS

Q.1

a) Study ITEM A and state

which survey has the lowest response rate; *(1)*

The survey with the lowest response rate is the British Social Attitudes Survey.

1/1

ii) which survey does not cover Scotland. *(1)*

The survey which does not cover Scotland is the British Crime Survey.

1/1

b) Study ITEM B and state

i) which women classified by the International Labour organisation as unemployed are excluded from the British government's figure; *(1)*

1/1

The women who are classified by the I.L.O. as unemployed and excluded from the British government's figures are females who are not receiving benefit.

ii) how many women were unemployed according to the International Labour Organisation. *(1)*

1/1

According to the I.L.O. 1.1 million women are unemployed.

c) Identify two secondary sources which may be useful to researchers studying poverty and explain why they may be useful. *(4)*

Rather weak. Explain why it could be useful

1 One secondary source could be statistics collected by other people e.g. people in poor housing. Voluntary organisations like "Shelter" collect information on poverty.

Good. 3/4

2 They could also use government statistics about the number of people who receive social benefits like family income supplement. This would give them an idea of the extent of poverty according to the government's definition.

d) Identify and explain two advantages a researcher may gain by undertaking a pilot study.   *(4)*

> The first advantage the researcher may gain is knowledge of how difficult or easy it is to use a particular research method such as structured interviews. A pilot study might show that a different method might work better.
>
> The second advantage which a researcher may gain is she is able to try out questions which she would like to ask and from the answers given be able to see whether the subjects understand the questions or misinterpret them.

Good explanation of 2 points, as requested. 4/4

e) Why should sociologists be careful when using official statistics in their own studies?   *(8)*

> Sociologists should be careful when using official statistics because some statistics such as crime figures show wrong information. For example the police only record reported crime and unreported crime remains undetected. Therefore the information they gather may be misleading.
>
> Also you must be clear who collected the information and if the government paid them. For example the government may use a relative definition of poverty and find more people are in poverty than if they use an absolute definition of poverty.

Rather thin – only 2 points explained. 4/8

Quite good over all. A little more explanation needed in parts. 15/20

ANSWERS TO EXAMINATION QUESTIONS

Q.2
Choose two advantages and two disadvantages and explain them, making sure they are applied to the issue of teenage motherhood.

Advantages include:

- being able to observe the effects of teenage marriage on children as they develop.
- being able to examine different influences such as class, marital status and number of children on the behaviour of teenage mothers.

Disadvantages include:

- the problem of keeping contact with subjects and ensuring that a representative sample is maintained. Single mothers may wish to discontinue the research if they later marry.
- completed research may tell you about teenage mothers in the past but may be no longer applicable to the present.

Q.3
a) Socialisation
b) Social values (or any of the other three headings)
c) i) Because it enables members of society to work together and cooperate in relative peace and harmony.
   ii) Personal achievement.
d) Through formal social controls by the police and courts. People will conform to avoid arrest and legal sanctions.

   Through informal social controls exerted by family and peers. We show our approval of desired behaviour and our disapproval of deviant behaviour.
e) The family.

   Children learn the culture of their society and the family. Their parents act as role models. Children are encouraged to behave appropriately by parental reward and punishment.

   The mass media.

   Children and adults spend many hours watching TV and being exposed to other mass media. This influences the way they see the world and helps to reinforce notions of right and wrong.

f) Young people may form sub-cultures to resist the order that schools try to impose of them. The school promotes values such as hard work and individual achievement. Some children cannot achieve the school's goals by hard work or do not want to achieve them as they do not see such achievements helping them in the future. They may develop a sub-culture with values such as having a laugh in order to resist the influence of the school. School counter cultures may be characteristic of working class boys.

g) The Scarman report claimed that the police in Brixton in 1981 stopped and searched black youth because they associated them with drug related crime and street robbery. This created a sense of grievance amongst the innocent, and perhaps the guilty, who saw the police as unfair and racist. When incidents between the police and the black community occurred many black (and white) youths were prepared to violently confront the police and take part in riots.

The riots further soured relationships between the police and the black community making further confrontations likely. This has been called a deviance amplification spiral. More vigorous policing may encourage more serious crime.

Q.4

There are lots of hints in the question. Do not try to include all of them. Choose say four major themes and explain and discuss them. You should define both socialisation and culture.

Example of cultural differences help to demonstrate that social behaviour is the result of culture rather than nature.

If you are interested in children who have been raised in isolation from other people there are a handful of famous cases some from the past may not be reliably documented. However Giddens quotes the case of Genie a Californian girl who was locked away from the age of one and a half to 13. When she was freed she was able to learn some normal behaviour but never progressed beyond the language development of a 4 year old. Psychologists would argue that she had missed learning during a critical period and could not compensate for this.

REVIEW SHEET

This Review Sheet covers the material in Chapter 15 (Religion and the Mass Media) and Chapter 16 (Methods and Themes).

■ List, and briefly explain, two ways in which religion might act as a form of social control.

1 _____

2 _____

■ How might religion suppress women?

1 _____

2 _____

■ Look back to Item B of Question 3, Chapter 15. Use the figures to:
1 Show the change in the Muslim's position within "Non-Christian Religious Groups" since 1970.

_____

_____

2 Show the change in the Jehovah's Witnesses position with the 3 Christian groups since 1970.

_____

_____

■ List 2 advantages of *covert* observational research.

1 _____

2 _____

■ List 2 problems of *covert* observational research.

1 _____

2 _____

■ Briefly explain:
1 A quota sample

2 A random sample

■ List 4 types of *secondary* sources of information.

1 _____

2 _____

3 _____

4 _____

■ List 3 main agents of Socialisation. Briefly outline how each one acts in this way.

1 _____

_____

2 _____

3 _____

_____

■ List 4 *causes of social change.*

1 _____

2 _____

3 _____

4 _____

■ Look back to Item A of Question 1, Chapter 16. Which survey is most reliable in terms of response?

_____

■ List the interests and language you have developed at school or college from your peers.

_____

_____

■ List separately the skills you have gained through informal and formal education. Compare your list with a family member from a different generation. (Examples might include cooking, swimming, driving, word processing, painting and decorating etc.)

_____

_____

_____

_____

_____

INDEX